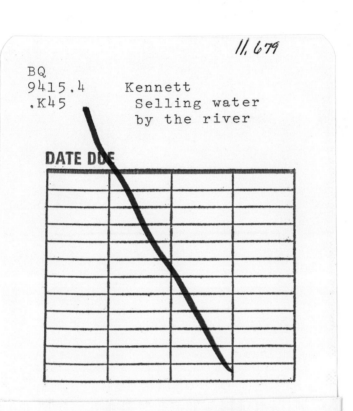

Selling Water by the River

49

Selling Water by the River

A MANUAL OF ZEN TRAINING

BY

Jiyu Kennett

PANTHEON BOOKS

A DIVISION OF RANDOM HOUSE, NEW YORK

Copyright © 1972 by Reverend Jiyu Kennett

All rights reserved under International and Pan-American
Copyright Conventions. Published in the United States by
Pantheon Books, a division of Random House, Inc., New York,
and simultaneously in Canada by Random House of
Canada Limited, Toronto.

Library of Congress Cataloging in Publication Data

Kennett, Jiyu, 1924–   Selling Water by the River.
1. Sōtō (Sect)   II. Title.
BL1442.S65K45   294.3'927   70–38836
ISBN 0–394–46743–4

Design by Kenneth A. Miyamoto

Manufactured in the United States of America
by The Haddon Craftsmen, Inc., Scranton, Pa.

FIRST EDITION

To my master, the Very Reverend Keidō Chisan Kōhō Zenji, late Chief Abbot of Sōjiji, Yokohama, and Archbishop of the Kanto Plains

Foreword

BY THE LATE CHIEF ABBOT OF SŌJIJI

IT WAS DŌGEN ZENJI who brought Sōtō Zen from China to Japan in the twelfth century, but it was not until Keizan Zenji became abbot of Sōjiji several generations later that the teaching spread throughout Japan. The reason for this is not far to seek. Dōgen had returned from China thinking that only the Chinese way of doing things was right, and as Reverend Kennett quite correctly points out, it is not possible to graft the customs and culture of one country onto another. When a religion is carried from country to country it is only the basic Truth that will survive; it is like a Japanese bride, who wears white at her wedding so her husband may realise that she is willing to be dyed to any colour, with regard to customs, ways and behaviour, that he may wish. When a religion is married, as it were, to a new country, it must be willing to be dyed in the same way as the Japanese bride. Keizan realised this and changed the customs, but not the Truth, to be in accord with Japanese thought; thus did Sōtō Zen become the bride of Japan and gain acceptance throughout that country, so that it now has more than fifteen thousand temples and is the second largest religious organisation in Japan.

But this expansion was impossible whilst Zen remained in its original Chinese state, since the Japanese people felt that a foreign religion was being forced upon them. The people of Western countries also, if Zen is ever to reach them properly, must colour it for themselves just as the Japanese did. Thus will Zen be reborn in the West. Like the Buddhist at rebirth, the new Zen will be neither completely new, being the same stream of Truth, nor completely old, as it will have new forms, ways, customs and culture.

Reverend Kennett has worked hard to make this book a manual suitable for Western people who are sincerely seeking true Zen but not trying to copy Eastern ways and manners. It is my sincere hope that all who read it will keep this fact in mind, for the Zen of the West must be born of Western priests in Western countries and not be spread by Japanese who know nothing of Western ways and customs. My blessings are with this book.

CHISAN KŌHŌ
Chief Abbot, Sōjiji Temple
Yokohama, Japan

July 1967

Preface

In 1186 military government, under Yoritomo Minamoto, was established in Japan, and with it came one of the greatest changes ever experienced in the history of that country. Up until that time the pleasure-loving aristocracy in Kyoto had written their poems, painted pictures, sung and forgot that the peasantry existed. Degeneracy was in the air. The Buddhist hierarchies had enjoyed political support in return for mysterious and beautiful ceremonies which were more or less devoid of genuine spirituality. Then, with the fall of the aristocracy, the temples and monasteries found themselves on their own, a prospect very few were able to adapt to.

But amidst all the turmoil a new spiritual force began to arise. In the year 1191 Eisai Zenji, a Japanese Buddhist priest, returned from China and established the Rinzai school of Zen. He had spent four years studying under Master Eshō. The new and vital school of Buddhism that he brought with him was like a beacon of light shining in the religious darkness of mediaeval Japan.

The *kōan* system of the Rinzai school was itself a fairly new development in the history of Zen. It was mainly through the eloquent master Daie Sōkō, in the early part of the twelfth century, that it had become widely used in China. The kōan exercise, with its shouting, kicking, crying and beating "performances," culminating in the sudden understanding of *kenshō*, attracted the young samurai of Japan, who quickly absorbed its methods into their own discipline.

Shortly before Eisai's death, a young trainee named Dōgen began studying under the aged master. Upon the death of his teacher, Dōgen, who was not satisfied even with the Rinzai teachings, found it necessary to travel to China in order to further his studies. There he found the "serene reflection" type of meditation being practised by the Sōtō school of Zen, and it is with the teachings he brought back to Japan that this book deals.

Sōtō Zen followed mainly the Indian tradition and was the religion of the ordinary person, man or woman. In his writings after his return, Dōgen proclaimed that there was no difference between the meditations of a man and a woman, a rich person and a poor one, everyone being able to find peace and freedom if he truly sought it. It is because of its simple, straightforward approach, the very opposite of the bewildering and, because of this, frequently useless approach of Rinzai, that I have chosen Sōtō, not to mention that whereas Rinzai is mainly suited to a small group of people with a specific type of outlook, Sōtō is suitable for anyone.

Under his Chinese master, Nyojō, Dōgen learned that Sōtō masters were not bound by any one system of teaching. Instead, they preferred to use kaleidoscopic teaching methods and to allow the kōan to develop naturally in the daily life of the trainee as his spiritual understanding ripened, rather than force his growth through the unnatural tension created by a fixed system of kōans. It was in 1227 that Dōgen returned to Japan to teach the "new" Sōtō system, so called despite the fact that Sōtō is the oldest of the three Zen schools.

During the years of his teaching Dōgen made one grave mistake. He reckoned without the fact that one cannot force the customs and culture of one country upon another, however modern and desirable that culture may seem to be. It is for this reason, and this reason only, that Sōtō Zen had to wait several generations before it was to enjoy widespread acceptance in Japan under the aegis of Keizan Zenji. But the times were ripe for a new and vital religion, Rinzai having by then degenerated into a means of artistic religious expression rather than being a source of real spiritual help for the masses who were in dire need of it.

Until the time of Keizan, Dōgen's Zen had clung to its Chinese heritage, thus alienating itself from the common people of Japan. Keizan brought the old ideas of Buddhism into line with the new spirit of the times—and in so doing exemplified one of Dōgen's greatest teachings—by his insistence that Zen could survive only if it came alive for the time in which its adherents were living. To this end he, like Dōgen, taught the most advanced forms of hygiene and living habits then extant, blending them with the culture of the Japanese people and the ancient spirit of Zen so that every act of daily life became an act of religious understanding. Through this simple process Sōtō Zen spread throughout the country until today it is the second largest school of Buddhism in Japan, its teachings keeping ever in step with the times and yet retaining their original spirit.

I commenced my Buddhist studies at an early age with the London Buddhist Vihara and later became a lecturer at the London Buddhist Society. It was while studying Buddhist history that I discovered that all the really great Zen masters appeared before the Sōtō and Rinzai lines separated, although there were many good masters later in both lines. I spent time in Malaysian and Chinese temples of the Rinzai school, both in Singapore and Hong Kong, but felt that its teachings did not go far enough. It therefore seemed only natural that I should devote my fullest energies to pursuing the Sōtō way. This I did for almost ten years, in Japan.

There is a Japanese saying that whilst Rinzai is for the generals, Sōtō is for the farmers. Whereas Rinzai Zen is much better known for its religious arts than for its genuine spiritual help for the ordinary man and woman, Sōtō Zen teaches the way for every living person, student, factory worker or executive, to find peace and freedom in everyday life. The farmer in his fields can apply Sōtō Zen to his daily life as much as can the queen of England or the president of the United States, and find complete peace of spirit without the stress or strain he would experience should he try to reach the same state through the Rinzai kōan method.

Bearing these facts in mind, Sōtō Zen is ideal for the present-day religious revival in America. Both Dōgen and Keizan were far in advance of their own day and age, and in some ways are still in advance of ours. What they wrote and taught is as applicable now as it was when they wrote it. Although the old forms of many of the ceremonies included here are still kept and performed intact, their meaning and spirit are abreast of the times in which we live, which vitalises them in a way no other religion at present extant seems able to equal.

At a time when the young are seeking a religion that means something to them personally rather than one that requires rigid adherence to doctrine and old rules, Dōgen's insistence upon finding freedom and perfection, peace of spirit, within oneself amidst the struggle of everyday life and within the structure and times in which one lives is as relevant as it was when he lived, and it is my certain knowledge of this that has led me to place the following work before the public.

Jiyu Kennett

Abbess of Shasta Abbey, California, and former Foreign Guestmaster, Sōjiji Temple, Yokohama

October 1971

Acknowledgements

I WISH TO ACKNOWLEDGE the very great help of Reverend Suigan Yogo in translating the writings of Keizan and most of the ceremonial. There is no doubt that this book could never have been written without his help and encouragement. I also make grateful acknowledgement to Reverend Myozen Miyagawa for her assistance in translating the works of Dōgen and part of the ceremonial.

The works of Dōgen and Keizan were translated from books in both my own and Reverend Suigan Yogo's libraries. The ceremonies are taken from the official handbook of ceremonial published by the Sōtō Zen Church in Japan; for the most part these ceremonies are exact translations, but one or two have been very slightly altered to make them more understandable to the Western mind. The translators have been very careful, however, to make certain that the original meaning and spirit are preserved.

In writing the history of Dōgen, I used Masaharu Anesaki's *History of Japanese Religions*, and the *Japanese-English Buddhist Dictionary* published by Daitō Shuppansha in Tokyo.

The poem versions of the Scripture of Kanzeon Bosatsu and the Litany of the Great Compassionate One, in Book IV, are based on the translations of these works to be found in Daisetz T. Suzuki's *Manual of Zen Buddhism*. Narada Thera's *Manual of Buddhism* supplied all the doctrinal material in Chapter 2, on essential doctrine, much of which I have quoted straight from Reverend Narada's book. The New American Library's Mentor edition of *The Teachings of the Compassionate Buddha*, edited by E. A. Burtt, provided much of the historical data for Chapter 3, on the growth of Buddhism, as well as some of the scriptural references. Reiho Masunaga's *The Sōtō Approach to Zen* (published by the Layman Buddhist Society Press, Tokyo), one of the few books on Sōtō Zen in English, supplied the translations of *The Most Excellent Mirror—Samādhi* and

Sandōkai that were used in composing the poem versions in Book IV.

I wish to thank the following authors and publishers for their kind permission to use copyright material:

Grove Press: From *Manual of Zen Buddhism*, by Daisetz T. Suzuki. Reprinted by permission of Grove Press, Inc. All rights reserved.

Narada Thera: From his *Manual of Buddhism*, printed by Thu Lam An Thu Quan, Saigon.

The New American Library: From *The Teachings of the Compassionate Buddha*, edited by Edwin A. Burtt. Copyright © 1955 by Edwin A. Burtt. Reprinted by arrangement with The New American Library, New York.

Charles E. Tuttle, Inc., Tokyo: From *History of Japanese Religions*, by Masaharu Anesaki.

Contents

Book I   The Stem of the Lotus

Book II   The Teachings of Dōgen Zenji

Book III The Teachings of Keizan Zenji

Book IV Scriptures and Necessary Ceremonial

Illustrations

Introduction

PEOPLE WHO have made only a cursory study of Zen have often said that it has little or nothing to do with original Buddhism, and that there is no connection whatsoever between the two. For this reason, I have arranged the material in this book in such a way that the basic doctrines of Theravāda Buddhism can be traced to their later development as doctrines—if such they can then be called—of Zen. Therefore, if it is the reader's wish to see how these doctrines develop, he should not read the book straight through but follow the order below, using the chapters of Book I as starting points.

Chapter 1. "The History of Buddha According to Zen Belief"
> The connection of this chapter with later ones is so obvious that no special suggestions for reading need be made.

Chapter 2. "Basic Original Doctrines Essential to Zen"
> Section 1 (Anattā) should be read in conjunction with Book II, "Shushōgi," section 1, and "Shōji," section 2.
> Section 2 (Karma) should be read in conjunction with Book II, "Shushōgi," section 2; and Book IV, Jūkai: Sange.
> Section 3 (Anicca) should be read in conjunction with Book II, "Ūji."
> Section 4 (Rebirth) should be read in conjunction with Book II, "Shōji"; and Book IV, Funeral Ceremony and Segaki.
> Section 5 (The Four Noble Truths) should be read in conjunction with Book II, "Shushōgi," sections 3 and 4; Book III, Kyojūkaimon; and Book IV, Morning Service: The Scripture of Great Wisdom.

Chapter 3. "The Growth of Zen from Basic Theravāda Doctrine"
> This chapter is primarily historical, but it can be tied in with Book II, "Shushōgi," sections 4 and 5.

Chapter 4. "The Necessity of Zazen"

This chapter should be read in conjunction with Book II, "Gyakudoyōjinshu" and "Bendōwa"; Book III, *Sankon Zazen Setsu*; and Book IV, Evening Service and Kessei: Nyudō-no-hai, Jōdō, Hossen.

Chapter 5. "The Necessity of Understanding the Heart of Kanzeon"

This should be read in conjunction with Book II, "Taitai-kōhō," "Shūryoshingi," "Fushukuhampō," "Bendōhō," and "Tenzokyokan"; and Book IV, The Scripture of Kanzeon Bosatsu, Jūkai: Sange, and Various Short Ceremonies.

Chapter 6. "Activity in the Heart of Fugen"

This should be read in conjunction with Book IV, Morning Service: *Sandōkai* and *The Most Excellent Mirror—Samādhi*.

Chapter 7. "The Heart of Monju"

This chapter should be read along with the *Śūraṅgama Sūtra* (not included here except for summary); Book II, "Gen-jokōan" and "Shushōgi," section 5; and Book IV, Morning Service: The Scripture of Great Wisdom.

Chapter 8. "What Are Kōans?"

This chapter should be read in conjunction with Book I, Chapter 2, section 5 (The Four Noble Truths); Book III, *Denkoroku* and *Kyojūkaimon*; Book IV, Morning Service: *The Most Excellent Mirror—Samādhi*, and Jūkai: Reading of the *Kyojūkaimon*.

Chapter 9. "Apostolic Succession"

This chapter should be read along with Book III, *Denkoroku*; Book IV, Ordination Ceremony, and Jūkai: Ceremony of the Ketchimyaku and Ceremony of Recognition.

There are many points in Chapter 1, on the life of Shakyamuni Buddha, which the reader may think unnecessary, but nothing has been included that is not made use of later on in Zen. For example, the story of the ascetic Asita and the baby Gautama, recounted in this chapter, became the basis for the custom in the Zen transmission ceremony of the master's mat first being placed over that of the disciple and later the disciple's mat over that of the master. The necessity of doing pure Zazen, or seated meditation, without indulging in ascetic practices—the true way of Sōtō Zen—is prefigured in the simple Zazen done by the child Gautama at the time of the ploughing festival. The Buddha's search for the answer to his questions concerning suffering became the first carrying around of a kōan, and his enlightenment became the first kōan solving. The three masters with whom he studied were the precedent for the Zen system of requiring all trainees to have three masters (that is, three official ones): the first for ordination, the second for Hossen and the third for transmission. I could go on listing the connections of Shakyamuni's life with Zen, but the reader will enjoy this study all the more for doing his own research as he reads the book through.

The foregoing information is for those who wish to read this book as an exposition of the historical growth of Zen. However, my main purpose in writing it was to provide a comprehensive work for those who wish to study Zen as a religion, with the intention of entering the priesthood. If this is the reader's aim, Book I then becomes the necessary foundation from which a layman should approach the subject; it will take him up through the Jūkai ceremonies, which all true laymen are obliged to undergo prior to entering the priesthood. Book I should therefore be read in conjunction with Jūkai, in Book IV. When this material has been thoroughly mastered—even though it may seem highly trivial to some—Book II should be worked upon, bearing in mind that "Taitaikōhō," "Bendōhō," and "Tenzokyokan" are the basis of the monastic rule in all temples. Problems that may arise during training are dealt with in "Gyakudoyōjinshu" and "Bendōwa." Since there is no doubt that every living person has his own personal kōan, which is a facet of the eternal kōan, no stories of masters and disciples are included here other than what may be gleaned from the *Denkoroku* in Book III. He who would be a true Zen monk must follow the rules laid down for the Order of Monks in "Taitaikōhō," "Shūryoshingi," "Fushukuhampō," "Bendōhō" and "Tenzokyokan" in Book II, do his Zazen with all his might and study the lives of the patriarchs in the *Denkoroku* in Book III, at the same time carefully studying and using the ceremonies, as applicable, of Book IV.

Although when speaking of Zazen in Book I I have tended to divide Zen into stages of realisation, I want it clearly understood that enlightenment is not realised piecemeal. Enlightenment is enlightenment; it is one and undivided and not realisable in portions. But the

five types, or stages, of meditation are talked about by most authorities, and I have seen fit to use the same method of explanation,
though I have said little or nothing about the first two stages. This
is because the first stage, *bompu* Zen, which is sitting simply for
the advantages to be gained from the physical standpoint, seems to
me so unworthy a reason for doing Zazen as to not be worth mentioning. One should not sit just for the purpose of physical fitness;
man is body and mind, not body alone. That sitting produces good
physical results is important *after* one has sat; it should not be made
the reason for sitting. For exactly the same reason, I have not discussed the second stage, *gedō* Zen, at length, since to sit for the
supernatural powers it will give one is not only wrong but completely
contrary to the teachings of Buddhism. I have talked instead about
how Zazen is done both mentally and physically, and about the sort
of mind to be cultivated during the time of training, adding a
detailed discussion of the three higher stages of Zen, which are the
finding of the heart of compassion, the heart of love and the heart
of wisdom, these being by far the more important aspects of Zen
teaching.

Another point is worth mentioning, and that is the difference between the ideal and the actual. As the *Sandōkai,* one of the most
important scriptures of Sōtō Zen, expresses it: "With the ideal
comes the actual, like a box and its lid; in darkness there is light, but
you will not understand it by one-sided darkness alone; in light
there is darkness, but you will not understand it by one-sided light;
the two go together like the sequence of steps in a dance." What I
have written in the following chapters represents the ideal; the
actuality in Zen temples in Japan is often quite different, and many
Western people are upset by this. If anyone who reads this book is
planning on going to Japan, he should digest this comment well. A
temple is a small world, and in it will be found every type of person
from the saint to the bottom-rank sinner, the former as holy as
it is possible to be and the latter as unrepentant as any in the
ordinary world. All types of situations will present themselves, and
these will be intensified by the fact that one is living in a closely
knit community where there is no escape from them as in the world
outside. All these things have to be accepted, and understood, as
manifestations of the eternal kōan: in other words, with the ideal

comes the actual, like a box and its lid! The ideal can only be upset by the actual if one permits it to be; if the trainee keeps his heart pure, and follows the instructions written in these chapters, nothing can harm him. This is important. Western people should also remember that since they are in the minority in Japanese temples, they will have many of the problems that minority groups encounter when living in a close community in a Western country, and must try to make allowances and adjustments accordingly. This is not meant to discourage the reader from going to Japan, but to warn him of some of the difficulties he will have to face when he gets there, not the least of which is cultural shock. Too many sincere people go to Japan with their eyes shut to such things. Both I and all my community want them to go with their eyes open.

In ancient China there was a famous female Zen master named Mo Shan, who had a large meditation hall full of male trainees. On one occasion a new trainee came to ask admission, and knowing that the master was a woman, made the following comment: "You are supposed to be a great Zen master. If that is true, I will stay and learn from you; if it is not, I will tear down your seat." As Mo Shan made no answer, the young man became uneasy. "If you are so great, why don't you turn yourself into a man instead of remaining a mere woman?" was his next comment. "I am I," Mo Shan replied. "I cannot change my shape. I am not a sorcerer." The young man bowed, took the lowest place and accepted her teaching for many years.

Mo Shan's words still hold true today. No one can change his shape, however much he may wish to; he must learn to accept it. Of course, it is possible to improve one's character, turn over a new leaf and realise the Buddha Nature; if it were not so, there would be no reason for Buddha to appear in the world. This is another of the meanings of "all is one and all is different," for we have to accept such things as sex, race, colour and features just as they are. My nose will never be flat like that of a Japanese and my eyes will always be grey and round instead of almond-shaped: I know this and I accept it. So, when I hear from my fellow Westerners that it is essential to follow Japanese customs such as eating with chopsticks and sitting Japanese-style on the floor if one would under-stand Zen, I know that their "religion" has degenerated into non-religion. The only value of sitting cross-legged on the floor in the original Zazen position—which incidentally is Indian and not Japanese—is that it provides the sitter with a firm base from which it is difficult to fall. But there is no reason why Zazen cannot be done successfully on a chair or stool with a really good-sized seat and no back. Western people should be content with their own customs and not practise one-upmanship on their friends by trying to prove that they have a smattering of the culture of the mysterious East. Zen study should make one normal, not abnormal.

From the moment I arrived in Japan more than ten years ago, I was constantly told that I must concentrate on the basic Truth and not worry about customs and culture, as the West can only make use of this Truth to build its own form of Zen. Yet many so-called Buddhists in Western countries are convinced that only an Oriental can teach them and that Oriental customs are essential to Buddhism. They despise their own nationals who enter the Buddhist priesthood, as well as their own culture, thinking there is something lacking in them that the Orient possesses. To such a one the Zen teacher says that white cows and brown cows are perfect as they are and need no improvement. I too was of the average Western opinion until some years ago. Chisan Kōhō, the late chief abbot of Sōjiji, pointed out to me that if a Westerner could not be a teacher, then obviously no Westerner could ever learn, since all were mistaking the finger pointing at the moon for the moon itself. If one gives this a little thought, the revelation is startling. A philosophy or a truth is transplantable, but customs and culture are not, and so that philosophy or truth must take on the customs and culture of the place to which it goes. After all, the moon colours the snows of Iceland in a different way than it colours the green growth of the tropics, though it is still the same moon. As the late chief abbot so rightly pointed out, Dōgen was a Japanese who brought Zen teaching back from China; China did not send someone to Japan to convert that country to Zen. There are some Japanese who become extremely angry when they hear Dōgen criticised as having made a grave mistake in attempting to transplant the Chinese form of Zen to Japan, and who swear that China and Japan have exactly the same culture. In many larger aspects this is true; but when one is living in a close community it is the small differences in customs that get on one's nerves, not the big ones, and there is no doubt that the smaller customs in the two countries are very dissimilar. I have lived in Chinese temples in Malaysia and Hong Kong, and I know.

When the West has truly learned Buddhist all-acceptance, it will cease to turn up its nose at its own nationals and be willing to learn from them in true Buddhist humility. In the words of the late chief abbot of Sōjiji: "When the West is ready, it will find for itself its true teacher. That person may have learned in Japan, but he or she will definitely be one of their own nation and not a foreigner to them. So long as they want a Japanese teacher, they will never understand Buddhism, for they are in duality in so far as they are seeing Japanese and foreigners as separate in the Buddha Nature instead of one."

My own comment on the subject is the same as that of Dōgen: "Do not travel far to other dusty lands, forsaking your own sitting place; if you cannot find the Truth where you are now, you will never find it." It took me a long time to discover that I had never needed to go to Japan in the first place.

One thing cannot be stressed too much, and that is the necessity of believing that the Buddha Nature exists in each and every one of us. Without such faith, it is impossible to arrive at any understanding of Zen; after all, if you do not believe that you have the potentiality of Buddhahood, you are never going to discover its existence. In brief, Zen Buddhism is a religion that needs faith, and not a philosophy. For those who believe, no explanation of what I have written here will be necessary, and for those who do not believe, no explanation is ever going to be sufficient. You *must* believe that Shakyamuni Buddha discovered his Buddha Nature for himself by realising his own innate enlightenment along with the universe from the beginning of time, and that because he realised it, you can realise it too.

1

The Stem
of the Lotus

All men know suffering, which is as the mud wherein the lotus takes root. All men know the lotus blossom which gazes at the heavens. Few men indeed know how to nourish the root of True Religion within themselves in the mud of ignorance that surrounds them, and fewer still know how to make the root flourish and grow in the dark water the long stem that is needed before the flower can bloom in the clear light of day. In these chapters I shall attempt to show how to grow the long stem of the lotus from the root to the blossom, for the stem of the lotus and Zen training are identical.

CHAPTER 1

The History of Buddha According to Zen Belief

ON THE FULL-MOON DAY of May, in 623 B.C., Prince Siddhārtha Gautama, afterwards Shakyamuni Buddha, was born in Lumbinī Garden at Kapilavastu, on the borders of Nepal, his family being of the aristocratic Shakya clan. His father was King Suddhodana and his mother Queen Mahā Māyā. Seven days after his birth his mother died. His mother's younger sister Mahā Prajāpatī, who was also married to King Suddhodana, became his foster mother. The ascetic Asita, an intimate friend of the king, visited the palace to see the child, and when the baby was brought out he placed his feet in Asita's matted hair. Foreseeing by this action the child's future greatness, Asita rose from his seat and saluted him with *gasshō*, as did also the king. After this Asita first smiled and then wept, for he knew that Gautama was the Buddha that was to come and that he, owing to his own prior death and rebirth in a formless realm, would not be alive to benefit from the Buddha's superior wisdom.

On the fifth day the child was named Siddhārtha Gautama, which means "Wish Fulfilled," and many learned Brahmans were invited to the palace for the naming ceremony. Among them were eight distinguished men, seven of whom, on examining the child's characteristics, raised two fingers to signify their belief that he would be either a universal monarch or a Buddha. However, the youngest and most learned, Kondañña, raised only one finger, thereby firmly declaring that the child would retire from the world and become a Buddha.

During the ploughing festival the future Buddha had an unprecedented mental experience, which served as the key to his enlightenment. This festival was arranged to encourage agriculture and both nobles and commoners, in gala dress, participated. The child was left on a screened and canopied couch beneath a rose-apple tree, to be watched by his nurses. At the climax of the festival the nurses

3

stole away to watch, and the child, sitting cross-legged and concentrating on the inhalation and exhalation of his breath, gained *samādhi*, one-pointedness of mind, which is the first ecstasy. The prince was so absorbed in meditation when the nurses returned that, struck with awe, they told the king, who came and saluted his son for the second time.

After an excellent education and a special training in the arts of warfare, Gautama married his beautiful cousin Yasodharā, both of them being sixteen years old. Thereafter they led a luxurious life, unaware of the life of tribulation led by most people outside the palace. So as to be able to enjoy his life to the full, Gautama had three palaces, each one for a different season, hot, cold or rainy. Renunciation of luxury and pleasure was not yet in his mind.

However, his contemplative nature and boundless compassion did not allow him to enjoy real pleasures as others did. He knew no woe, but he had a deep desire to witness the way of life of humanity in general, even amidst his own comfort and prosperity. His search for knowledge led him one day outside the palace, where he began to see the darker side of the life of men. First he saw a decrepit old man, then a diseased person, later a corpse, and finally, a dignified hermit. The first three of these sights showed him the inexorable nature of life and the universal sickness of humanity. The fourth showed him the means of overcoming this and the way to attain calm and peace. Realising the uselessness of sensual pleasures and the value of renunciation, he decided to leave the world. It was after this decision that he heard of the birth of his son and, regarding the child as an impediment rather than a blessing, named him Rāhula, "Hindrance."

He now realised that the time was ripe for his departure, and after ordering Channa, his favourite attendant, to saddle his horse Kanthaka, he stood on the threshold of the princess's chamber and cast a dispassionate glance at his wife and child. Yet his compassion so dominated him even at the moment of parting that he stole away at midnight, attended only by Channa, to become a penniless wanderer at the age of twenty-nine.

After travelling for a long way he stopped to rest on the far bank of the river Anomā, and there shaved his head, giving his garments and ornaments to Channa to take back to the palace. Then, adopting the simple yellow garb of an ascetic, he began to lead a life of voluntary poverty as a homeless beggar.

He commenced his search for calm and peace by studying with Ārāda Kālāma, an ascetic of repute, who after his pupil had attained the third Arūpa Jhāna, or the Realm of Nothingness, regarded him as his equal. Gautama was not satisfied, however, with mere mental concentration, and went next to Udraka Rāmaputra, with whom he attained the final mental stage of the Realm of Neither Perception nor Non-Perception. Since in those days the sages could proceed no further in mental development, the teacher invited his pupil to take full charge of all his disciples.

Finding that there seemed to be no one competent to teach him, since all were enmeshed in ignorance, Gautama gave up looking for external help from teachers, realising that Truth and peace are to be found within oneself and not gained from another. Thereafter he wandered in the district of Magadha, arriving eventually at Uruvelā. Hearing of his renunciation, Kondañña, who had foretold his destiny at his naming ceremony, and four sons of the other sages who had been present at the same time, Bhaddiya, Vappa, Mahānama and Assaji, also renounced the world and joined him. Asceticism was practised very severely in ancient India, and Gautama, now called Shakyamuni, practised all forms of austerity to such an extent that his delicate body was reduced almost to a skeleton. But the greater his torments the further his goal receded, the only result being exhaustion.

Then came the demon Māra, suggesting to his mind that he live a life of merit which would involve him in sacrifices and celibacy. But the future Buddha would not be tempted, knowing that sensual desires, aversion, hunger, thirst, craving, sloth, torpor, fear, doubt, distraction, obstinacy, profit, praise, honour, false fame, the extolling of oneself and contempt for others were the army of Māra. Resolving that it would be better to die in the battle against such things than to live vanquished by them, he dismissed these thoughts from his mind and made firm his determination to reach Buddhahood.

It was after this decision that Shakyamuni abandoned self-mortification as futile and adopted the Middle Path between asceticism and indulgence, for he now realised that the way to enlightenment was the one of simply sitting which he had discovered as a child. He therefore took food, which so disgusted his five fellow ascetics that they deserted him on the spot, saying he had become self-indulgent. After a substantial meal offered by the woman Sujātā, he resolved just to sit.

Seated under the famous pipal tree at Buddha Gayā, with his mind tranquil and purified, he developed the supernormal knowledge of the true way to the destruction of passions, and comprehending things as they truly are, realised his original enlightenment, exclaiming, "I was enlightened simultaneously with the universe." He was then thirty-five years old.

He was born human, and he lived and died as a man. Yet although he was human and neither deified nor immortal, he became an extraordinary man. He must not be thought of as an incarnation of Vishnu or of any other god, and his personal salvation cannot save others. "You yourselves must make the exertion; the Buddhas are only teachers," was one of his sayings. "Remember thou must go alone; the Buddhas do but point the way," is another famous quotation. Instead of placing an unseen, almighty god over man and making him subservient to such a belief, Shakyamuni Buddha raised the worth of mankind. Selfless service and the equality of all men are the cornerstones of his teaching.

CHAPTER 2

Basic Original Doctrines
Essential to Zen

1. ANATTĀ (No-Soul)

Apart from mind and matter, which constitute this so-called being that we know as man, there is no immortal soul, or eternal ego, with which we are gifted or which we have obtained in some mysterious way from a mysterious being or force. The Buddhist doctrine of rebirth should be distinguished from the theory of reincarnation, or that of transmigration, for Buddhism denies the existence of an unchanging or eternal soul. The forms of man or animal are merely the temporary manifestations of the life-force that is common to all. "Being" is only a concept used for conventional purposes. Birth is simply the coming into being of a psychophysical existence. Just as a physical state is conditioned by a preceding state as its cause, even so the coming into being of this psychophysical life is conditioned by causes anterior to its birth. As one life-process is possible without a permanent thing passing from one thought-moment to another, so a series of life-processes is possible without anything to transmigrate from one life to another. This body dies, transmitting its life-force to another, without anything transmigrating to the other that is recognisable as a separative entity. The future being there will be conditioned by the present life-force here. The new being is neither absolutely the same as its predecessor, since their composition is not identical, nor entirely different, being the same stream of life-force which, like electric current, can be tapped when a bulb is inserted, so as to give light, but is unseen when the bulb breaks until a new one is inserted. Just as with electricity there is no lack of current when a bulb breaks, but merely the necessity for a new bulb, so with rebirth there is a continuity of a life-force which manifests itself in birth and seems invisible in death: just that and nothing more.

2. KARMA (Action or Deed, Either Good or Bad)

The law of moral causation; action and reaction in the ethical realm; karma includes both past and present actions. It is not fate, not predestination imposed by some mysterious power to which we must helplessly submit. It is one's own doing which reacts on one's own self, so it is possible for us to direct the course of our karma. *Karma* is action, and *vipāka* is its reaction: thus, cause and effect. Karma, being a law in itself, needs no lawgiver. It operates in its own field without the intervention of an external, independent ruling agency. Inherent in it is the potentiality of producing its due effect. The effect already blooms in its cause. Karma, good or bad, is caused by not knowing things as they truly are, and ignorance and craving are the chief causes. "No doer is there who does the deed, nor is there one who feels the fruit": this can be understood clearly after deep and true meditation thereon. Our will, or ego, is itself the doer of karma, and feeling is itself the reaper of the karmic fruit. Apart from these mental states, there is none to sow and none to reap. Karma is not stored somewhere either in the consciousness or in the body. Being dependent on mind and matter, it manifests itself at the opportune moment and is an individual force which is transmitted from one existence to another. Not everything is due to karma; otherwise a person would always be bad if it was his karma to be bad. Seasonal phenomena, the order of germs and seeds; the theory of cells and genes; the order of act and result; natural phenomena such as gravitation and other similar laws of nature; the order of mind and the psychic law, such as the processes of consciousness and arising and perishing of consciousness: all are laws in themselves. Karma, which is the third of these five universal laws, helps, with the other four, to account for diversity in the world. Karma gives hope, self-reliance, consolation and moral courage to a Buddhist. It teaches individual responsibility and explains the problem of suffering, the mystery of so-called fate and predestination in other religions, and above all, the reason for the inequality of mankind.

3. REBIRTH

Past karma conditions the present birth, and present karma, in combination with past karma, conditions the future birth. As stated earlier, rebirth must be distinguished from reincarnation or trans-migration since an unchanging or eternal soul is nonexistent; since there is no individual "I" to think, then there is nothing to be re-born.

4. THE FOUR NOBLE TRUTHS

As stated in Chapter 1, Shakyamuni Buddha saw old age, dis-ease, death and the priestly life when he went outside the palace. His search was undertaken for the purpose of discovering how man-kind could be released from the suffering engendered by the first three of these, and the means for undertaking that search showed itself to him in the form of the fourth, which is why he entered the priestly life. In the Four Noble Truths he discovered the answer to his problem and, inadvertently, enlightenment.

The first of these Truths is that of the existence of suffering. Birth, decay, death, sorrow, lamentation, pain, grief, despair, not to get what one wants and existence itself as the world knows exist-ence: these are suffering. All these things are karmically acquired. The Three Characteristics, *anicca* (transiency), *dukkha* (suffering), *anattā* (self-lessness), can be understood by experience but cannot be adequately explained in words; the three warnings, sickness, old age and death, must come to all, and the beginning of the wheel of existence is inconceivable.

The second Truth is that of the origin of suffering, which is craving, and this can be threefold. It can be sensual, spiritual or material. Whereas the first is clear, the other two need some explana-tion. Spiritual craving is the desire to be reborn in some state better than the one we now occupy, such as in a heaven; material craving is the outcome of the delusive notion of a more or less real ego which is annihilated at death and which stands in no causal relation with the time before and after death. This craving arises as a result of the senses and consciousness. The doctrine of Dependent Origination may be regarded as a detailed explanation of the second Truth.

The third Truth is the extinction of suffering; thus Nirvāna is pos-sible in this life, for it is the control of greed, hate and delusion. It is the constant cleansing of oneself, even after one has realised one's innate enlightenment, and before it, the dropping of all desires, ideas and notions with which one has filled one's mind and thus created waves on the sea thereof which prevent one from seeing clearly the reflection of the moon of one's true self. When we have utterly discarded all this rubbish we realise the realm where there is neither solid nor fluid, heat, motion, this world nor any other world, sun nor moon. In this state there is neither arising nor passing away, standing still, being born nor dying; neither foothold, development nor basis. This is the end of suffering. There is something that is unborn, unoriginated, uncreated, unformed. If there were not, the realisation of our true nature would not be possible. But we must never cease from meditation—and indeed, Shakyamuni Buddha never ceased from it either—for should we do so, then we shall begin again to fill the pond of the mind with our own ideas and notions, likes and dislikes, and in so doing destroy once more the moon of our true self. It is for this reason that no true trainee ever says that he has understood Buddhism; nor does he say he does not understand it; he simply goes on training himself eternally, always becoming Buddha every moment of his life, which turns, therefore, into every minute enlightenment or every minute Zen. He is neither conscious of it nor unconscious of it. He trains in Buddhism for the sake of Buddhism, just as Shakyamuni Buddha carried his begging bowl and wore his robe every day of his life after his understanding, as well as doing his meditation.

The fourth Truth is the Eightfold Path which leads to the cessation of suffering. Since most people indulge in one of two extremes, either sensual pleasure or self-mortification, suffering exists. Buddha avoided both extremes and found instead the Middle Path that leads to true peace of mind, which is called Nirvāna. Since this Path is explained more fully in the *Kyojūkaimon* later on, I will simply give the names of the so-called steps here: right understanding, right thought, right speech, right action, right livelihood, right effort, right mindfulness and right concentration.

5. ANICCA (Impermanence, Change)

All things change, all life grows old, decays, being ever changing. This doctrine includes the total separation of all moments one from another, leading ultimately to the void of the Scripture of Great Wisdom and Dōgen's "Ūji."

The foregoing doctrines are among the basic teachings of Theravāda, the earlier form of Buddhism. There are many other doctrines and beliefs in early Buddhism which arose either directly out of original Hindu teachings or from some other source, but the foregoing, which are strictly what Shakyamuni Buddha taught, are all that are necessary for the study of Zen.

CHAPTER 3

The Growth of Zen from
Basic Theravāda Doctrine

ZEN HAS BEEN called a transmission outside the scriptures and
this is true, but this does not mean that the scriptures are to be
ignored, especially by the very beginner who knows nothing of Buddhism. In order to understand Zen, one must possess a thorough
knowledge of the basic Theravāda doctrines given in the preceding
chapter, as well as some knowledge of the life history of Shakyamuni
Buddha and the way in which his teachings grew and were ex-
panded into what is now called Mahāyāna Buddhism. Therefore I
am presuming that the reader has thoroughly examined the two previous chapters, and that upon this knowledge we can now build our
study of how Zen thought grew.

But remember that though some Zen scholars have attempted to
explain and defend their position with rational, philosophic argument, they were not looking at Truth with a philosophical eye; theirs
was the heart of faith. To put it more plainly, if you try to understand Zen from a rational, philosophic point of view, no argument is
ever going to be good enough: alternatively, if you try to understand
Zen intuitively, using the heart of faith instead of the argumenta-
tive mind, no explanation of what I am about to say will be necessary.

It follows from this, then, that Zen is an intuitive *religion* and
not a philosophy or a way of life.

Although in this chapter I shall deal largely with philosophical
and religious arguments, these are not the object of Zen. Metaphysics is just so many dead words; to the Zen trainee the only thing
that matters is putting the teachings of the Buddha into practice and
training himself in the same way as he did. Therefore, after this
one chapter, I shall abandon metaphysics and philosophy and go
into the realm of practical application.

In the preceding chapter we examined some of the basic beliefs of Theravāda Buddhism. This earlier form of Buddhism also emphasised the necessity of the trainee's renouncing the world to pursue wholeheartedly the path of the Arahant—one who has cast off home, family, comforts and ordinary life so as to escape the chains of birth and death that bind him to Samsāra, this world of patience, and so gain the complete peace of Nirvāna, irrespective of whether anyone else can follow him. The Theravāda idea was that the Arahant had done everything for others that could be done by giving them a glowing example to follow—in another life, if not in this. How, then, did this body of belief give rise to the ideal of Mahāyāna Buddhism, which taught that the enlightened person should not enter Nirvāna until he can take every blade of grass with him? This is a difficult question to answer. Doubtless national temperaments had something to do with it, but a comparison of the Theravāda and Mahāyāna viewpoints concerning Shakyamuni Buddha gives us the main clues.

The Theravāda Buddhist sees in Shakyamuni a man who cleansed himself utterly from all attachments, a pioneer who discovered the way to escape the sufferings that all beings undergo in transitory existence, and for whom it was natural to take the reward of Nirvāna when he had attained enlightenment. It seems to have escaped their notice that the Buddha remained in the world for forty-five years afterwards for the purpose of helping suffering mankind. The Mahāyāna Buddhist, on the other hand, sees not so much the pioneer as the prince who gave up a life of luxury in order to pursue the discovery that might save all mankind, and did this out of pity for the world and not for the sake of his own peace of mind. In the Mahāyāna view, his willingness to share his great discovery with the world is proof that he truly understood the oneness of all beings and was no longer caught up in the desire for self-enjoyment, as would have been the case had he decided to enter Nirvāna without a thought for others. This true love for the world, which later on I shall call the heart of Fugen, is the hallmark of spiritual perfection. To return to serve all beings with bliss-bestowing hands became the aim of the Bodhisattva—the enlightened person who, having reached Nirvāna, decides not to enter into it until he can take all beings with him. By this it may be seen that the Bodhisattva ideal was exemplified in the life of Shakyamuni Buddha himself and was not, as some Theravādins claim, a later addition to the original doctrine.

But the way that this change of aspiration is explained by the Mahāyānists is most interesting, and touches upon the very basis and core of the teaching of Zen. Among the specifically Mahāyāna sūtras, which were written after the Buddha's death to explain some of his teachings more succinctly and are not recognised by Theravādins, there is one called *The Lotus of the Wonderful Law,* wherein the Buddha is shown as teaching only as much truth at a time as the individual disciple could understand. As each group of disciples developed spiritually, he taught them higher truths. The teachings of Theravāda were for the beginner and those of Mahāyāna for the disciple who had made greater progress. This means that the Buddha was aware of the higher truths—indeed, they were inherent in the early teachings and can be seen in them—but because the disciples were not yet ready for them, they could not yet be fully revealed. It was only to Makakashyo, who smiled upon seeing the flower the Buddha held, that he revealed the highest truth of all, in silence. This intuitional transmission, which was from heart to heart, was in fact outside the scriptures and was the reason that Makakashyo became the first Zen patriarch.

It may be argued that in revealing the Truth only so much at a time, the Buddha was deliberately deceiving his disciples. The *Lotus Sūtra,* however, disproves this in the parable of the householder who had three sons in a burning house. When the sons refused to leave the house for the sake of the great present he had to give them, the father offered them instead the little things that he knew they wanted and so was able to entice them out. Then, when they were safely at the gate, he gave them only the big present that he had for them originally. The parable poses the question, Did he deceive them? The sūtra has this to say:

> Even as that father at first attracted his children by the three carts, and afterwards gave them only a great cart magnificently adorned with precious things and supremely furnished, yet that father is not guilty of falsehood, so also is it with the Tathāgata; there is no falsehood in first preaching Three Vehicles to attract all living creatures and afterwards in saving them by the Great Vehicle only. Where-

fore? Because the Tathāgata possesses infinite wisdom, power, fearlessness, and the treasury of the laws, and is able to give all living creatures the Great Vehicle Law; but not all are able to receive it. Śāriputra! For this reason know that Buddhas, by their adaptability, in the One Vehicle define and expound the Three.*

This idea of "giving only as much food, and of the right kind, as the baby can take" is carried to extremes by Zen Buddhist teachers in Japan, as will be seen from the following chapters.

The Bodhisattva ideal has too often been neglected by students of Zen, especially in the West, where the metaphysical and philosophical as well as mystical elements have attracted people rather more than the deep understanding that service to mankind might be another name for Zen training; therefore, it is important that a few more points be made concerning it. A Bodhisattva is obviously someone who has transcended the opposites of self and other and is no longer concerned about his own salvation. The thing that is difficult to grasp is that he is not *consciously* concerned about the salvation of others, either; he simply does what has to be done for the sake of doing it. I hope to make this clearer as I proceed, for it is a very important point. A Bodhisattva is not just an ordinary do-gooder in the Christian sense of the word. He remains in the world as an ordinary person, devoting himself to leading others gently and compassionately with only as much teaching as they can manage at a time, which may mean nothing more than setting them an example, because it is the natural thing for him to do. But it is more than just setting an example, for he has realised his eternal oneness with all men; he suffers as they suffer without being conscious of a difference between them and himself, although he has himself overcome the causes of suffering. And it is because of this that he continues to train himself endlessly so as to overcome everything that stands in the way of his deepening his oneness with all men; this oneness gives him increased power in their service, including the service of his enemies.

But one question has always puzzled beginners in Buddhism: What is Nirvāna? From the altered viewpoint of the Bodhisattva,

* E. A. Burtt, ed., *The Teachings of the Compassionate Buddha* (New York: New American Library, Mentor Books, 1955), p. 147. Paraphrased slightly.

this question becomes all the more important. If Nirvāna is that state into which one enters after attaining enlightenment, as in the case of the Arahant, what happens to the Bodhisattva who, after all his efforts, deserves it just as much but can never enjoy it because of his compassion for others? Obviously, if the Theravāda view is retained, there can be no Nirvāna for the Buddhas and Bodhisattvas. But as the Bodhisattva proceeds through the stages to Buddhahood, he gradually realises that Nirvāna is a state of mind leading to true spiritual perfection rather than a reward in the hereafter. This state of mind has perhaps best been described by Meister Eckhart: "And a man shall be free, and as pure as the day prior to his conception in his mother's womb, when he has nothing, wants nothing and knows nothing. Such a one has true spiritual poverty." This is when compassionate oneness has so transcended all thought of self that not even the oneness exists. So, just by being a Bodhisattva one is already in Nirvāna, Nirvāna and Samsāra not being two different states of existence. In fact, nothing is outside Nirvāna, and later we shall see that even Nirvāna does not exist. By giving up Nirvāna for the sake of others, one finds oneself in Nirvāna in its true spiritual meaning.

This true spiritual state, then, is the Nirvāna with which Zen is concerned. Although I have always said that Zen represents the closest of the ten Chinese Mahāyāna schools to the original Theravāda, the idea of the Bodhisattva and this altered concept of Nirvāna are a long way from the Theravāda viewpoint. However, the basic doctrines of Theravāda and the Precepts—that is, the teachings of the Buddha himself—remain the same fundamentally, Zen representing an amplification thereof in many ways and the *Kyojūkaimon* being distinctly an extension of the original Precepts.

Certain of the Mahāyāna philosophers, two of whom were direct descendants of Makakashyo, gave reasoned arguments concerning causality and Nirvāna to justify their altered conception in the Mahāyāna ideal. Aśvaghosha, Nāgārjuna, Asanga and Vasubandhu were amongst the most noteworthy of these, but remember that they were men of the spirit and not just men of letters. The intuitive heart of faith is all-important if one wishes to understand what they are trying to convey in words. Their purpose being religious rather than metaphysical, their words were written in order to free energetic intellects from the mental blocks they had set up to bar their own path to spiritual understanding. Nāgārjuna does this by blowing concepts of reason to pieces, and he is willing to do this even with basic Buddhist ideas if they are only concepts, as in the case of Nirvāna. Vasubandhu works on the destruction of physical reality and shatters the concepts of atom and of perceptual qualities, leaving as real only such subjective impressions as can exist in the mind. These metaphysical arguments lead quite naturally to the study of the true nature of mind, which, when realised intuitively, is the intellectual aspect of enlightenment.

That ultimate reality is absolute mind is made clear in certain passages from the *Śūrangama Sūtra*, which poses the following four questions: (1) Where is mind, as functioning through vision, located? (2) If it has no location, how do we determine its reality and nature? (3) To be able to view that which is changing implies a power to view that which is changeless. (4) The power of vision, though changeless, is not, as such, absolute. What, then, is absolute and why?

These theories and metaphysical arguments show how the great Zen patriarchs endeavoured down through the centuries to clarify the nature of reality, the intellectual aspect of enlightenment, which has always been the most intriguing and attractive part of Zen teaching from the Western point of view. But ultimate reality transcends what can be expressed in words. Since universal mind alone is real, one must abandon seeking for anything. This universal mind is realised only by ceasing to search and by discarding all theories, ideas and concepts that one knows and believes in. This is the flash of enlightenment explained in philosophical language; later I will explain how it is done through training. However, even in this moment one must realise that mind itself and the means by which it has been explained are a contradiction in themselves, for the real Truth lies beyond any kind of verbal expression. Shakyamuni Buddha knew this, and this was the reason he never gave answers to certain questions. For the same reason, the Zen teacher will give such answers to a student's questions as will discourage him from asking them altogether. This is to teach him that his difficulty lies in his need to ask questions, which shows that his state of mind is still one that clings to reason. It is this very reason that he must abandon in order to perform the leap to perfect freedom.

This leap requires a trust in the heart—that is, intuition instead of reason—but it does not separate us from the world of the senses. It is simply that, as Shakyamuni Buddha taught, the clear water of the mind has become ruffled by the winds of thought and reason; when we have quietened them we perceive that the Buddha Light has never ceased to shine upon the water. Here again, we are using imagery to express Truth. It is we who threw all the dirt into the water and set up the winds that disturbed it; only we can still the winds and throw out the dirt. But remember that this water image is only a means of representing an inexpressible truth, for the nature of mind must be grasped intuitively and not intellectually. As Hui-nêng so aptly puts it:

> The Bodhi is not like a tree,
> The mind is not a mirror bright;
> Since there is nothing from the first,
> Where can the dust alight?

CHAPTER 4

The Necessity of Zazen, or Meditation Practice

THAT A LIVING CREATURE who is in possession of true faith in Buddhism shall be able to bring to fruition the seed of Buddhahood latent in each and every one of us, three things are necessary. Such a person must realise with his whole being, possess, and exhibit in his daily life:

> The heart of Kanzeon, which is the bringing to fruition of the seed of Great Compassion to be found within us;
> The heart of Fugen, which is the bringing to fruition of the seed of Great Love to be found within us;
> The heart of Monju, which is the bringing to fruition of the seed of Great Wisdom to be found within us.

Only then can that being return to the world with the bliss-bestowing hands of Miroku, the Buddha who is to come. These three, Compassion, Love, Wisdom, are like three great drums which, although silent, thunder nevertheless across the world when our whole being expresses them. These three are the keys to the gateless gate of true freedom, and it is only ourselves that prevent us from unlocking it, for it was in fact never locked. It is only that we, by clinging to our ideas of right and wrong, of good and evil, our likes and dislikes, our prejudices and concepts—in other words, by making choices—have created clouds that hide the brightness of the moon of our true self. When we sweep away these clouds, we discover that the moon has never ceased shining: what prevented us from seeing it was our belief that we were right in our attachment to opinions and that everyone else was wrong. Therefore the first scripture to be recited during morning service in a Zen temple is that of Kanzeon, for Compassion, like a mother, brings forth the child of Wisdom whose father is Love; a love which is non-possessive in the worldly sense and all-embracing in the spiritual. So the first duty of a layman in studying Zen is to find and bring forth the heart of compassion. We will consider first the method of meditation by which this is done, and in the next chapter, the viewpoint that goes to make up the exhibition of the heart of Kanzeon. Most people who wish to study Zen want to start with the philosophical side, but this is wrong. As I said in the previous chapter, the Bodhisattva mind is the first thing to be cultivated by all who wish to study, and in leaving the metaphysical and philosophical side to the very end I am copying Shakyamuni Buddha, in the scripture of *The Lotus of the Wonderful Law,* by giving the trainee only what is good for him at the present time.

Zazen, or seated meditation, teaches the realisation of our true mind, and once one has this realisation, the mind never again changes back to its old state. Remember that this is not an attempt at stilling the mind, for that is an impossibility. It is true that we quieten down the winds of thought by allowing no thought to disturb us, but it is not possible to stop thinking, nor would it be advisable. We simply notice that thoughts arise and that they disappear.

A quiet room in your own home in which you will not be disturbed is the best place to select if you cannot go to a meditation hall. It should not be too bright or too dark, nor too hot or too cold. Generally speaking, it is best to meditate when the body is slightly cool rather than warm. You will need a large square cushion—about two to three feet square—on top of which you will need another smaller round one, about eight inches in diameter and eight inches high, like a ball; if this is not available, use a square cushion doubled up to make it twice its height. Do not wear anything that is tight or constricting in any way. Trousers, socks, tight skirts and other similar articles of clothing are all to be carefully avoided, as is clothing that is too short, such as mini-skirts. The Japanese, both priests and laymen, if they are not wearing special robes, use what is called a *hakama,* a wide pleated skirt with large slits at the sides under which one can place the hands if one is attacked by insects. It allows the legs to be crossed in comfort without any unnecessary constriction of the circulation.

It is, of course, best if one can sit in the lotus position, in which the legs are crossed with each foot placed on top of the opposite thigh, but this is not possible for all people. Some can manage what is called the half-lotus, in which only one foot is placed on top of the opposite thigh; others use what is known as the Burmese position, in which the legs are not crossed but the knees are bent out to either side with one foot placed in front of the other. This last is very much favoured by Western people, who are likely to find the lotus position intolerable after a short time. There are other positions which a good teacher can show one if these are all too painful. It is also possible to use a chair, but remember that if the body becomes tired, it may not be able to keep its stability unless it is sitting on a wide base such as provided by the three positions just described; there is also the danger of swollen feet if they are left dangling for an indefinite period. In teaching Westerners in Sōjiji, I found that although the initial pain of the lotus position is excruciating, it is in the end perhaps worth the effort for the facility it gives later on in sitting for long periods. The secret of training oneself to sit in this position is not to do it for too long a period at first. After all, Zazen is not an endurance test, despite the fact that it seems to have become so in certain Japanese Zen temples. Dōgen Zenji, who brought this method of meditation from China to Japan, expressly warned against excesses of asceticism, saying that Zazen was to be regarded as "the comfortable way." Five minutes a day done properly will lead, in about three to six months, to being able to do twenty to forty minutes not only in comfort but with serenity of mind. One should increase the amount of time gradually and not force the body to do what it is incapable of doing. The result of such forcing is invariably the same: the trainee eventually loses interest in doing Zazen for fear of the pain.

In the beginning the knees will rise of themselves from the cushions and you will have to repeatedly push them down again. This is a non-volitional action due to muscle spasm. I can remember watching my left knee rise from the cushions in Sōjiji despite my using every muscular effort to prevent it. Most teachers realise that this action is involuntary, but there are some who do not and who consequently tend to punish rather than help the trainee. In large Zen temples the trainee is taught the necessity of sitting still by being hit with the kyosaku, or "awakening stick," if he moves. Usually this stick is in the hands of a capable person who realises the possibility of involuntary movements and so does not punish the

offender, but occasionally it finds its way into the hands of a beginner in the disciplinarian's office, with unfortunate results. Be that
as it may, the important thing is to sit as still as possible, and if
one must move, to give up sitting for a few minutes and then go
back to it again. Just as Shakyamuni Buddha gave up unnecessary
asceticism, so must we modern trainees not try to do the impossible.
This does not mean that we do not strive to conquer our bodies—
we do, but gradually and in such a way as to cause the least strain,
for a strained body leads to a strained mind.

Having settled the legs comfortably, place the left hand, palm
upward, in the right with the thumbs touching each other lightly
so that the two hands together look like a slightly flattened oval.
This is the procedure for a right-handed person, the purpose being
to repress the active side of the body with the passive; a left-handed
person would place his left hand in his right. Opinions differ with
regard to this, but I have found, at least for Westerners, that it is
the best practice to follow. Since one wishes to gain the highest degree of tranquillity possible, the more active side of the body must
be tranquillised by the opposite one.

The most important physical thing to remember is that the spine
must at all times be erect. This does not mean a stiff erectness, which
indicates pride and is as much to be avoided as a sloppy posture,
indicating dejection. The state of the body shows the state of the
mind, and obviously neither pride nor dejection is the proper frame
of mind in which to do Zazen. Make sure that the small round
cushion is only under the tip of the spine at the back, and bend
the body forward so as to position the buttocks correctly; then
sway from side to side, beginning with large swings and ending
with small ones, seven or eight times, rather like a pendulum finding its place of rest, until your body positions itself automatically
in its natural erectness. This should have the effect of making the
body completely weightless from the waist up. The ears and the
shoulders should be in one straight line and the nose in a straight
line with the navel. The mouth must be closed with the tip of
the tongue lightly touching the top of the mouth behind the teeth.
The eyes must be open, since to close them encourages sleep,
dreaminess and sometimes hypnosis. Since the last-named is completely incompatible with Zen meditation, it is to be absolutely dis-

couraged. The eyes should be lowered, not focussing on anything in particular, but resting on a point on the ground that is natural for the range of vision of the trainee concerned. I have heard it said that this must be at least three feet away, but since some of us are longsighted and others shortsighted, it is not possible to lay down a firm rule on exact distance. Just allow the eyes to rest naturally on a spot on the ground a short distance from the body, thus causing them to be automatically lowered but not closed; this will prevent both eyestrain and fatigue. Also, be sure that the head is erect at all times and that you breathe quite naturally through the nose. The spine must stay absolutely erect, since if it slumps, the digestive and other functions will be interfered with, resulting in trouble of mind as well as discomfort of body, not to mention a painful back. You should sit facing a wall or curtain, as this will prevent your mind from dwelling on the beauty of the scenery or on objects in the room. Do not focus your attention on anything, least of all on folds in the curtain or knots or cracks in the wall. This last happened to one of my trainees to such an extent that he could not sleep at night for fear of seeing the huge knot opening up and swallowing him.

When you are completely comfortable, take two or three deep breaths. Both inhalation and exhalation should be slow and taken through the nose. This will tend to quieten your mind and allow your breathing to settle down quite naturally. For the purpose of learning concentration at this early stage, the best training is to work on counting incoming and outgoing breaths. This will help keep out thoughts of a reasoning nature and point the mind in one direction only; it will also begin to calm down the thought-waves. Under no circumstances go further than ten in your counting. When you reach this number, start from the beginning and go up to ten again. At first, count both inhalations and exhalations; then as your power of concentration grows, count only inhalations. Thoughts will, in fact, run through your mind, but will do you no harm so long as you do not try to hold on to them or to push them away. Many people still think that Zazen is a means of stopping all conscious thought; although some schools of Yoga do actually aim at this, it is not the purpose of Zen meditation. You cannot stop hearing things, and you cannot stop seeing them if they are within your range of vision; they will form thought-patterns in your mind however much you work on counting your breaths. This will not impede you in the least unless you try to analyse these patterns and so set up discrimination, which will again set the waves of thought going in your head. You must understand that none of these things are, in themselves, obstructions to Zazen. Many people misunderstand this and so set up mental blocks which are hard to get rid of. Just concentrate on your breath counting and do not worry about stray thoughts, words, sounds and sights. It is advisable not to sit too close to the wall or too far away from it: two or three feet is a good distance. Natural sounds, such as those of birds, insects and water, and the sounds of mechanical motors will not bother you in the least, but human voices, radios and the like can be very distracting even to experienced sitters, so choose a place that is far from such noises. When in Malaysia I was unable to find a single temple where I was not constantly disturbed by such noises, which were usually very loud. All were unsuitable for meditation, at least for people who had not been sitting for several years. Of course, it is possible to get to a state where no noises whatsoever distract one, but this is not the case at the stage of which I am writing.

It goes without saying that the room in which one sits must be clean and tidy and preferably contain flowers and incense. Zazen should never be done in bed unless one is a bedridden invalid, since the psychological approach is then all wrong. The ideas of cleanliness, purity and freshness are all-important in Zazen practice, and the above-mentioned things tend towards this. I personally find that I do my best Zazen after bathing, for then I am freshest. However, when I was in Sōjiji it was not possible for priests in their junior years to have a bath more often than once every five days, according to the rules, and still they had to do their Zazen every day. Since I was a woman and, during my junior years, the women's bathroom had not yet been built, I frequently had to do without a bath for as long as two months, which has proved to me that although personal freshness is a definite aid to meditation, it is not absolutely essential. The present-day trainees in Sōjiji are much more fortunate, for there are now large modern bathrooms for both men and women and the old rule is no longer so strictly enforced. The important thing is to make yourself as clean and tidy as you possibly can under the circumstances and not to wear nightclothes or anything dirty. Since man is body and mind, purity of body goes a long way towards making purity of mind.

The best times to do Zazen are just before dawn and just before dusk, but these times are not available to all people. A dark curtain, or a small light in a dark room, can create the same effect as these times of day. If I were asked which time is best I would definitely say early morning, for the mind is then freshly awakened from sleep, clear, bright and well rested. There is also less probability of disturbance, since few people are early risers. Any time before a meal is a good time, but you should never practise sitting after one for at least half an hour, as it is important to allow the digestive processes to work naturally.

If you practise regularly for only five or ten minutes a day, without straining your body, you will soon want to extend the time you spend in sitting because of the increased feeling of bodily health as well as the great peace of mind you will enjoy. Once you begin to experience bodily discomfort, stop sitting; otherwise you will grow tired of doing Zazen and come to dread the time when you think you should be doing it. I myself have experienced this and know what it can be like when one is forced to sit by some over-zealous "teacher." It was only a supreme effort of will on my part which made me continue—and a change of the so-called teacher! The average layman, not being in an actual monastery, is not perhaps going to have either the same incentive or the same will-power. Even in a big monastery, one does not normally sit for longer than forty-five minutes at a time without a short break. This is because the strain of keeping the mind taut in the beginning is very great, and this lessens the value of the actual sitting. Five to ten minutes done really well is worth a whole day done badly.

The usual system, after sitting for about forty minutes, is to do *kinhin*, which is a form of walking meditation, or some work such as gardening or cleaning the house, still keeping one's mind in the same tautness and in silence. According to legend, this type of walking meditation was done by Shakyamuni Buddha himself when he spent one day after his enlightenment walking round the Bodhi tree. Here again, Zen is trying to emulate the ancient system of Shakyamuni Buddha. If one does follow a system of so much sitting, so much walking and so much work, it is possible to do "everlasting Zazen" in such a way that one finds the meditation hall is with one wherever one goes. This, in fact, is the aim of the ancient system of Zen training, and the reason for the numerous activities which many Western people decry as not being in the spirit of, or being a hindrance to, meditation. Dōgen Zenji himself said the same thing to the cook-priest whom he met on the ship on his way to Mount T'ien-tung in China, and was roundly scolded by the old Chinese for "not beginning to understand the aim and purpose of Buddhism" (see Book II, "Tenzokyokan"). The conversation ended with the old man telling Dōgen to come to Mount T'ien-tung and learn it. In the next chapter I will explain how manual work helps to cleanse the mind of its impurities and bring about the change of heart that is essential for spiritual growth.

Do not eat too much: I cannot stress this too strongly. Dōgen Zenji taught that one should eat only two-thirds of one's capacity, and that it should be all vegetable since meat leaves acid in the blood which is not good for the body. From his writings, I do not doubt that he would have used most of the vegetables to be found in the West today; however, he recommends that oil, which is heating to the blood, be avoided since the body must be cool, and also onions and garlic, which tend to act as an aphrodisiac when one is meditating. Since the aim is to still the waves of thought as much as possible, obviously pains from acid indigestion and discomfort from overheated blood and sexual desire are to be avoided at all costs. These three foods—meat, oil of the variety employed in fried foods, and onions—as well as alcohol are therefore taboo in all the really good training temples in Japan at the present time. One can, however, take milk and similar products in moderate quantities.

Whilst on the subject of food, I should perhaps say there is a theory that wrong eating can cause the hallucinations and visions which sometimes beset people in training. These phenomena are called in Japanese *makyo*, or "devils of the objective world," but I am not at all sure if bad eating does cause them. Opinions differ. All the authorities agree, however, that they can be caused by bad sitting and incorrect breathing. Dōgen Zenji himself, in his writings on Zazen practice describes how the body may feel hot or cold, glasslike and hard, heavy or light, if the breathing is not well harmonised with the mind. He also says that one may experience sensations of sinking or floating, feel hazy or alert; seem able to see through solid objects as if they were transparent; or perceive one's body as a translucent substance. One may also see Buddhas and holy beings, receive penetrating insights or suddenly understand difficult passages of the scriptures, but all these abnormalities are simply a proof of not having properly harmonised one's breathing with one's mind. If not regulated early, they may turn into such things as visions of gods, sounds of heavenly voices, or miracles seemingly worked by oneself, which to some may be desirable but to a Zen trainee are only proof that he has got himself caught up in *gedō* Zen, the second and more dangerous stage of meditation through which all must pass. Although such phenomena may produce a feeling of well-being in their own way, they should be understood only as figments of an overstrained mind and thus not truly religious. We have had proof of this in the faith-healers who have abounded in the world from time to time; the miracles of Christ are just another example of what can be done with advanced gedō Zen. In principle, anyone who can get someone else to have sufficient faith in his powers of healing can work miracles. Miracle-working and mass hallucination are indeed by no means unknown or uncommon in Zen, there being many stories of miracles performed by the Zen priesthood. But the Zen trainee passes such things by, setting no store by them although he may be able to do them, for he knows they are morbid states of the imagination of others and nothing more. They are no better than dreams which vanish for ever on awakening. To hold on to them is to become a prey to superstition. Too much asceticism can cause visions also, as I know to my own cost. Anything that causes the body to live abnormally is likely to result in a corresponding psychological state. This explains how some Christian saints, after rigorous ascetic practices, have had visions of God and angels. This did not mean they were any nearer heaven, but simply that they had punished their bodies excessively and their minds were creating a balance to make them stop. Their minds were simply giving them the sort of images they wanted to see. Shakyamuni Buddha tried asceticism in the beginning and called the visions that beset him "obstructing devils." It was only after he abandoned these excesses and just sat that he realised the Truth. The hallucination of Christ's disciples after the Crucifixion, who saw Christ "risen from the dead," as they thought, is easily explained by the overwrought state of their minds at the time. In fact, this type of mass hallucination is quite well known in Eastern religious circles, being nothing out of the ordinary. The danger comes when we attach importance to such things. So if makyo appear, just ignore them, correct the faults in your sitting, breathing and mode of life as much as you possibly can, and then continue to do your Zazen as if nothing had happened. If once you think that you are becoming holy as a result of visions, all progress will stop completely.

When ending your period of Zazen, rest your hands, palms upward, on your knees and sway from side to side in the opposite way from what you did when you first sat down—that is, begin with small movements and end with large ones, seven or eight times. Get up slowly and gently and commence to do your kinhin. Begin by making a fist of the left hand, with the thumb inside, and covering it with the right hand. The hands should not be held tightly against the chest wall; instead the arms, held loosely, should form an oval at the level of the chest, with the elbows extended. The body must always be erect with the eyes still in their naturally lowered position, not closed nor looking too far ahead of the feet. Continue to count your breaths as you walk, beginning with the left foot. Walk calmly and slowly, with great dignity. Do not walk absent-mindedly. A step of not more than six inches at a time should be taken. Walk first on the heel and then along the side of the foot, ending upon the toes, so that the foot digs itself into the ground, as it were. This is done for five to ten minutes after each period of thirty to forty minutes' sitting. Remember that this is moving Zazen; it is not done for the purpose of stretching the legs, as some people think. This completes the actual explanation of the physical side of Zazen. In the next chapter I will speak of the mental attitude to be cultivated by the beginner.

CHAPTER 5

The Necessity of Understanding the Heart of Kanzeon

AT THE BEGINNING of Chapter 4 I said that it was necessary for a layman to find and bring forth the heart of compassion, and I then went into the physical method of doing meditation for this purpose. Now I want to talk about the mental attitude to be adopted in daily life, as well as in Zazen, for this same purpose.

In the *Kanzeon Sūtra* there is the following passage: "Mujinni Bosatsu said to the Buddha, 'World-honoured One, how does Kanzeon visit this world of patience? How does he preach the Dharma to all beings? What is the extent of his skilful means?' The Buddha said to Mujinni Bosatsu, 'O good man, if there are beings in any country who are to be saved by Kanzeon's assuming any form from that of a Buddha down to that of a human, animal or devil, Kanzeon will manifest in the form of such a being and preach them the Dharma.'"

Originally, in India, Kanzeon was called Avalokiteśvara and was definitely male, but on being brought to China, the concept of Kanzeon, or Kannon, became female. Instead of being the idea of the seed of compassion within each and every one of us, Kanzeon became the goddess of mercy. How did this come about? The answer lies in the fact that the Chinese found Buddhism, in its early form, not suitable for spreading among the masses as a means of salvation, presupposing as it did the perfection of the individual rather than salvation for all. With the growth of the Mahāyāna ideal, new sūtras were written to expand the old doctrines, and the Mahāyāna ideal itself became embodied in the cosmic Buddha Amitābha and the compassionate Bodhisattvas, especially Kanzeon. It is believed that Amitābha, or Amida, achieved Buddhahood on condition that all who sincerely call on his name shall go, at death, into his Western Paradise, where they will continue to liberate themselves under more encouraging and happier circumstances than they enjoyed on earth.

In other words, Shakyamuni Buddha was no longer thought of as a historical figure but as one incarnation of a transcendent cosmic reality, Buddha Nature, which is working at all times and in all worlds for the salvation of all sentient beings. Amida became the celestial example of Buddhahood. Kanzeon, the all-merciful, became the goddess who helped to guide the faithful on their road to the Pure Land of the Western Paradise. From this it will be seen that whereas Pure Land, or Shin Buddhism as it is called in Japan, tends more towards the devotional attitude of faith, the Zen attitude is one of intuitive knowledge of the existence within oneself of the Buddha Nature. For Zen, Kanzeon remained an image embodying the characteristics of mercy and compassion which the Zen trainee must find within himself, a seed which he must fertilise and cultivate to good growth through Zazen. There is room in the world for both viewpoints, the devotional and pietistic and the intuitive, although I have heard it said by some that Pure Land and Zen are incompatible. My own view is that in the deeply spiritual knowledge of religion, they represent opposite ends of the same tunnel, and that according to one's temperament and character, one goes in at the entrance of one's own choice. Although they are externally very different, it is impossible to say which end of the tunnel is the right one, since this can only be decided by the individual concerned. At all events Zen temples do not recite the *Amida Sūtra,* but they do recite the *Kanzeon Sūtra* for the purpose of cultivating the seed of compassion in the trainee.

The statues of Kanzeon in Japan appear female until, on looking at them closely, one realises that they are neither male nor female but something which is beyond both. This is because if someone truly realises the heart of Kanzeon, he becomes a new creature, beyond the opposites of male and female, right and wrong. Therefore in every large Zen temple there are two meditation halls, one for laymen and one for *unsui,* a word which translates as "Zen trainees." The statue in the laymen's meditation hall is that of Kanzeon, for laymen have not as yet learned to transcend duality and, until they reach the heart of Kanzeon, are still in the world of patience where the opposites of male and female, right and wrong, exist. The statue in the unsui meditation hall is that of Monju, Great Wisdom, and those who enter there are no longer conscious of male and female, right and wrong, like and dislike. They are unsui, free as the clouds and strong and gentle as water, with the determination of both to wander across the universe in search of truth and wisdom, swirling all obstacles from their path as they go, for they have undergone true rebirth.

When a layman arrives to study, he is taken to the laymen's meditation hall and shown the statue. He is told that he must become like Kanzeon Bodhisattva whom it represents: all-compassionate, all-seeing, all-helpful. Just as the statue has a thousand arms to help in all places at once and a thousand eyes to see where the help is needed, so the lay student must search within himself for a means to benefit mankind throughout the world. He must find within himself the strength of a thousand arms and the sight of a thousand eyes. He must so cleanse his heart that no attachment to anything of his old selfish self remains, and he does this by the power and training of the meditation I described in the previous chapter. But he must not train for the sake of helping others only, nor for the sake of helping himself; he must train just for training's sake and nothing more. In some ways this type of meditation could be called brainwashing, for it is a constant criticism of oneself in the minutest details, but it is brainwashing with the difference that it is done by one's own wish and not by that of another.

The motive for coming to a Zen temple is all-important. It was Shakyamuni Buddha's love for the world that made him go in search of the cause of suffering, old age, decay and death; and at a later date he trained simply for training's sake, albeit in the service of mankind. Those who wish to study Zen should consider this point carefully. The purpose of Zazen is *not* to think about gaining anything; this will become clearer as I progress. Shakyamuni Buddha had already found the heart of Kanzeon prior to setting out on his journey. He was, in fact, already half-enlightened. Too many people nowadays want to study Zen solely for the benefit of themselves, and without the Bodhisattva mind, which is the heart of Kanzeon and Fugen, they will never achieve it. All the pictures of the East warn that this is so, if one has the eyes to see them clearly. Always Kanzeon appears as a mother pouring out the waters of mercy upon the sea of the world, and behind her walks her little son, Miroku, the Buddha who is to come. Those who seek only wisdom and are unwilling to seek for the heart of Kanzeon will never find either, for their basic motive is selfish.

It is for this reason, then, that a Zen student must first find his true heart, the heart of Kanzeon, before he can be allowed to enter the great meditation hall of the unsui. He will be expected to meditate from three in the morning until nine at night; he will be watched minutely and his slightest action regulated. Since he must be of impeccable moral character, the smallest infringement of the Precepts will bring down strict censure. But all meditation is not just sitting. If one places one's slippers correctly—and this is the first thing to be taught a newcomer to a temple—it becomes a form of meditation. Slippers must be placed neatly together, with their backs to the door, so that they do not offend the eyes of others or get in their way when entering and leaving the room. This is the first attitude of mind to be cultivated: the thought of order, tidiness and other people's comfort. The small ceremony performed by oneself prior to bathing has the same purpose. The words of the prayer are, "I am about to cleanse my body; I pray that I may cleanse my heart." When the bath is over the prayer becomes, "I have cleansed my body, I must work hard to cleanse my heart." In the bathroom itself strict rules govern the folding and placing of the clothes on the necessary rails and shelves; they must be folded so as not to to offend anyone's sight and so as not to occupy too much room, lest there be no room for others. No soap must be used in the bath, since it is communal, and no towel or face-cloth is allowed to be placed in the water. All washing must be done at a separate washing place outside the bath, in a special position, and the water disposed of in such a way that it does not soil the feet of others. Only then may the actual bath be entered. When in the bath one must sit in the Zazen position with one's washcloth upon one's head so that it will not be in others' way. All bathing, like everything else, is done in silence since one must consider that others are working hard on cleansing their own hearts and do not wish to be disturbed by idle chatter. There is a special small ceremony prior to the use of the lavatory, and also one after it; a special position of the body must be used, not the conventional one, so as to remind one that all habits of mind and body must be changed completely if one is to understand the Truth of Zen. One must make no noise in walking, and stand and sit in attitudes that are neither arrogant nor disrespectful to others. One must sleep on one's right side, with one's head on a meditation cushion instead of a pillow, and the coverlet must be tied with two strings round one's body, lest during the night someone in the meditation hall should awaken and be disgusted by the sight of a body in an unsightly position or partially uncovered. Since all sleep in the meditation hall together, this is a wise precaution. The *tenkien,* or senior on night duty, who walks around the meditation hall with a lantern to make certain that all is well, carries a kyosaku and is empowered to thrash any sleeper who is uncovered or partially uncovered during the night. This is one of the strictest rules of the temple.

The prayer before meals also reveals the Zen idea of considering others rather than oneself (see Book II, "Fushukuhampō"). When the eating is over—and it must be done in silence so that all may consider the necessity of eating as explained in the prayer—the washing-up water is passed round. Each trainee must wash up in his own bowl and later make an offering of the washing-up water by drinking it whilst reciting in his mind the prayer, "I am going to give this water to the hungry ghosts so that they too may be filled." So nothing is left; the bowls are polished clean, reminding the trainee that just as the bowl is immaculate, with nothing left in it, so must he himself become. The bowl from which one eats, which is also the begging bowl, is called "the round head of the priest" in Zen terminology, and it must always be pure and immaculate, empty of all defilement. Meal taking is a very important thing in Zen: within it can be found all the teaching of Zen Truth. The housework must be done in the same spirit. One does not think only about cleaning one's own living space but helps all others to clean theirs, for the mind is such that he who cleans up for himself alone is selfish; one takes the Bodhisattva vow for all other beings as well. The garden is cleaned and tended in the same way, and periods of meditation in the meditation hall are interspersed with manual labour in the garden, kitchen and house. These periods must not be regarded as chores but as a means of doing moving meditation. The chief cook and his assistants must live and think in such a way that they can see the Buddha Body in a stalk of cabbage and cherish it just as much when handling it in their cooking. He who regards anything as clean or unclean, holy or unholy, is still in the realm of the opposites and thus very far from the Zen way of life. Herein lies a grave difficulty for the beginner who understands that one must work hard to reach immaculacy of mind and then is shocked out of it by a teacher who does some wicked act so as to teach him not to cling even to immaculacy. In order to teach his pupils, friends and acquaintances, a teacher will often resort to strange and even fantastic methods, appearing sometimes unreasonable, angry, grumbling, cajoling, dishonest or even mad. Whenever the teacher behaves strangely, one must remember that he is holding a mirror in front of the person being taught; that person should study himself carefully and not criticise the teacher, however bewildering and worldly his behaviour may seem. If he is licenced to teach, he knows what he is doing. Dōgen Zenji does not tell us this much in words, but from the many references in his writings and especially from his "Tenzokyokan," or "Instructions to the Chief Cook," I strongly suspect that he got far more understanding from his wanderings near or work in the kitchen than from a good many other places. Some Zenists even go so far as to say that the monastery's under-standing of Zen can always be tested by a careful study of the chief cook, whose character must be so kaleidoscopic as to be able to embrace all Buddhism in a grain of rice. Doing one's washing is another important thing for a Zen trainee. Here it is very obvious that cleaning up one's own dirt is synonymous with throwing out the stupid ideas and notions that one has in one's head. Mending clothes, tidying oneself up and shaving heads each have their own appropriate spiritual meanings within the same scheme of thought. Thus every aspect of life is made into a meditation on how to think of others and purify oneself. Each one of us also has something that he must cure—a secret vice, a rasping voice, heavy footfalls, unsightly dress; anything that can offend others must be carefully attended to. Never for a moment must one consider oneself only.

In the beginning one concentrates on counting one's breaths when meditating, but later, as problems present themselves, such as pains in the legs and other portions of the body, sights that may be disturb-ing, and sounds that distract, one must learn to deal with them by neither trying to hold on to them nor to thrust them away. One should simply observe that they arise and disappear.

Gradually the trainee will become aware that his powers of concentration are growing, and the peace within him will deepen. He will begin to ask questions as to what Kanzeon is and how she actually appears. He will realise that Kanzeons do not always appear as ladies in white dresses but sometimes as judges who punish to make one better, doctors who employ a knife which is painful in order to cure, teachers who are cruel to be kind to their pupils. The true meaning of compassion is often misunderstood.

Many people also misunderstand the role of the *inō* priest, or disciplinarian, whose thankless job it is to see that the temple rules are kept and to mete out punishment to all offenders, however slight their offences. He also has the job of beating all trainees twice a month with his kyosaku to encourage them to greater efforts and to teach them that praise and blame are but two sides of the same coin. He is the embodiment of the saying, "The kindest Kanzeon is to be found in hell." Do not misunderstand the use of the words *heaven* and *hell*; both places are here and now and of our own creation. Gradually, as the trainee's meditation deepens, he will discover that it is a joy to be alive and that all people, irrespective of colour, race, sex or religion, always have been and always will be one. When this moment comes, right and wrong, male and female, like and dislike will cease to exist, and he will find himself bathed in a joy that seems to fill the universe. From this point there is neither self nor other, and he trains for training's sake.

Without realising it, the trainee will have become the living incarnation of Kanzeon and proved the truth of the scripture that says Kanzeon can be seen in any form from that of a Buddha to that of a human, animal or devil. He will have been reborn in heaven upon earth, and that heaven will always be with him, for it is in fact his own discovery and his own creation.

CHAPTER 6

Activity in the Heart
of Fugen

UP TO NOW it has been possible to write of things that are easily comprehensible to the ordinary mind, for the reaching of the passive state, described in the preceding chapter as the heart of Kanzeon, can be understood without difficulty as a sign of spirituality, and indeed, for some people spirituality need go no further. If it does, it is not spirituality to the minds of some. This is because the world does not clearly understand the true meaning of the words *activity* and *stillness*. Spirituality might be described as activity in stillness or stillness in activity. Let me make this clearer. Just to be passively peaceful and serene may be very nice for the person concerned, but it is not particularly useful to anyone else, except perhaps as an example of what can be achieved with self-discipline. From the Zen point of view something more practical must take place, which I call passive activity, and this is extraordinarily difficult to describe.

If we are truly to fulfil the Bodhisattva vow, we must do something more practical than be passive about everything; we must exhibit dynamic activity in the way we teach others, and this dynamic activity is often very painful to the pupil. This is because the Zen mind, if it has truly understood the heart of Kanzeon, compassion, and the heart of Fugen, love, is going to think quite differently from the way the world thinks, and it is also going to behave quite differently. This strange behaviour has often acquired Zen teachers bad characters, bad reputations and many difficulties, but if the teacher is a true one, he will accept all of this simply because he knows that what he did was done from the standpoint of no-self for the purpose of teaching others.

It follows logically from this that the pupil must have absolute faith in the teacher, for otherwise he will always be criticising his actions in his own mind and will not be able to develop the trust between master and pupil which is absolutely essential before transmission can occur. It also means that he must study very carefully the true meaning of the words *love* and *compassion*. Compassion means to be merciful, but true mercy does not necessarily wear a white dress and look like a beautiful lady, as I said before; nor does its active side, love, necessarily express itself in gentle action. Every doctor knows that when patients are suffering from hysteria it is better to slap them than to make a fuss over them; this is not cruelty but kindness. The Zen teacher is in the same position as the doctor in this respect. He must first diagnose the spiritual "illness" from the trainee's questions and then administer the cure for it, and he will not be gentle in the way he does it. Obviously, then, without blind faith in the teacher the pupil will get nowhere. The teacher, for his part, must put up with the bad reputation he acquires, including accusations of ill-treatment, since this is the logical karmic consequence of his own actions, despite the fact that he was doing what he did for the benefit of others. It is this fact alone that makes what may seem a right action into a wrong one and a wrong one into a right one. For the teacher understands the doctrines of anicca (change) and anattā (no separative self), and from the former he knows that what may be right now will be wrong later on, and again at a later date right again. This swing of the pendulum is often misunderstood by the worldly mind; I have known students completely bewildered and even driven away from the study of Zen because they could not understand the two-facedness—as it seemed to them—of the teacher who one minute said one thing and the next its exact opposite, and who sometimes imputed things to the student that he had never said or done and literally turned black into white and then back into black again. It is easier for an Oriental to get away with this kind of teaching than it is for a Western teacher. Whereas the average Western student will accept two-facedness from an Oriental, whitewashing the contradiction with the thought that it is inexplicable and part of the mysterious East, when faced with the same behaviour in a Western teacher he has no way of rationalising it and so ends up either hating and distrusting the teacher or walking completely out of Zen. If he took the trouble to look a little harder at the problem, he would realise that for an Oriental student with an Oriental teacher the problem is exactly the same, with this difference: the Oriental student does not try to rationalise the behaviour of his teacher; he simply accepts it, however irrational it may seem to him. The Western student, with his sharpened critical faculties, has great difficulty in trusting a teacher to this extent and so is hardly ever capable of surmounting the problem. But if the student from the West is seeking true religion and not Eastern mysticism and culture, he must learn to trust his teacher completely, for the teacher is seeing beyond the opposites to the true heart of the matter; that others cannot see this heart as clearly as he can is a source of grief to him and he wishes deeply that they may share with him the joy of knowledge and true freedom. The lot of a Zen teacher is an extremely lonely one, and he is often forced to grieve very deeply, not for himself but for the misunderstanding of others.

In the *Denkoroku*, or *Book of the Transmission* (see Book III), which is simply the explanation of how the Truth was transmitted from patriarch to patriarch in the Buddhist apostolic line, each individual patriarch had a besetting fault—or sin, as a Christian would call it. As one reads the book through, one gradually discovers that the patriarchs were no better and no worse than present-day people; yet all of them trusted their teachers implicitly once they had found them. Each patriarch represents a type of person to be found in the world at the present time. In one respect almost all Westerners come under the same category as the second Indian patriarch, Ananda, in that they love argument and are proud of their erudition. As a warning to my fellow Westerners I would like to point out that it took Ananda almost five times as long as it took anybody else to realise the Truth of Zen simply because of his clinging to books and knowledge. Keizan Zenji, who wrote the *Book of the Transmission* early in the thirteenth century, says the following therein:

> I know well that the very Truth is not in the clever and the erudite, nor is it in those who gain worldly rank. This is the proof. Ananda followed Makakashyo as a servant for twenty years [before enlightenment]. He was born on the same night that the Lord [Shakyamuni Buddha] was enlightened. . . . he liked erudition and, because of it, was not enlightened. Shakyamuni Buddha, however, concentrated his mind and so was enlightened. I know well that erudition dis-

turbs enlightenment; this is the proof. Therefore the following saying is in the *Kegon Sūtra*: "A poor man who counts another's treasure cannot have his own. Erudition is like this." If you wish to understand the Truth really, you should not like erudition. Concentrate your mind hard.

Ananda was always thinking there must be something other than the *kesa*, or monk's robe, that was given at the transmission. There *had* to be something mysterious—just giving a kesa was too ordinary. Keizan continues:

> The Truth cannot be gained by erudition. Although a person is clever and has sharp ears and can understand every (Chinese) character in the sūtras and doctrines, he is counting another's treasure if he cannot understand their real meaning. This is not because there is no meaning in the sūtras and doctrines. . . . Therefore, in Japan they understand the meaning of the sūtras by words and so they cannot understand fully. Of course, the Truth should be thought of sincerely. If Ananda as the disciple of Buddha could understand the sūtras and doctrines of the Lord, who is unable to follow? However, after spending many years as the servant of Makakashyo and being enlightened, he repeated the sūtras and doctrines. We should know this. If you want to become one with the Truth, as one fire combines with another fire, throw away selfish opinions, old emotions, arrogance and obstinacy, and learn the true mind of the Lord with the naive mind of a child. . . . You yourself are the manifestation of Truth. If you can realise Truth you disappear at once. As this is so, we should not look for it outside ourselves.

Because of this solemn warning I have eschewed erudition as much as possible in this book. All those of my readers who love book-learning are earnestly advised to take the comments of Keizan to heart, for these are far truer than they will ever realise this side of Zen understanding.

To make all the foregoing clear, it would be appropriate for me to do what other writers on Zen have done and quote stories of the Zen teachers of old to prove my various points, but any intelligent reader can get the appropriate books and work out this side of Zen for himself. Concerning the people who criticise the actions of teachers, I have this to say. Zen teachers are excellent actors; they have to be. They can give an extremely convincing and accomplished performance, even to the extent of changing colour when simulating anger, without being agitated in the slightest within themselves. Just as the ocean is undisturbed in its depths by the storms that sweep its surface and create gigantic waves, so is the heart of the licenced and trained Zen teacher. Students who suffer from the notion that such a teacher is exhibiting emotionalism had best plumb the depth of their own emotions before criticising the mirror that the teacher is holding up before them, for just as the mirror is undisturbed by the reflection upon its surface, so is the Zen teacher undisturbed by the reflection in his actions of what the students are exhibiting in front of him.

Now it is extremely difficult, even after reaching the stage of understanding compassion, for a trainee to reach the point where he can exhibit the correct behavioural traits of a teacher. This is because in reaching the stage of compassion, he has been, as it were, climbing up a side-branch of the tree rather than the main trunk. He has reached passivity, which all can comprehend; hereafter he must swing to the opposite branch, activity. The way in which a trainee is forced to make the change is again somewhat cruel to the ordinary thinking mind. When one is given the kyosaku to carry, not just for routine purposes of serving as *jikidō*, or monitor, in the meditation hall, but as a junior teacher, one knows it has been decided that it is time for one to learn to become active. Many people find it almost impossible to use the kyosaku for some time after being handed it, for it is now their duty to be cruel to others in order to be kind. In some Zen temples there is a picture of a trainee being thrashed with the title, "Deeds of the Utmost Kindness." In the religious sense this is true, but looked at with the discriminating mind it appears cruel. To put him in charge of a bunch of raw trainees is another way of teaching activity to the third-stage trainee, who can then no longer sit as he wishes in the meditation hall; he has to learn to find that meditation hall just as much in hell as in heaven. So both the trainees and the teacher are always being taught; this is one of the meanings of "endless training," or training for training's sake.

At this stage—and indeed, at most of the others—the teacher's task is a thankless one. Since a true Zen teacher is in any case beyond the necessity of thanks, this does not much matter, but those who wish to study Zen should consider this point well, for they are likely to acquire a bad character from those who misunderstand what they are trying to do when giving genuine teaching. If the trainees on whom they practise have not complete faith in them, they may well find themselves with a bad reputation. If they are true teachers this will not worry them in the least. Since Shakyamuni Buddha was content with only a tree under which to live and nothing more, he could teach as he wished; once one requires the financial support of others, limitations are placed upon one's teaching methods. The "Shushōgi," the most popular of all the Zen scriptures in Japan, has this to say: "When you meet a Zen master who teaches the Truth, do not consider his caste, his appearance, shortcomings or behaviour. Bow before him out of respect for his wisdom and do nothing whatsoever to worry him."

It is said that there is plenty of room at the top of the tree of fame, and there is certainly plenty of room in the rarefied air of fourth-stage and fifth-stage meditation. Few indeed are those who have the courage to complete their training and fearlessly cast off both friends and enemies for the sake of giving true teaching. Also, to shock a person out of the passivity of the third stage of compassion, which is in some ways akin to madness or living death, can be not only difficult but dangerous since one is, so to speak, resurrecting him. This stage, which is that of many priests and some laymen, is so comfortable and enjoyable that it does not seem possible that there could be anything better. Yet there is a greater experience, and a joy and freedom beyond the powers of imagination.

The true teacher can tell when the trainee has reached the heart of Fugen by watching his actions and his reactions to the situations the teacher is bound to create as a result of his teaching methods, and the proof of whether the trainee truly loves mankind with the heart of Fugen is given when, in the face of all opposition, distrust and misunderstanding, he is willing to carry on in the path that he has chosen, truly caring nothing for material things, fame, fortune, reputation, honour, life or death. The person who thinks that a teacher can tell by just looking at a trainee whether or not he has had a realisation of the Truth is completely mistaken; the only way any teacher can tell if a change has taken place in one whom he is training is by observing that change over a long period of time. Teachers are not sorcerers, they are human beings, and those who go around imputing almost magical powers to Zen masters deserve a sound box on the ears for doing a grave disservice to a great, deep and wonderful religion.

CHAPTER 7

The Heart of Monju

WHEN SHAKYAMUNI BUDDHA saw the morning star and realised the Truth, he uttered the following words: "I am enlightened, and always have been, simultaneously with the beginning of the universe." This saying has not received enough attention from those who would study Zen, and yet it is all-important, for within it lies one of the greatest of all clues to understanding Buddhism.

When I first asked my former master how to go about my studies, he told me quite simply, "Expect nothing, seek nothing, just live." This, to someone who had travelled round the world in order to study, did not seem at the time an adequate answer; yet my master spoke nothing more than the literal truth. The analytical and critical mind of Western man desires something more, and it is this analytical and critical mind that Zen seeks to remove. For this to happen, one must come to an understanding of what is real "mind" and what is misconception.

In the last two chapters I talked about the ways in which Zen teachers train their pupils to go beyond duality to unity, then back again into duality through activity in stillness. Now I want to speak of the way that both activity and stillness, compassion and love, dissolve into wisdom, which is the immaculacy of nothingness, leading to being able to just live, expecting nothing, seeking nothing and knowing nothing—the acme of perfection of spiritual poverty which possesses the universe. To do this we must consider the philosophic and spiritual way of thinking that produces the activity of both compassion and love, as well as the true meaning of the words *mind* and *enlightenment*.

In the *Śūrangama Sūtra*, as stated earlier, four main questions are posed: (1) Where is mind, as functioning through the senses, located? (2) If it has no location in such senses, how do we determine its reality and nature? (3) To be able to view the changing implies that we are also able to view the changeless, and (4) although the power of the senses is changeless, they are not, as such, absolute. What, then, is absolute and why?

Without going into a long and detailed explanation of these questions, I will summarise them quickly. If mind were located within the senses, obviously a blind or a deaf man would not be in possession of a mind as far as these senses were concerned, yet the blind and the deaf both have cognisance of darkness and silence. As this is so, mind cannot be located in the senses. However, that which sees and hears perceives things undergoing changes; it notices that the hand becomes wrinkled with age, that leaves wither and fall; yet that which has cognisance of these things does not of itself change. The fourth question is the all-important one: The power of the senses, though changeless, is not, as such, absolute. What, then, is absolute and why? The illustration given by Buddha in the same sūtra is an excellent one, so I will quote it in full.

Although we exercise the power of sight through the medium of this very sight-power, seeing still does not depend on this sight-power; even whilst "seeing" we may be still at a distance from "true sight"; nor by the exercise of sight do we necessarily exercise the power of "true sight." Consider a man whose eye is afflicted with a cataract. At night, when the light of the lamp shines before him, he thinks he sees a round shadow encircling the flame, composed of the five colours interlacing with one another. Are these beautiful colours in the lamp or in the eye? If they are in the lamp, then why does not a man with healthy sight see them? It is in the sight of the person concerned, then, as it is the result of an act of vision; so what name shall we give to the power that produces these colours? We must conclude that the object looked at, the flame, is dependent on the lamp, but that the circle is the result of imperfect vision. Now all such vision is connected with disease, and to see the cause of the disease (that is, the cataract) is curative of the disease. Therefore, what you and other creatures now see is the result of an original fault of sight, of the cataract, on the true and ever-glorious power of sight which I possess. If the ordinary power of sight be a cataract on the eye of my true sight, it follows, as a matter of course, that the pure and bright mind of my true knowledge in seeing all these unreal associations is not afflicted with this imperfection; *that which understands error is not itself in error;* therefore, having laid hold of this true idea of sight, there will be no further meaning in such expressions as "hearing with the ears" and "knowing by the sight." This faculty which we and all the twelve species of creatures possess, and which we call sight—this is the same as the cataract on the eye—it is the imperfection of true sight; but that true and original power of vision which has become thus perverted and is, in its nature, without imperfection—that cannot properly be called by the same name.*

The obvious deduction from all this is that mind only is absolute Buddha, shining brilliantly and perfectly in everything, manifesting itself in all things and at all times, and this universal mind, which is Buddha, can only be realised by leaving behind all reason, analysis, belief and knowledge which it knows and trusts in. This awakening to reality can be achieved only by Zazen and by the intuitive understanding which the teacher is always exhibiting to the pupil. But here again we have a difficulty, for the very fact that mind has been explained in such a way as above, which is the teaching of the Ōbaku sect of Zen, is in itself contradictory, the real Truth lying beyond any kind of verbal explanation or expression—which means, of course, that there is no mind as explained above.

Ōbaku teaches that the mind is a mirror bright. Sōtō teaches that the mind is not a bright mirror since there never was anything from the beginning. However, it is necessary to know this Ōbaku belief, for it leads naturally to the Rinzai and eventually to the highest of all, Sōtō. There is only one way to understand what I have written here and that is to do Zazen and get your own realisation. I can tell you that fire burns, but you will not know what I mean by "burns" unless you put your hand in the flame for yourself. I cannot give you my understanding; you must find your own. Although Shakyamuni Buddha was aware of these facts, he gave the beginnings of these teachings only, out of sheer compassion for others, hoping that as people progressed in knowledge and understanding they would come to greater realisation.

It was for this reason that the understanding of Makakashyo, the first patriarch after Shakyamuni Buddha, was transmitted silently in the famous story of the flower and the smile; no words were

* From "Ultimate Reality Is Absolute Mind," in E. A. Burtt, ed., *The Teachings of the Compassionate Buddha* (New York: New American Library, Mentor Books, 1955), pp. 193–94. Slightly paraphrased. Emphasis added.

capable of expressing that which they both knew. The great Chinese teacher Ōbaku Kiun puts it rather well:

If students of the Way desire to become Buddhas they need not study anything whatsoever of the Dharma. They should only study how to avoid seeking for, or clinging to, anything. If nothing is sought, the mind will remain in its "unborn" state, and if nothing is clung to or known, the mind will not go through the process of destruction. That which is neither born nor destroyed is the Buddha. The eighty-four thousand methods for counteracting the eighty-four thousand forms of delusion are merely figures of speech for attracting people towards conversion. In fact, none exist. Relinquishment of everything is the Dharma and he who understands this is a Buddha, but the renunciation of *all* delusions leaves no Dharma on which to lay hold. If the student of the Way wishes to understand the real mystery, he need only put out of his mind attachment to anything whatsoever, especially his own opinions and criticisms. To say that the real Dharmakāya of the Buddha is like the void means that it actually is void and that the void is the Dharmakāya [conception of cosmic Buddhahood]. The void and the Dharmakāya do not differ from each other, neither do sentient beings and Buddha, the phenomenal world and Nirvāna, or delusion and Bodhi. When all such forms are left behind, that is Buddha. Ordinary people look outward whilst followers of the Way look into their own minds, but the real Dharma is to forget both the external and the internal. The former is easy enough, the latter very difficult. Men are afraid to forget their own minds, fearing to fall through the void with nothing to which they can cling. They do not know that the void is not really void but the real realm of the Dharma. This spiritually enlightened nature is without beginning or end, as old as space, neither subject to birth nor to destruction, neither existing nor not existing, neither defiled nor pure. . . . It cannot be looked for or sought, comprehended by wisdom or knowledge, explained in words, contacted materially or reached by meritorious achievement. If a man, when he is about to die, can only regard the five aggregates of his consciousness as void . . . if he can only awake to this in a flash and free from the remaining entanglements of the Triple World [past, present and future] he will indeed be one who leaves the world without the faintest tendency towards rebirth. If he should behold the lovely sight of all the Buddhas coming to welcome him and yet feel no desire to go towards them, if he should behold the devils and evil forms surrounding him and yet have no fear, remaining oblivious to self and at one with the Absolute, he will indeed achieve the formless state. [This is not only true of the time of death but also during Zazen; Shakyamuni Buddha experienced these very "temptations" and rejected them all.] When analytic thinking concerning the past, present and future does not take place, it is called complete relinquishment of the Triple World. Since the time when the Buddha entrusted Makakashyo with the Dharma until the present day the transmission has been from mind to mind, yet these minds are identical with each other. In fact, however, mind is not really mind and the reception of the transmission is not really reception. *When the Buddha was alive he wished to preach the True Vehicle, but people would not have believed him, scoffing at him instead.* Hence a transmission of mind cannot be made through words, and any transmission in concrete terms cannot be that of the Dharma. So the transmission is made from mind to mind and these minds are identical with each other. On the other hand, if the Buddha had said nothing, that would have been selfish. So he adopted the expedient of preaching the Three Vehicles [that is, only revealing as much as people could understand at any one time]. None of these vehicles represents the real Dharma, so it is said that there is only a One Vehicle Way, for wherever there is division into this or that, there is no Truth. However, there is no way of expressing universal mind (which is no-mind). Therefore the Buddha called Makakashyo to the Seat of the Law on which he sat and commanded him to practise this branch of the Dharma separately, saying that when a silent understanding of it is obtained, the state of Buddhahood is reached.*

I have paraphrased this considerably because of its great length and in order to make it clearer in places for Western minds. But the question that all those who read it will be asking is, "How and when does one reach this state of understanding and what is the standard by which the teacher judges the pupil's ability?" This is one question, not two, and is easily answered. When the pupil is just living, without thought of self or other, doing that which has to be done without fear or elation, taking notice of neither praise nor blame as a result of his actions, the teacher will know that he has, in fact, refound his original true self. He will be living in the same way as a top spins: whilst he is seemingly in motion outside, yet his centre will be still and unmoving. When this stage has been

---

* From "Ultimate Reality Transcends What Can Be Expressed in Words," in Burtt, ed., *Teachings of the Compassionate Buddha*, pp. 198–201. Paraphrased.

reached and the master and disciple behold each other face to face, they will know that their minds always have been and always will be one, just as they are one with the mind of Shakyamuni Buddha and all the Buddhas of the past, present and future. (Please note the similarity of the teaching here to that for Zazen: do not try to think and do not try not to think; just sit. Here he who exhibits true Buddhahood neither clings to anything nor pushes it away, he just lives; in Zazen is the key to the whole of Buddhahood.) But this past, present and future too are nonexistent, for time also has been transcended, and as this is so for those who have the instantaneous perception of true understanding, the very time that you are reading this *now* is none other than the time when Shakyamuni Buddha smiled at Makakashyo in India, and *you* are Makakashyo; it is the time when Hui-Nêng was transmitted at midnight, in secret, and *you* are Hui-Nêng in ancient China; it is the time when Dōgen looked upon Koun Ejō in Japan in the twelfth century, and *you* are Koun Ejō. If you want the Truth as much as a hanged man wishes to loosen the rope round his neck, you will understand these words instantly and know that *you* yourself *are* Buddha, always have been and always will be; you are enlightened in all ages simultaneously with the whole universe. To those who realise the heart of Monju, not only is duality transcended in unity but the very unity itself is also transcended and the truth of Meister Eckhart's words proved for all time: "And a man shall be free, and as pure as the day prior to his conception in his mother's womb, when he has nothing, wants nothing and knows nothing. Such a one has true spiritual poverty." Bodhidharma put in this way:

> The nature of the mind, when understood,
> No human words can compass or disclose.
> Enlightenment is naught to be obtained,
> And he that gains it does not say he knows.*

This is true spirituality and true enlightenment, but do not stay with unity any more than you stay with duality, for if you do you will be the embodiment of the saying: "[And he who thinks that he is Buddha,] there he sits upon his throne, unseen by any save himself."

* *Ibid.*, p. 203.

Every philosopher knows that to reach perfection is to reach an ending from which one must start again at the very beginning. So he who reaches Buddhahood is Buddha because he is himself and nothing more. He is not pretending to be holy or unholy, nor is it his problem if others dislike him or worship him for being the way he is. He just does what has to be done and nothing more, without ever saying that he is Buddha or that he is not. He is always becoming Buddha and leaving Buddhahood behind every moment of the day; he cannot hold on to Buddhahood any more than you who read this can hold on to the moment when you read the words I have just written.

They who know never say they do or do not know; they just live. Despite the thanklessness of his task, the Zen teacher has his compensations, but he does not know them for compensations since he is unconscious of them as such. He just goes on, making himself as perfect as possible as he goes, doing that which has to be done.

The last stage for the trainee is, after reaching the heart of Monju, to return to the world with the bliss-bestowing hands of Miroku, the Buddha who is to come. In Daisetz Suzuki's *Manual of Zen Buddhism* is the following passage:

> *Entering the City with Bliss-bestowing Hands.* His thatched cottage gate is closed, and even the wisest know him not. No glimpses of his inner life are to be caught; for he goes on his own way without following the steps of the ancient sages. Carrying a gourd he goes out into the market, leaning against a staff he comes home. He is found in company with wine-bibbers and butchers, he and they are all converted into Buddhas.
>
> > Bare-chested and bare-footed, he comes out into the market-place;
> > Daubed with mud and ashes, how broadly he smiles!
> > There is no need for the miraculous power of the gods,
> > For he touches, and lo! the dead trees are in full bloom.*

It is the duty of every trainee to share with the world the glory of his own understanding, and this is done in many ways; he is not confined to any one method. Remember that Kanzeon reveals herself in the world in all walks of life and spheres of activity. The

* From "The Ten Oxherding Pictures," by Kaku-an Shi-en, in D. T. Suzuki, *Manual of Zen Buddhism* (New York: Grove Press, Evergreen Books, 1960), p. 134.

trainee may take up the work of a doctor or a nurse, a teacher, hotelkeeper or servant, but his nature will be so different from that of ordinary men that all the world will notice and want to copy him. So just by being an Arahant he is, in fact, a Bodhisattva. By this gentle method of teaching, which is devoid of proselytising, he will gradually lead others away from the idea of personal gain to higher things; thus Kanzeon manifests herself at all times in the world of patience.

CHAPTER 8

What Are Kōans?

IT IS ESSENTIAL to do Zazen if we would understand the world we live in with anything deeper than the superficial comprehension of the average person, and this is not a matter of doing anything out of the ordinary, since all religions have practised contemplation in some form throughout the centuries. Even dogs and cats love to sit quietly for long periods of time. However, most Western people, being intellectually oriented, are plagued by either fear or boredom during such periods if they have nothing specific to think about, and this is the main reason why the Rinzai system of kōans appeals to the average Westerner: it gives him something to think about.

This is a completely wrong use of the kōan and of Zazen. It was Daie Sōkō, born 1089, who advocated the use of kōans during Zazen as preferable to the old method of quiet sitting, known as *shikan taza* in Japanese, in which he himself had been trained, as had indeed all the great masters up until that time, including Rinzai himself. Since Daie Sōkō is known to have been brilliantly intellectual, I strongly suspect that he found the older method of meditation too difficult to practise, for it is the intellectual types who seem to have difficulty in practising quiet sitting (see the chapters on Ananda and other intellectuals in Book III). Since the whole purpose of Zazen is to quieten down the thought-waves so that one may realise one's True Nature, the present-day approach of many Westerners to kōans, of seeing how many they can solve like puzzles, is utterly wrong. In Japan I have so often seen, with disgust and sadness, a snobbish pride taken by these people in telling their fellow trainees how many kōans they have already solved and what "heights of understanding" they have reached. It must be clearly understood that the sole purpose of kōan training was, and still is, to lead the trainee to a true understanding and keeping of the Precepts: that is, to the exhibition of enlightenment in daily life.

This last sentence may come as a considerable surprise to those who have a mistaken idea of what constitutes Zen "freedom," about which so much has erroneously been said. Alan Watts has very expertly listed the six types of kōan in his book *The Way of Zen*, so there is no need for me to do so, but I do wish to explain how kōans are used to teach the Precepts in Sōtō Zen. Generally speaking, they are applied only when a trainee exhibits a need for a specific type of kōan.

It is perfectly true that Sōtō Zen does not make it a rule of training that every trainee must "solve" a matter of three hundred or so kōans before being given his master's seal of approval, and this for the very simple reason that kōan training is not for the purpose of gaining seals or anything else but solely for teaching the trainee the true meaning of Buddhism. Because the connection between kōan technique and the teachings of Buddha is obscure, many people have with some reason believed in the past that Zen is not a branch of Buddhism at all, and I for one do not blame them, for I have never yet seen any book which explained the connection between the two. It would be wrong, however, to believe such nonsense, for Zen is of the very essence of Buddhism. Without Zazen, Buddha could never have reached enlightenment; the very first kōan was Shakyamuni Buddha's own. After seeing the four sights (see Chapter 1) and realising the need to find the cause of suffering and remove it (the very first kōan), he sat under the Bodhi tree doing Zazen until the kōan was solved with the Four Noble Truths. Thereafter he taught the Four Noble Truths and the Eightfold Path; the whole of his forty-five years of service to mankind was an extended explanation and applied use of the answer to his own kōan, and this answer we call his enlightenment. The whole of the present kōan system is geared for the trainee's benefit in so far as it teaches him how to walk the Eightfold Path and solve all the problems he meets with on the way. But to use kōans as puzzles or, worse still, to believe that they must all be solved and then graduation will be automatic, is a waste of time. Sōtō Zen uses kōans only when they are applicable to a situation, and never more often than necessary.

Alan Watts speaks of the sixth stage of kōan study as the study of the Precepts themselves, the other five stages being used to bring the trainee to a fit state of mind for studying them. This point should be carefully noted. Let me try to make it clearer. *The Most Excellent Mirror—Samādhi* says that when a trainee asks a question, a matching answer always comes from the Zen master, who uses all varied means when teaching, even to saying that black is white, because the delusions in the trainee's mind are all topsy-turvy. In other words, because the trainee has no idea of what Buddhism *really* is—that is, the *true* use and keeping of the Precepts—his early attempts at answering questions are rejected by the master although the trainee may have and frequently has given the right intellectual answer to the kōan set. The teacher refuses the answer because the pupil's spiritual growth is not great enough, as yet, for it to receive the seal of the teacher's approval. Each time the pupil comes to the teacher with his answer it is rejected; and each time the pupil comes back with the same answer, frequently in different wording, with greater conviction than he had in the beginning, until he eventually explodes the answer and comes to the teacher no longer caring whether the latter agrees with him or not because he *knows* with his whole being that his answer is right.

The important point to remember here is that the master always gives matching answers to the trainee's questions; in other words, it is the pupil that makes the running and not the teacher, the latter acting only as a mirror reflecting the actions and reactions of the pupil. This is the master's reason for sometimes making black white, although he knows that this only muddles the trainee more. If a pupil is already in a muddle and is deliberately made by a skilful teacher to see that his thinking and behaviour are muddled, he can do something about himself.

This system is excellent as a means of character training for the Eightfold Path. When a trainee first comes to a temple, he knows the beliefs and basic tenets of Buddhism, the Ten Precepts and other necessary doctrines, but he only knows them in his brain and not deeply in his blood and bones. All kōans are carefully geared to the harmonising of the opposites of right and wrong, which are eventually transcended, leaving the person free of all attachment in every sense of the word. This means that by the time the trainee has undergone the strict moral training of the temple for several years, his character is beyond reproach—if his teacher has given him an excellent example—and he keeps the Precepts because it is his nature to do so and not because an external deity has made it incumbent upon him to keep them. Here again the connection of Zen training with the old Buddhist Precepts is exemplified. The moral codes of most religions are enforced by a deity from outside, but the Buddhist takes the moral discipline of Buddhism upon himself. Because an external deity is lacking, conviction of the Truth of the Precepts must be generated from within the trainee; thus the conviction-stimulating kōans. When the teacher sees that the pupil has made the Buddhist moral code his natural way of life, he knows that the latter has finally taken the Buddha, Dharma and Sangha for refuge in the true meaning of the words and is therefore just as enlightened as were Shakyamuni Buddha and the patriarchs. One has to live Buddhism, to be Buddhism, and to do this the Precepts must flow through one's veins as the very lifeblood. Just as we do not notice the coursing of our blood but permit it to flow unhindered, so the Buddhist lives the moral code of the Precepts, unhindered by them and not hindering them. The flashes of understanding—the *kenshō*—that come at various times, as a result either of meditation on a kōan or simply of sitting quietly without one, deepen the trainee's character and enable him to take the Precepts more completely to himself, but it is above all else the example of the teacher in living the Buddhist life which brings the trainee to the final state where his character is so purged of all greed, hate and delusion that he is the walking embodiment of Nirvāna. However, once it is second nature to constantly exemplify the Precepts, one is not conscious of doing so and so is not conscious of being Buddha. Therefore Buddha recognises Buddha when the trainee sees that the master is himself living Buddhism, and the master recognises the pupil as Buddha when the latter keeps the Precepts with no smell of holiness and no taint of evil, for Buddha then walks, sleeps, sits, eats and works in him without any knowledge of Buddha and any attachment thereto. He is spiritually autonomous. Many can reach this state successfully without kōans of the orthodox type at all—having their own private one, perhaps—but the intellectual usually needs them. Rinzai forces the kōan book on everybody; Sōtō studies the individual and artistically suits the kōan to his needs.

In order to bring the students to this level of acceptance of the Precepts, it is imperative to raise conviction to its highest peak, and the first thing every pupil must be certain of is his own possession of the Buddha Nature. Hence the use of the early types of kōan, which smash up intellection about such matters. It is important to find the Buddha within animals and inanimate things. Once the certainty of one's own Buddha Nature has been established beyond doubt, the stream of Buddhism has been entered and one is free to progress, deepening one's understanding as one goes with each successive kōan. But it must be understood that the solving of each kōan is not a separate gaining of enlightenment but a deepening of original enlightenment. Enlightenment is not obtained piecemeal; it is one and undivided. A shallow glimpse is no less enlightenment than is a deep one, and the fact that we all possess the Buddha Nature from the beginning of all things proves that we are already enlightened anyway and have only to train ourselves in order to realise it. This is not to say that merely knowing one possesses the Buddha Nature is equivalent to being enlightened—some critics of Sōtō Zen have claimed this as its most glaring fault—for to have something with no real knowledge of possessing it is the same as not having it; the *knowledge* of possession must be awakened. One has to know of this possession, and still train, in order to realise it to the full. When a student is not convinced of his possession of the Buddha Nature, his faith therein can be encouraged and then turned into certainty of knowledge with the whole of his being by the use of a kōan.

The reader may ask, How is it then that a teacher, when using kōans, may on occasion do evil acts if the whole purpose of the kōan system is to teach the pupil the correct understanding of the Precepts? The answer is that it is impossible to harmonise right and wrong unless one knows fully what right and wrong represent. One cannot know heaven without also knowing hell; one cannot understand them without transcending both. Most people are bound by the moral code of their religion, but Buddhism teaches its followers how to be freed by their moral code. This does not mean that immorality is countenanced and encouraged. Unless one knows with one's whole being that an act is evil, one does not understand evil; unless one knows with one's whole being that an act is good, one does not understand good; unless one knows with one's whole being that a good act and a bad act partake of both a Buddha and a devil action, being the reverse and obverse of the same coin, one does not understand that the kindest Kanzeon is to be found in hell and the worst devil occupies the highest heaven. The four types of kōan between the first and sixth teach these things in detail to those who need it, and the teacher must accept the karmic consequences of any evil act he may do in order to teach the transcendence of good and evil to his pupils. Only after this paradox has been transcended can the pupil fully understand the Goi theory (fifth-stage kōans) and the Precepts, for only then will he know how to keep these Precepts without being either bound by them or attached to them. It is as bad to keep the Precepts out of attachment to morality as it is not to keep them at all; it is good to break them in order to teach the immorality of morality to those still suffering from attachment to morality. The grave danger of the Precepts is their liability to create spiritual pride; hence the need sometimes of an evil act on the part of the teacher. Eventually the Precepts are so transcended that there is morality in immorality to such an extent that even the Precepts themselves do not exist and the pupil is instead the very living embodiment of them. Such a person will live a moral life, but he will not be able to explain to anyone the reason why, since it will be his nature to live so. This is the true keeping of the Precepts.

CHAPTER 9

Apostolic Succession

So FAR AS I can discover, no one has ever yet talked about the priestly ranks to be found in Sōtō Zen, nor have the various terms and titles used been explained. Since these are a source of much controversy in Western countries, I have decided to devote a whole chapter to them.

First and foremost, the term *tokudō* must be explained. This is the most misunderstood word in Zen terminology. Strictly speaking, *tokudō* means "ordination," but the Japanese have stretched it to include the meanings and equivalent status of Christian baptism and confirmation without employing a qualifying word to differentiate between the three meanings. Since this is so, many Western people return to their own countries from Japan suffering from the idea that they are priests when in fact they are only confirmed laymen. The blame for this must be laid squarely at the door of the Japanese; after all, if you insist on having only one word to mean three different things, you cannot blame the unfortunate foreigner who looks it up in his dictionary, reads that it means "ordination," interprets this in the Christian sense because it is so understood in his own culture, and goes away thinking he is a full priest. It is important to counteract such misunderstandings and prevent recurrences in the future, though doing so is a bit like locking the stable door after the horse has bolted; I know of at least three confirmed laymen who are going around dressed as priests and performing various ceremonies. A fair way of judging whether the ceremony you have undergone is that of a layman or a trainee priest is to ask if you are expected to shave your head, wear robes and enter a training temple. If the answer is no, then you can safely take it you are a confirmed layman and not a priest, even if the priest who performs the ceremony looks up the word in his dictionary and tells you otherwise. To become a confirmed layman, you agree to keep the Precepts and are given a small *rakusu,* or token kesa, to wear; it is perhaps this last which misleads people more than the actual terminology, since the kesa has always been the badge of the Buddhist priest. If you plan on going to Japan, it would be wise to make exhaustive enquiries of any priest at whose temple you may receive tokudō, since to say you are a priest when you are not one upsets the Japanese considerably, and no one wants to be branded a religious fraud—especially when he is innocent.

Next, let us look at the words *monk* and *nun.* In Zen temples the Japanese again have only one word for both of these: *unsui.* This word is made up of two Chinese characters, the first of which means "cloud" and the second "water." Their combined meaning is as follows: an unsui is a person, male or female, who wanders across the world as free as a cloud in his search for Truth, yet has the strength of an ocean to wash away the mountains that stand in his or her way. This is obviously a very different meaning from that usually given to the words *monk* and *nun* in countries with a Christian culture or background. A monk or nun lives a dedicated life in the service of God under vows of poverty, chastity and obedience, but the unsui takes no such vows; his only vow is that of the Bodhisattva: "However innumerable beings may be, I vow to save them; however difficult the teachings are, I vow to master them; I vow to cleanse my own heart." There is another difference: in Zen both male and female unsui are expected to become members of the priesthood; they are not supposed to be content with being unsui. This brings into focus the difference between Christian and Buddhist monasticism; the former does not permit nuns to become full priests, but in Zen the female unsui is expected to become a priestess of a temple. The ideal set forth in the Buddhist scriptures is that male and female are alike in the Buddha Mind and so men and women can go up the ranks of the priesthood equally. Unfortunately, Japanese custom (or prejudice, whichever word you prefer) gets in the way of the women far more often than it should, with the result that there are not nearly as many full priests among them as there should be and those who have made it have much poorer temples than the men. Prejudice apart, the ideal is complete equality of the sexes, and a woman, if she is energetic and resourceful, can go all the way up the seven ranks of the priesthood; quite a number of my friends have done so. Before the war the obstacles placed in a woman's way were so great as to be almost insurmountable. However, with the influx of new ideas from outside Japan, life has become a lot easier for the female members of the priesthood, and a really determined woman, if she is willing to put up with slights from male priests, can become a full priestess. This is perhaps easier for Western women to achieve, since they possess more tenacity than do their Japanese sisters.

Because of the great difference in meaning between the English words *monk* and *nun* and the Japanese *unsui*, the former are never used to describe Zen trainees in this book. Scholars argue between "trainee" and "seminarian" as translations of *unsui*, but I feel sure that the former is far closer to the true meaning, since "seminarian" does not adequately describe the actual activities of the temple unsui. Perhaps the best solution would be to keep the Japanese word *unsui* and carry it over into the English language, since no one English word can really convey its true meaning.

With regard to the words *priest* and *priestess*, the Japanese language presents no such difficulties. *Oshō* literally means "priest" and *ni-oshō* means "female priest," or "priestess." These terms are applied to unsui who have reached the fifth grade of the priesthood, and cause no complication once they are truly understood. It is, of course, the duty of every member of the priesthood to serve his fellow men to the best of his ability, and this may involve him in performing duties that are not of a particularly priestly nature, such as working in commerce or industry. Since every priest or priestess was at one time an unsui, this is another reason why the word *unsui* cannot be translated as "monk" or "nun."

Let us now look at the various ranks of the Sōtō Zen priesthood. These are seven in number.

1. *Jūkai Tokudō*. This is equivalent to a layman's confirmation in the Christian church, and so not strictly speaking a rank of the priesthood. Whilst it is not incumbent on every Buddhist layman to undergo this ordination ceremony, it is imperative for all aspirant priests to do so.
2. *Tokudō*. This signifies ordination to the priesthood as a trainee.
3. *Shusōshō*. This is the rank of chief junior, which means the trainee has reached a certain level of understanding, can re-

cite all the scriptures, lead all the other trainees in the temple in debate and perform various ceremonies. The new chief junior undergoes the ceremony of Hossen.

4. *Transmission.* Once this ceremony has been performed upon an unsui it is impossible for him to leave the priesthood, for he has then been joined to the apostolic line of his own master. The transmission ceremony is secret and is therefore not included in this book, although Reverend Suigan Yogo and I have translated it into English. Those who would understand the apostolic line and the transmission should study the *Denkoroku* (Book III) in detail.

5. *Zuisse.* This is a special congratulatory ceremony, held only in the head temples of Sōjiji and Eiheiji, at which trainees receive their certificates of priesthood. However, the ceremony itself is not obligatory and many young trainees save themselves the expense of travelling to the head temples by paying a sum of money to the head office of the Sōtō Zen Church and taking the examination to prove their ability to perform certain ceremonies, notably those of funeral, wedding and Segaki. The ceremony was instituted by imperial command and is therefore of little use to Western trainees, who naturally are not subject to the emperor of Japan; for them it is sufficient to take the test from their teacher.

6. *Shin Zan and Kyoshi.* The kyoshi is the divinity degree bestowed by the temple in which the new priest underwent his training. After receiving it, he may perform the ceremony of Shin Zan, or "ascending the mountain," as the new abbot (priest) of a temple.

7. *Kessei.* The four ceremonies of Kessei are included in Book IV and are performed when a priest has a disciple whom he has trained from tokudō to shusōshō. Strictly speaking, the term *kessei* refers to the training period of a hundred days, held twice a year in spring and autumn, during which the priesthood undergoes its strict discipline. Nowadays it is used somewhat loosely to mean the four principal ceremonies mentioned above, which are then not spread out over a hundred days but compressed into a space of less than a week.

Often children are registered as future priests at a very early age, perhaps at birth. Here again the word *tokudō* is a misnomer in that it implies simply a paper registration in an office of something that may never become actual fact. Should a young person be so registered he can take Jūkai Tokudō, if he does not want to be a full priest when he grows up, or he can merely keep Jūkai, which is something like attending church for a few days non-stop. It is possible to do the two simultaneously; the second is renewable each year, and many people come year after year for that purpose. Both involve living in the temple for about a week under exactly the same discipline as that of the priesthood and attending ceremonies (see Book IV, Jūkai). Those who only attend Jūkai and do not undergo Jūkai Tokudō do not attend the actual confirmation ceremony, nor do they receive the token rakusu. It is usual for people to take the priesthood tokudō, or unsui ordination, after Jūkai Tokudō, but sometimes the priesthood ordination is done first. This is not a good practice, since it puts the cart before the horse, but fathers often resort to it who wish to ordain their own sons without going to the great expense of holding Jūkai Tokudō in their own temples. The unfortunate young unsui whose ceremonies are done in this order is made to do all the menial tasks in a training temple until the next Jūkai ceremony, which always takes place in spring. After this ceremonial error has been corrected, he can continue his training normally.

Like Shakyamuni Buddha before him, the trainee has two masters from whom he learns prior to finding his *honshi*, or "true master," with whom he will undergo the transmission ceremony. The first master is regarded as the trainee's father in Buddhism, since he gives him birth into the family of the Buddhas at ordination, a new name in religion and the opportunity to be set free from the world of patience, Samsāra. It is the first master's duty to teach his new disciple the scriptures, to correct his morals in accordance with the Precepts, to feed, clothe and otherwise watch over his welfare as a parent watches over a child, providing him with financial aid at all times. It is this last fact that makes it so extraordinarily difficult for Western people to get themselves ordained by Japanese teachers. To be financially responsible for a boy or girl in the teens or early twenties who is a member of your own nation is one thing, but to become so for an adult foreigner of whom you know little or nothing is a very different matter, and some priests have been badly treated by unscrupulous foreigners in the past. Also, it is not easy for a priest to make an adult foreigner, of whose language he is not certain and whose Japanese is probably bad, to behave as is required of all Japanese disciples, doing all the chores of scrubbing, cleaning, cooking and waiting on the priest's wife and children as if he or she were a servant in the priest's house, whilst being scolded and sometimes beaten. Such behaviour is easier when one is young, but even twenty-year-old Westerners have difficulty adjusting to this sort of thing, and Japanese teachers are incapable, it seems, of understanding that an adult cannot be treated in the same way as an adolescent. As far as they are concerned, the disciple is a baby Buddha who, having just been born, must be taught accordingly. In the religious sense this is a good practice, but it becomes ludicrous when it is carried over into everyday life to such a degree that the adult person is treated in the same way, physically, as a small child. I know there are some types of Western mentality to which this appeals at least for a short time, but never for very long. For all these reasons, it is extremely difficult to get one's head shaved and be ordained into the priesthood in Japan if one wants it done by a Japanese, and the very small number of teachers who do do it are not all exactly out of the top drawer, their aim often being to show off the number of foreign disciples they have rather than to give those disciples a genuine insight into Buddhism. One of their favourite occupations is forcing foreign disciples to appear on television or in newspaper interviews for the teacher's, or temple's, own glorification. The effect of such publicity on the trainee is terrible, since the very last thing a sincere student wants is anything of the sort whilst undertaking his search for Truth. Such banal personal questions as the publicity media ask are frequently rude in the extreme and tend to turn the unfortunate student into an insincere public show rather than a true trainee. I say this with considerable feeling, for I myself was gravely subjected to this sort of thing until the late chief abbot of Sōjiji found out about it and stopped any further interviews. Those who wish to go to Japan to study should consider this information carefully. I was lucky enough to find a true friend and teacher, but many are not.

At the end of a year or a little earlier, the trainee can become a *shusōshō,* or chief junior. If he is being taught by his own father, a much longer time may elapse. The shusōshō's qualifications are as described earlier in this chapter. The period of time that he is in charge of various ceremonies and debates is one hundred days. For this special training period he takes his second master—or should do so. In practice it is frequently the first master who performs not only the duties of the second but of the third as well.

The next grade is that of transmission. There is no way of gauging when this will take place, since it takes as long as it does for a person to become truly converted and to find his true spiritual potentiality, the Truth of Zen. Under no circumstances can the ceremony be performed until this stage is reached. However, it does not *always* take a long time, and age and sex have no effect upon it. The majority of transmissions take place between the ages of twenty-five and forty-five, although there are exceptions. You will find, if you go through the *Denkoroku* (Book III), that this was true in ancient times as well as now: Shakyamuni Buddha was approximately thirty-five, Christ about the same age, and Dōgen twenty-eight. The only people who took a really long time to arrive at realisation were the ones who loved book-learning and argument. Unfortunately, a good ninety-five percent of all Westerners studying Zen fall into this category. I cannot emphasise the danger of book-learning too strongly. Like Keizan, I too say that erudition is a grave hindrance to Zen understanding.

There is an interesting historical link between the life of Shakyamuni Buddha and the present-day transmission ceremony in the placement of the mats belonging to master and disciple. The history of Shakyamuni Buddha (see Chapter 1) tells of his being brought as a child to the ascetic Asita and placing his feet on the latter's head, thus indicating that he would be the greater. In the transmission ceremony the mats of master and disciple are placed, first, so that the top edge of the master's mat overlaps the disciple's very slightly as they bow to each other; later on, the side edge of the disciple's mat is placed over the master's as they bow side by side to the altar. The text of the ceremony says, "Although the disciple stands beneath the master's feet, he must also stand on the master's head." This means that if Buddhism is to remain a living religion, the disciple must be greater than his master. In Japanese, Shakya-muni Buddha is called the Dai Honshi, or "Great True Teacher," and the title given to the transmission master is Honshi, or "True Teacher"; for the Zen trainee he stands in the place of Shakyamuni Buddha as his representative and descendant in the apostolic line. It is the honshi who ratifies the trainee's final realisation of Zen Truth. There is a grave danger here in that people may think they cannot reach the Truth of Zen without a honshi, though nothing could be further from the meaning of Zen. After all, Shakyamuni did not have a honshi; he made his own way to realisation, and he was a man, not a god, from the beginning of his life until his death. He was not gifted with any power that we do not have ourselves. So long as we believe that he possessed the Buddha Nature and follow the system of meditation he taught, we can rediscover that same Buddha Nature without any outside help; all we really need is to have sufficient belief in ourselves. Once again I quote: "Remember thou *must* go alone; the Buddhas do but point the way."

The honshi may act as a catalyst for his disciple in achieving his realisation, but we should remember the many stories of persons who arrived at their realisation as a result of some inanimate object: in these cases the object was the catalyst. Although such a realisation must afterwards be confirmed by the honshi, he can do nothing more than provide that confirmation; he cannot literally get inside a person to "inspect" his Buddha Nature. Only intuition and observation over a long period of time will tell the teacher when the disciple is truly ready for transmission. It is debatable which of the two, intuition or observation, is the more valuable, since a person may realise Zen Truth and still have a long way to go towards perfecting himself. Intuition tells both master and disciple of the meeting of mind with mind, of heart with heart, the flowing of the two into one and the one merging into the immaculacy of nothingness. This intuition apart, the disciple may still not be ready for transmission for some time after his realisation because his character training is not finished —though in this sense no disciple is ever ready for transmission, since a perfect character is impossible. However, a real kenshō will make the training process a thousand times easier for both master and disciple.

Because of the importance of character training—and herein the master's observation comes into play—the honshi must at all times set an example of being as perfect as possible within the Precepts, and it is the disciple's duty to copy his good points and not his mistakes. All masters, being human, make mistakes, and some make them deliberately so as to ensure that the disciple does not stay with immaculacy but learns that there is nothing holy or unholy anywhere. At the same time, knowing that he is imperfect, the master must continue his own training. In addition to this, he must be perfectly himself, sometimes performing a seemingly evil act in order to teach the disciple the *true* meaning of right and wrong. The only *practical* value of a honshi is that he can, after observing the trainee over a long period of time, affirm or deny the latter's understanding by either giving or withholding the sealed silken certificates of transmission and performing or not performing the actual ceremony. The sad thing about most Western people in Japan is that they are hunting for a "God the Father" figure who will teach them everything, instead of doing what Shakyamuni Buddha did. They should understand that all things are teaching at all times if one is truly looking for teaching. Anything or anyone that creates the realisation of Zen Truth for a person is both Buddha and honshi. If the reader is searching for a special person as a master, he will get nowhere, for he is very definitely in the world of the opposites; he is saying that one thing is Buddha and another is not.

Do not think that the patriarchs in the apostolic line in the *Denkoroku* were so different from yourself. First there was Makakashyo who, being a deeply spiritual type, could understand things easily by intuition. But next came Ananda, who was so busy running around in erudite circles in his own head that it took him years and years to accept a very simple fact—one that was just too simple for his erudite brain to believe it was true. Shōnawashyu carried around a personal psychological problem concerning clothes and so was the prototype of the present-day psychological problem cases that come to Japanese temples. Mishaka liked playing with sorcery until he found something better to do in religion. Bashumitsu was probably one of the worst drunkards the world has ever known until he too accidentally met a true priest; up to that time he had thought drink the finest thing there was—simply because he knew of nothing better. Such human failings do not prevent a person from reaching sainthood so long as they are not clung to with a closed mind; it is the willingness to believe there may be something better that makes spiritual growth possible. All these people had to admit to themselves that perhaps they were wrong; they had to do *sange suru*—admission and acceptance of being at fault—before they could make any progress spiritually. If the reader wants to study Zen seriously he should take a good look at himself, decide that he does not think much of what he sees, and do sange suru too.

The other ranks, with the exception of Kessei, are of little use to Western people since they are part of Japanese custom rather than original Buddhism, and so no deeper explanation is made of them here. Kessei is useful in foreign countries both as a ceremonial form, since it comprises the ceremonies needed for the testing of both a teacher and a shusōshō, and as a certification of their ability. The West needs to keep the teaching of Zen in its original purity, and for this, gorgeous ceremonies such as Zuisse are quite unnecessary. The degree certificates issued by various training temples are valuable in some ways, but there is no reason why, after Western training temples are established, similar certificates could not be issued in English with examinations in the same language. Such certification would be far more valuable than one in Japanese, since the language difficulty is insurmountable for many Westerners.

The title of Roushi (spelt Roshi by some authorities) is much misunderstood in the West. Since it means "Reverend," it is often applied as an honorific by people when greeting a priest. Most priests are not too happy with the term, since it has the connotation of old and useless as well as noble; they prefer, instead, the last half of the word, or its second Chinese character, which is *shi* or *sensei*, meaning "teacher" in Japanese. There are many titles in Zen with exactly the same meaning as Roushi, one of the most used being Zenji, which means literally "Zen Master."

In both Rinzai and Sōtō the title Roushi should be conferred by a master only upon a really worthy disciple. However, there is a difference in the way it is used by the two schools. After receiving the title from his master, a Rinzai priest is always called by it, but a Sōtō priest is not necessarily. Although the Sōtō priest's master may think him worthy of the title because of his spirituality, others may not have the same opinion. This does not mean that the priest concerned is a bad one; there are priests who are good for some trainees and not for others. A Sōtō priest may be a roushi to his master and to no one else. The Sōtō practice has the advantage of keeping roushis from temptations to which, being only human, they may succumb. Remember that although a priest may have understood true spirituality and become a roushi, he is still as subject to making mistakes as the next man. For this reason, Dōgen wrote in the "Shushōgi" that it is wrong to consider a priest's shortcomings if he is teaching true religion; one's duty is to be grateful and not to criticise, remembering that perfection is impossible.

This chapter was written to clarify many points about which there seems to be much misunderstanding in the West. Whilst I realise that this short explanation is inadequate, I hope I have at least made it clear that anyone who has been to Japan and received an "ordination" there had best consider what that ordination really means, unless he has spent many years going up the ranks just described. Only if he has gone through them all is he really a priest of the Sōtō Zen sect *in Japan*. In Western countries, it is sufficient to have gone up as far as transmission, since we are not trying to follow in the steps of the Japanese but in those of Shakyamuni Buddha.

BOOK

The Teachings of
Dōgen Zenji

INTRODUCTION TO THE TRANSLATIONS

DŌGEN ZENJI was born in Japan in 1200 and entered the Buddhist priesthood at the age of twelve. He studied Tendai Buddhism on Mount Hiei, but finding the studies there unsatisfying from the religious point of view, he went to Kenninji in Kyoto, where he studied Rinzai Zen under Eisai (1141–1215), the founder of Rinzai in Japan, and subsequently under Eisai's disciple Myozen. In 1223, Dōgen left for China with Myozen, again because he could find no real depth in the Rinzai teachings. He studied much in various temples in China, and eventually received the transmission from Tendō Nyojō Zenji, the abbot of Tendō-Zan. Returning to Japan in 1227, he stayed for a time at Kenninji but left there in 1230, feeling that he was not yet competent to run so large a monastery, and retired to a small temple, where he began work on his famous writings. In 1233 he became the first abbot of Kōshōji. In 1244 Hatano Yoshishige offered him the opportunity to become founder of Daibutsuji (later Eiheiji), at which temple he died in 1253. He is known in Japan as Eihei Dōgen Zenji, or by his posthumous title of Kōsō Jōyō Daishi.

Dōgen Zenji brought with him from China both the transmission and the teachings of the Sōtō Zen school of Buddhism. Sōtō, which is the oldest of all the Zen schools and of which both Ōbaku and Rinzai are derivatives, is perhaps the only school of Mahāyāna Buddhism to retain some of the original Indian elements of Theravāda Buddhism. The main teaching of the Sōtō school that Dōgen brought with him was that no words or scriptural text can adequately express the Spirit of Buddhism and therefore those who are bound by such words and scriptures can understand nothing of the Truth transmitted by the Buddha himself to his first disciple, Makakashyo, who had in his turn handed it on, from mind to mind, down the line of patriarchs and disciples to the present day.

The following writings must be understood as Dōgen's exhortations to his followers to be earnest and strenuous in their training; his own sentiments on this subject are clearly expressed. Serenity, simplicity and purity were his ideals, and his whole life was a living expression thereof. Those who would follow in his footsteps must live immaculately pure lives within the Precepts of the Buddha without being in any way bound by them; thus morality becomes the norm without being hindered by either moral codes or rules and regulations. Purity of life and thought, harmony within the community, and the destruction of all rules and regulations that did not lead to the complete freeing of the mind to commune with the One Mind of the Buddha were absolute essentials for all his followers, and at the heart of the teaching, as the lodestone to which all returned, was silent meditation during which one just sat as had the Buddha, in utter serenity of contemplation, mind communing with the Buddha Mind. Theology, as far as Dōgen was concerned, was of no importance whatsoever. His was an intuitive method of spiritual training which resulted in a lofty transcendence over worldly cares and desires, thus eliminating suffering and the attachment thereto of which the Buddha speaks in the Four Noble Truths. There is no doubt that Dōgen's way was hard to follow, for he was a somewhat puritanical mystic, but there is equally no doubt that he inspired Japanese Buddhism with a new spirit.

Dōgen's major works are the *Shōbōgenzō* (*The Treasury-Eye of the True Teaching*), of which the "Gyakudoyōjinshu" is the best-known part; the *Eiheikōroku;* and the *Eiheishingi.* The following translations, all from the *Shōbōgenzō,* are not literal, for the very good reason that were they so this book would lose much of its true feeling and flavour. I have tried instead to give the religious fervour with which Dōgen obviously wrote its full value. The whole of the *Shōbōgenzō* is not given here, but I assure the reader that nothing of real value for the study and understanding of the religion has been omitted, the missing chapters being simply amplifications of those here included. The *Eiheikōroku* and the *Eiheishingi* are, at the moment, in the process of translation.

Shōbōgenzō
THE TREASURY-EYE
OF THE TRUE TEACHING

TAITAIKŌHŌ

How Junior Priests Must Behave in the Presence of Senior Priests

A taikō is a senior member of the priesthood, male or female, who has been in training for a period of five years or more longer than the priest in his presence. Since they have spent much time in training they are very excellent in their understanding of Buddhism, and all junior members of the priesthood must show their respect for these senior ones in their daily behaviour. This code of behaviour of sixty-two rules is excellent for juniors of the present day to follow.

1. The kesa must be worn and the mat carried at all times when a senior is present.
2. The kesa must not be worn merely as a covering for the shoulders in the presence of a senior. One of the scriptures says: "If all we do is cover our shoulders with the kesa in the presence of the Buddha, priests and seniors we shall fall into the worst of hells."
3. Clasp your hands respectfully when you see a senior; do not allow them to hang down.
4. Sit upright without leaning back when in the presence of a senior and never stare at him.
5. Do not laugh loudly, suddenly or with disrespect in the presence of a senior.
6. All seniors must be served with the same respect as you would accord your own master.
7. Be grateful for all teaching given by a senior. Be attentive and do not require its repetition.
8. Always show humility when with seniors.
9. When with a senior, never scratch or hunt vermin.

10. Do not spit or blow your nose when with a senior.

11. Do not clean your teeth or rinse your mouth when with a senior.

12. Always wait for a senior's permission before sitting down in his presence.

13. Do not sit on any raised surface whereon the senior may sit or sleep.

14. Never touch a senior when near him.

15. A senior of five years has the rank of ācārya. One of ten years has the rank of upādhyāya. This is the law of Buddha and you must remember it well.

16. Never sit down before the senior permits you, and then clasp your hands. Sit down respectfully and upright, showing no sign of laziness or disrespect.

17. Never lean to right or left when with a senior. This is gross impoliteness.

18. Show humility when giving information to a senior, and never say all you wish to.

19. When with a senior, never give a large yawn. If you must yawn, cover your mouth.

20. Never touch your face, head or limbs when with a senior.

21. Do not sigh heavily but behave yourself with respect when with a senior.

22. Stand as if at attention when with a senior, if you must stand.

23. If a senior enters the room in which you are sitting with another senior, stand and bow respectfully.

24. If there is a senior's room next to yours, never read scriptures loudly.

25. Never give information on religion to others without the direction of a senior, no matter how many times you may be asked.

26. Always give truthful answers to seniors' questions.

27. Be careful to neither disappoint nor anger a senior, and look at him straight when addressing him.

28. Never bow to another junior when you are with a senior.

29. Never receive reverence from another in the presence of a senior.

30. Work faster than the seniors at laborious work and slower than they at that which is agreeable, if you are living with them.

31. Never be slow in giving respect to a senior whenever you meet one.

32. Always ask the meaning of scriptures or the Vinaya if you are fortunate enough to become acquainted with a senior; you must never be contemptuous of him or idle in his presence.

33. Should a senior become ill, it is your duty to nurse him.

34. Never jest in the presence of a senior, either about himself or his room, and do not indulge in idle chatter.

35. Never criticise or praise a senior in the presence of another senior.

36. Do not show contempt for a senior by asking frivolous questions.

37. Shaving the head, cutting the nails or changing the lower garments must never be done in the presence of a senior.

38. No junior may go to bed before all the seniors in the house have retired.

39. No junior may take food prior to seniors.

40. No junior may bathe prior to seniors.

41. No junior may sit down before a senior does.

42. If you meet a senior you must bow and follow him; you may only return home when he directs you to do so.

43. If a senior becomes absent-minded, be respectful when refreshing his memory.

44. If a senior makes a mistake, do not sneer at him, either publicly or in private.

45. When entering a senior's room, snap your fingers three times to announce your entrance.

46. When entering a senior's room, never do so through the centre of the doorway, for this indicates pride; always do so by either the left or right side of the door.

47. If you go regularly to a senior's room, always enter and leave by the side of the door; never go boldly through the centre of the entrance.

48. Do not take meals before a senior has taken his.

49. You may not stand up before a senior does.

50. If a benefactor or donor comes to see a senior, you must sit down, erect, and listen politely to the sermon that the senior may give; you may not leave the room abruptly.

51. Do not scold others in the presence of a senior, not even if they deserve it.

52. If a senior is present, do not call to others from a distance.

53. If you take off your kesa, do not leave it in a senior's room.

54. No junior may criticise a senior's sermon or lecture.

55. Do not clasp your hands around your knees if a senior is present.

56. Do not bow to a senior if he happens to occupy a less important seat than you at some function or meal.

57. Always come out of your room before bowing to a senior.

58. You must never bow to a senior if you are sitting on a chair and he is sitting on the floor.

59. If the senior has teachers, be mindful thereof.

60. If a senior has disciples, be as respectful to them as you are to him; never waver in your respect to a senior.

61. When one senior is with another senior, the seniority of either is of no account to the other.

62. For you, seniors will always exist; there will always be someone senior to you, both when you are a first-grade unsui and when you become a Buddha.

The foregoing code of behaviour represents the True Body and Mind of the Buddhas and patriarchs. If you do not realise this to the full, the Pure Law will disappear and the Way of the Buddhas and patriarchs will be laid waste. Only those who have done good works in former existences will be able to comprehend the value of this behavioural code; it is the very perfection of Mahāyāna.

SHŪRYOSHINGI

Trainees' Hall Rules

The behaviour in the trainee's hall must be in accordance with the Precepts of the Buddhas and patriarchs as well as with the teachings of the scriptures of the Theravāda and Mahāyāna, paying especial attention to the rules of Hyakujō. He states in his rules that our every action, whether great or small, must be in accordance with the Precepts of the Buddhas and patriarchs. Therefore we must read the Vinaya and other scriptures there.

The scriptures of the Mahāyāna and the words of the patriarchs must be read when in the hall. One must meditate deeply on the teachings of the old Zen masters and try to follow their teachings.

Nyojō Zenji, my former master, once said to his trainees, "Have you ever read the scripture delivered by the Buddha on his death-bed? Within this hall we must love each other and be deeply grateful for the opportunity of possessing a compassionate mind, which enables us to be parents, relatives, teachers and wise priests; because of this compassionate mind our countenances will for ever show tenderness and our lives will for ever be blissful. We must never speak ill of another even if his language is coarse. We should speak tenderly to such a one, gently pointing out his fault, rather than defame him when he is not present. When we hear something of value we should put it into practice; by so doing we gain great merit. How fortunate it is that we are together. How fortunate it is that we in this hall have been able to make the acquaintance of those who, in former lives, performed good works and have thus become the treasures of the priesthood. What joy! Amongst the laity there is a great difference between related and unrelated persons, yet the Buddhist brotherhood possesses greater intimacy than most persons have with themselves. Zen Master Enan, of Ōryūzan, once said, 'The fact that we are in this boat is due entirely to our good deeds in past lives; that we are blessed with the opportunity of spending the training period together in the same monastery is equally due to the same cause. Although we are now in the position of master and trainees, one day we will all be Buddhas and patriarchs.' "

We must not disturb others by reading scriptures or poetry in a loud voice when in the hall. Nor may we hold a rosary when in others' presence. Herein all that we do must be gentle.

Visitors must never be permitted to enter the hall, nor may they be conversed with there, whatever their occupation. Those who must speak to shopkeepers must do so elsewhere.

Never talk idly or joke when in the hall. However great is the desire to laugh, it must not be indulged; we must always remember the four views of Buddhism: that there is impurity of body, pain in sensation; that mind is transient and things have no ego; we must always remember to be devoted to Buddha, Dharma and Sangha. How can there be pleasure in a world wherein life is as transient as that of fish in a tiny pond? We must not chatter with fellow trainees. If we live an energetic life, we can train our minds to become as mountains despite many others around us.

One must never leave one's place to look at books which others may be reading. Such behaviour is an obstacle both to one's own progress and to that of others in the study of Buddhism. Than this there is no greater misfortune.

If the rules of the trainees' hall are broken, the guilty one must be duly warned by the seniors if the offence is of a trifling nature; if it is serious, the disciplinarian must deal with the offender suitably after hearing the facts. Beginners and those who have entered the priesthood late in life must be warned compassionately and respectfully. Whether or not they will obey this warning will depend upon the depth of sincerity of the mind of the individual trainee. The Temple Rules state that speech, deeds and actions must obey the trainees' hall rules. Seniors must show an example to juniors, leading them as a parent would lead his own child. This behaviour is in accordance with the Mind of the Buddhas and patriarchs.

Wordly affairs, fame, gain, war, peace, the quality of offerings, etcetera, may never be discussed in the hall. Such talk is neither significant nor useful, pure nor conscientious, and is strictly forbidden. It is to be understood that since the Buddha has been dead for so long a time our ability to gain enlightenment is too feeble to speak of. Time flies as does an arrow, and life is transient if we are slow in training. Wherever trainees may be from, they must make titanic efforts to train themselves, just as if their heads were to catch fire, they would make titanic efforts to extinguish the flames: time is precious and must never be wasted in idle chatter.

One must not pass in front of the holy statue in the hall, either from the right or the left, nor may one take notice of or speak about another's presence or absence; it is also forbidden to look at another's seat.

One may not lie down, stretch the legs, lean against the woodwork or expose one's private parts when on one's seat, for such behaviour is disturbing to others. The old Buddhas and patriarchs sat beneath trees or in open places, and we should remember their very excellent behaviour.

Gold, silver, other money and clothes may not be hoarded in the hall. The old Buddhas made this clear in the Precepts. Makakashyo, the First Patriarch, when a layman, was a thousand times richer than King Bimbisāra; in fact, his wealth was greater than that of all the sixteen countries of the time put together. However, once he left home and entered the priesthood, he wore ragged robes and had long hair, going begging until his death on Mount Kukkutapāda. Always the funzoe of the trainee served him for clothing. One should understand this very clearly. Since Makakashyo was thus, we trainees of a later generation must be careful of our manners.

When speaking to another in the hall, it must be in a quiet and polite voice. No noise must be made with slippers, and noses may not be blown loudly; others must not be disturbed by spitting, loud coughing or yawning; one must learn the teachings of the Buddhas and patriarchs and not waste time with poetry. Nor may we read the Buddha's teachings loudly in the hall, for this is rude to others.

If someone is impolite he must be warned by the disciplinarian; however important a senior is, he may not behave rudely or impolitely to others.

If one loses something, such as a robe, a bowl, or anything else, the following notice must be exhibited on the board specially provided therefor: "Trainee . . . . lost . . . . on . . . . at . . . . . I beg that whoever may find it shall exhibit a notice similar to this saying that it has been found." A great priest once said that although one may be guilty in the sight of the law of the world and be punished, in the law of Buddhism one is beyond such punishment; therefore we must not make judgements or guesses of our own that may be detrimental to another's character: the matter of dealing with lost articles must be in accordance with the rules of the temple. If anyone finds a lost article, the fact must immediately be announced by a notice to that effect.

Worldly, astrological or geographical books, heretical scriptures, philosophy, poetry or scrolls may not be left in the hall.

Bows and arrows, military equipment, swords, armour and other weapons are not permitted in the hall. If any person is found to be in possession of a sword, he must immediately be expelled from the temple. No instruments for immoral purposes are permitted within the temple.

Musical instruments may not be played, nor dancing performed, in or near the hall.

Wine, meat, garlic, onions, scallions and horse-radish may not be brought into the hall.

When there are many in the hall, juniors must be quick to do laborious work; it is not, however, necessary for seniors to be so: this is traditional. Juniors must be slower than seniors in doing enjoyable work, for this is the True Law of the Buddhas.

All sewing must be done behind the hall. During this time no idle chatter is allowed, for thoughts must for ever be upon the Buddhas and patriarchs.

Since the hall is for training only,, no ill-mannered person is permitted either to enter or to lodge there; nor may those who are weak-minded, even if good-mannered, sleep there or wander about for fear of disturbing others.

Worldly affairs and commerce may not be dealt with in the hall.

These rules are the Precepts of the Buddhas; in Eihei Temple they must be observed for all time.

FUSHUKUHAMPŌ

Mealtime Regulations

"When one is identified with the food one eats, one is identified with the whole universe; when we are one with the whole universe, we are one with the food we eat." This comes from the *Vimalakīrti Sūtra.* Therefore the whole universe and a meal are identical in quality.

If the whole universe is the Dharma, then food is also the Dharma: if the universe is Truth, then food is Truth: if one is illusion, then the other is illusion: if the whole universe is Buddha, then food is Buddha also. All are equal in all their aspects. "Both concept and reality are equal as they are in the eye of the Buddhas, there being no difference between them whatsoever." This comes from the *Lankāvatāra Sūtra.*

"If the universe is seen to be the realm of the spirit, there is nothing outside the realm of the spirit. If it is seen to be Truth, then there is nothing other than Truth. If it is seen to be the equal essence, then there is only essence. If it is seen as 'different appearance,' then there is only 'different appearance.'" These are the words of Basō.

Here "equal" is not relative but absolute, meaning the Buddha's Wisdom. There is no difference between the whole universe and the Truth when they are seen with this Wisdom Eye, for the very manifestation of Truth is that equalness. We are, therefore, the personification of the universe when we eat, but this is a fact that only the Buddhas fully understand. The universe is the personification of Truth. When we eat, the universe is the whole Truth: in its appearance, nature, substance, force, activity, cause, effect, relatedness, consequence and individuality. So the Truth manifests itself when we eat, and when eating, we can realise the manifestation of Truth. The correct mind when eating has been transmitted from one Buddha to another and creates ecstasy of both body and mind.

When the bell rings for the end of morning Zazen, breakfast is taken in the meditation hall, each trainee remaining in the same place that he occupied for meditation. The drum is then struck thrice and the bell eighteen times to announce to all the trainees that it is time for breakfast. In city temples the bell is rung first, and in country ones the drum is beaten first. At the sound of the drum or the bell, those facing the wall turn round to face each other across the tan, and those who work outside the meditation hall cease to do so, washing their hands and returning thereto with dignity. After hearing the three slow strokes on the wooden han, they enter the hall in silence and without looking about them. No speaking is permitted in the hall.

Whenever a trainee enters the hall he must make gasshō, which means that the tips of the fingers must be just below the tip of the nose. If the head is dropped, tilted or kept upright the fingertips must always be in alignment therewith, and when making gasshō, the arms must be kept away from the chest wall and the elbows away from the sides. When entering the hall through the front door, all except the abbot must enter by the left side, irrespective of where their seats may be, using the left foot as they pass the left pillar of the door lintel. The abbot enters the hall by the right side of the door or straight through the middle of the doorway. In either case he enters with the right foot first, which is the traditional manner, bows to the statue of Mañjuśrī, turns right and sits in his chair. The chief junior trainee goes through the gaitan and enters by the left side of the front entrance. If trainees enter by the rear door, those

whose seats are in the right half of the hall enter by the right side
of the rear door, using their right foot first, and those in the left
half enter at the left side, using their left foot first. They bow to
the east behind the statue of Mañjuśrī and go to their seats.

Seats in the meditation hall are allotted according to the date
of ordination, the date of admittance to the temple or the work done
by the trainee. However, during the training period of ninety days,
the first of these three considerations is the one always taken into
account.

When he wishes to sit on the tan, a trainee must first bow to his
own seat, which means that he bows to his neighbours' seats, turn
round clockwise and bow to the trainee on the opposite side of
the tan, push the left sleeve of his koromo under his left arm with
his right hand, the right sleeve under the right arm with the left
hand, lift the kesa in front with both hands, hold it with the left
hand, put his feet together, sit down on the edge of the tan and
remove his slippers. He next presses on the tan with his right hand,
lifts first the left leg and then the right, pushes his body backwards
on the seat from the edge so that he is not sitting on the part used
as a table, sits upright and places his left foot on his right thigh.
The kesa is then spread over the knees so as to hide the inner robes
from others' eyes. Robes must never be allowed to fall over the edge
of the tan, and enough space must be left between the seated trainee
and the edge for the food bowls to be spread out, this space being
regarded as pure. The three reasons for this are called the "Three
Purities": (1) the kesa is laid there, (2) bowls are spread there, (3)
heads point towards there during sleep.

The director, disciplinarian, cook, general maintenance, and abbot's attendant priests sit on the right side of the gaitan, and the
guestmaster, bathhouse, sickroom attendant, librarian, outdoor,
and teacher priests sit on the left side of it at this time.

After the wooden fish [mokugyo] has been struck three times
all must be in their seats, and no one may enter the hall thereafter.
The umpan, which is hung outside the kitchen, is then struck several
times to tell the trainees to rise, collect their bowls from above their
seats and carry them to the pure place in front of their seats; all do
this at the same time. All stand up quietly, turn to the right, bow
reverently to the name over their seats, make gasshō, hold up the

bowls with both hands, taking care that they are neither too high nor too low, turn to the left with the bowls near the chest, sit down and put the bowls to the left behind them. All trainees must be careful not to disturb their neighbouring trainees by bumping against them with any part of the body or turning so fast that the holy kesa flies out and scrapes their faces or shaven heads.

After this the senior who is in charge of the statue of Mañjuśrī offers it boiled rice, making gasshō, accompanied by a serving trainee who carries the rice box. He then bows to the statue, removes the crêpe cover from the mallet found behind it, returns to the front of the statue with his hands in gasshō, bows again, turns to the right, leaves the hall and goes to his own seat, passing the tan of the officers in charge of the eastern half of the temple.

After three strokes on the drum, the bell is struck seven times in front of the meditation hall. The abbot then enters and the trainees immediately rise from their seats. The abbot bows to Mañjuśrī and the trainees and sits down in his chair. The trainees then take their seats again. When they are settled, the attendant priest who has followed the abbot to the hall and is waiting outside it bows immediately, enters, places a table in front of the abbot's chair, bows and leaves the hall. The abbot's bowls are placed upon this table. The trainees, sitting upright and in a straight line, place their bowls in front of them. The disciplinarian enters, bows to Mañjuśrī, offers incense, bows again and walks to the mallet, making gasshō. After the wooden block has been struck once with the mallet, the trainees unfold their bowl covers.

In order to set out the bowls one must first make gasshō, untie the knot on the bowl cover and fold the dishcloth to an unobtrusive size, twice crosswise and thrice lengthwise, placing it, together with the chopstick bag, just in front of the knees. Spread the pure napkin over the knees and put the dishcloth, with the chopstick bag on top of it, under the napkin. The cover is then unfolded and the farther end is allowed to fall over the edge of the tan, the other three corners being turned under to make a pad for the bowls to be placed upon. The lacquered-paper table-top is taken in both hands, the under fold being held in the right hand and the top one in the left, and is unfolded as if to cover the bowls. Whilst holding it in the right hand, take the bowls with the left and place them in the centre of the left end of this table-top, thereafter taking them out from the large one separately, in order, beginning with the smallest. Only the thumb of each hand is used for removing them so as to prevent any clattering. When the meal is a small one, only three bowls are used. The chopsticks are then taken out of the bag, followed by the spoon; when the meal is over they are put in in reverse order, but the bowl-washing stick remains in the bag. The chopsticks and the spoon are placed with their handles to the right on the table-top in front of the bowls. The bowl-washing stick is then removed from the bag and placed between the soup bowl and the pickle bowl, with its handle pointing to the edge of the tan. All trainees then wait for the offering of rice to the spirits of the departed. The empty chopstick bag is folded in three and replaced under the napkin on top of the lacquered divider, the latter being on top of the dishcloth.

When the meal has been offered by a donor, the sickroom attendant priest enters the hall carrying the incense burner, followed by the donor. After offering incense to Mañjuśrī, he leads the donor all around the hall. At this time the donor holds his hands in gasshō and keeps his head bowed. The trainees make gasshō, without speaking, laughing, looking from side to side or moving their bodies, just sitting calmly and quietly.

The disciplinarian then strikes the wooden block once and recites the following:

> We take refuge in the Buddha,
> The completely perfect scriptures,
> The patriarchs and Bodhisattvas
> Whose merit is beyond all understanding.

> Today a donor has offered food. I pray you all to understand well his reasons for doing so, which I am about to read to you.
> *(The statement of the donor is read.)*
> I have read the donor's reasons for his offering, and I call upon the Buddhas and Bodhisattvas to witness its sincerity, for they are endowed with holy eyes which can see beyond both self and other. Now let us chant the names of the Ten Buddhas in chorus.

The disciplinarian and the trainees make gasshō, chanting as follows:

> The completely pure Buddha, Birushanofū, Dharma itself;
> The complete Buddha who has been rewarded for his previous training;
> Shakyamuni Buddha, one of the many Buddhas who has appeared in the many worlds;
> Miroku Buddha, who will appear in the future;
> All the Buddhas in all directions and in the Three Worlds;
> The great and excellent Dharma Lotus Scripture;
> Holy Monju Bodhisattva;
> The great and wise Fugen Bodhisattva;
> The great and kind Kanzeon;
> All the Bodhisattvas and ancestors;
> The Mahāprajñāpāramitā.

The disciplinarian continues:

> In the beginning the mallet will strike the Buddha on the foot;
> Later it will strike him on the head.

If the meal is an ordinary breakfast or lunch the disciplinarian will again strike the wooden block, saying:

> Having taken refuge in the Three Treasures
> All will be able to grasp them perfectly.

When the names of the Ten Buddhas have been chanted, the disciplinarian strikes the wooden block once. In order to show that a true trainee will be willing to offer food to all other creatures, the chief junior makes gasshō and chants the following verse loudly:

> *(For breakfast)*
> The ten benefits bless the breakfast gruel
> And all trainees profit greatly therefrom;
> Since these wonderful results are limitless
> Pleasure is ours for eternity.

> *(For dinner)*
> Since I will give Three Merits and six tastes
> To all the Buddhas and the priests
> All sentient beings within the universe
> Will enjoy this offering.

When the chief junior is not present, the priest next in rank chants the foregoing verses. A trainee then enters and says in a loud voice, "Breakfast is served." This trainee must enter the hall by the left of the door, bow to Mañjuśrī, bow to the abbot, bow to the chief junior, stand near the left side of the front door, bow to Mañjuśrī again and make gasshō. The words must be spoken clearly and no errors made in their announcement, since if these words are pronounced incorrectly the meal cannot be taken. Should this happen, the announcement must be made again. The chief junior bows to the food in front of him and meditates, and then he and all trainees start to eat. If a donor has offered money or food, the disciplinarian comes from behind the statue of Mañjuśrī, bows to the chief junior and asks him to give thanks for the gift. The disciplinarian strikes the wooden block once, and the chief junior recites the thanksgiving verse loudly:

> The two kinds of alms, material and spiritual,
> Have the endowment of boundless merit;
> Now that they have been fulfilled in this act of charity
> Both self and others gain pleasure therefrom.

The rice must be served carefully and never in a hurry, for if the serving is hurried, they who receive the food will be flustered; it must not be served slowly, however, for then the recipients will become tired. The rice must be served by those whose duty it is to act as waiters; no one who is sitting on the tan may serve himself. The first person to be served is always the chief junior, the abbot being served last. During the serving the hands of others and the rims of bowls must never be soiled with either soup or gruel. In order to indicate how much they wish to receive, those sitting on the tan must hold a spoon in their right hand, with the bowl towards the chest and the handle towards the serving trainee. The handle must be moved up and down gently two or three times when enough has been placed in the bowl, and the body bowed slightly. The amount of gruel received depends entirely upon this. The spare hand must never hang down when a soup bowl or other bowl is being put down; it must be kept in a one-handed gasshō. Trainees may not sneeze or cough whilst receiving food. However, if either is unavoidable, the trainee must turn his back to the others present before doing so. The Precepts of Buddha must always be followed whenever one carries the rice box.

One must be respectful when receiving gruel or rice, for the Buddha himself said that we must receive food with respect. This fact must be carefully remembered. When receiving food the bowl must be held up horizontally with both hands underneath it. Only the correct amount of gruel or rice may be placed therein; there must never be so much that some is left uneaten, and those who are doing the waiting must be notified when enough has been received by the lifting of two fingers of the right hand. When the food has been received, it must not be consumed greedily by seizing a spoon or chopsticks from the trainee doing the serving, nor may a trainee receive food from a serving trainee to whom he has lent his own spoon or chopsticks for the purpose of dishing it out. It was said by one of the ancestors that one must have the correct mind when receiving food, holding the bowl horizontally. Both the rice and the soup bowls must be filled and the rice, soup and other food taken in regular sequence. Food may not be eaten with the knees drawn up. Should a serving trainee be in so great a hurry that even a grain of rice or a drop of soup is spattered in another's bowl, the serving must be done again. The bowls may not be held up nor may the trainees take food until the disciplinarian has struck the wooden block to announce that the food has been served.

When the block is struck the trainees make gasshō, bow to their food and recite the Verse of the Five Thoughts:

> We will first share the merits of this food with the Three Treasures of the Dharma;
> Second, we will share it with the four benefactors, the Buddha, the president, our parents and all people;
> Third, we will share it with the six lokas;
> With all of these we share it and to all we make offering thereof.
> The first bite is to discard all evil;
> The second bite is so that we may train in perfection;
> The third bite is to help all beings;
> We pray that all may be enlightened.

We must think deeply of the ways and means by which this
food has come.

We must consider our merit when accepting it.

We must protect ourselves from error by excluding greed
from our minds.

We will eat this food lest we become lean and die.

We accept this food so that we may be become enlightened.

Rice offerings for the spirits of the departed may not be made
before this verse is finished. To make this offering, seven grains of
rice are placed on the handle of the bowl-washing stick or the edge
of the lacquered table-top. The offering is always made with the
thumb and middle fingers of the right hand. If the food served is
rice cakes, noodles or buckwheat, a ball the size of a small coin
should be taken from the bowl and placed as above; if the meal
consists only of gruel no offering is made, although there was a time
when this was actually done; however, no spoon or chopsticks were
used for the purpose. After the offering all trainees make gasshō
and keep silent.

The following is the correct way to eat breakfast. The gruel is received in the largest of the set of bowls, which is then replaced upon
its holder. After a few seconds' wait the second bowl is taken with
the right hand, placed on the left palm and held there by the top
of the thumb, which is turned slightly inwards. The spoon is taken
in the right hand and seven or eight spoonfuls of gruel are transferred from the first bowl to the second, the latter being held on the
left side of the former. The brim of the second bowl is put to the
lips, and gruel may be taken with the spoon. All the gruel is thus to
be eaten up by repetitions of this sequence. Should gruel be left in
the first bowl, the second bowl must be replaced upon the table, the
first bowl taken, and the gruel consumed with the spoon. The first
bowl is then cleaned with the bowl-washing stick and replaced upon
its holder. The second bowl is picked up and any gruel left therein
consumed; the trainee must then wait for water to be brought for
washing up after cleaning it with the bowl-washing stick.

The following is the correct way to eat lunch. The first bowl is
raised as high as the mouth and rice is put therein. This bowl may

not be left on the table nor may it be put to the lips. The Buddha said that food must be eaten with respect and never with arrogance, for should we have an arrogant appearance, we are only equal to children or harlots. The upper part of the bowl is regarded as pure and the lower part as defiled. The first bowl is held with the fingers underneath and the thumbs in the brim, the second and third fingers only being on the outside and the fourth and fifth being kept away from the bowl entirely. This is the correct way to hold the bowls.

In far-off India Shakyamuni Buddha and his disciples used neither chopsticks nor spoons, simply making the rice into balls with their right hands. We present-day Buddhists must remember this fact. Many heavenly deities, Cakravartī Rāja and emperors did likewise. We must understand that this was the ancient way. Only sick monks used spoons; all others ate their food with their hands. In India they have neither seen nor heard of chopsticks. They may only be seen in use in China and certain other countries, and it is only because of local custom that they are used in Zen monasteries. The Buddhist Precepts must be followed at all times, however, and the custom of taking food with the hands has long since died out. Since there are no teachers left whom we can question about the old traditional way, we use a spoon, chopsticks and bowls.

When picking up or replacing bowls, spoons and chopsticks, no noise may be made, nor may rice be stirred in the middle with the spoon. Only sick trainees may ask for extra food; the extra bowls may not be filled with rice, nor may a trainee look into a neighbour's bowl or disturb him. Lunch must be eaten carefully; large lumps of rice may not be crammed into the mouth, nor may balls be made and thrown into the mouth. Not even a grain of rice that has fallen on the table may be eaten; the lips may not be smacked whilst chewing rice and it may not be chewed whilst drinking soup. The Buddha said that tongues must not be long nor lips be allowed to be licked whilst taking food. This must be studied well. The hands may not be waved whilst eating; the knees may not be held with the elbows nor the food stirred. The Buddha said that food may never be stirred as if by a cook, thus leaving the hands soiled, nor may it be consumed noisily. He also said that food may not be piled up like the mound on a grave or the bowl heaped full; that soup may not be poured upon food as if to wash it within the bowl; that other food may not be mixed with that in the bowl; that other food may not be mixed with rice and held in the mouth after the manner of monkeys.

Meals may not be taken either too quickly or too slowly in the meditation hall. It is very impolite to eat everything up so fast that one sits and watches others eat with one's arms folded. Noise may not be made with bowls or spittle swallowed before the serving trainee announces "Second helpings" in a loud voice. No rice may be left uneaten or anything else asked for. It is not permitted to scratch the head during a meal; dandruff must not be allowed to drop into the bowls and the hands must not be soiled. The body may not be shaken; the knees may not be raised or held; yawning is not permitted, nor may the nose be blown loudly. If a fit of sneezing comes on, the nose must be carefully covered with the hand. If any food becomes jammed between the teeth, it must be removed with one hand covering the mouth from the sight of others. Fruit seeds and other similar waste must be put in a place where it will give no offence to others, a good place being on the lacquered table-top in front of the bowl, slightly hidden by the bowl's rim; others must never be allowed to become disgusted by such a sight. If anyone tries to give food or cake that is left over in his bowls to another, it may not be received. No serving trainee may use a fan in the meditation hall during the heat of summer, especially if a neighbouring trainee feels a chill. If a trainee feels that he has a chill coming on, he should tell the disciplinarian and take his meal elsewhere. If a trainee wishes to ask for something, he must do so quietly. If, at the end of the meal, any food remains in the bowl, it must be wrapped in the dishcloth. The mouth may not be opened wide, nor may rice be eaten in large spoonfuls; rice may not be spilled into the first bowl nor the spoon soiled. The Buddha said that one may not wait with one's mouth open for food nor speak with one's mouth full. He also said that trainees must not try to get extra food by covering the food in their bowls with rice or by covering the rice with other food. Careful notice must be taken of this advice. The Buddha also said that tongues must not be smacked at mealtimes, lips may not be licked, or food blown upon to warm or cool it. This must also be carefully remembered. After breakfast all bowls must be cleaned with the bowl-washing stick. If each mouthful is ladled carefully three times before eating, it will become of a suitable size. The Buddha said that when eating, rice-balls must be made neither too large nor too small.

The whole of the bowl of the spoon must be put completely into the mouth when eating lest food be spilled. No food or rice may be spilled upon the napkin. If any food is found upon the napkin it must be given to the serving trainee. If any unhusked rice is found in the rice in the bowl, it must be husked and eaten. It may not be thrown away, or swallowed without being husked.

In the Scripture of the Three Thousand Manners it says that if something unpleasant is found in the food it may not be eaten, nor may its presence be made known to any neighbouring trainee; nor may the food be spat out. If any rice should be left in the bowl, it must not be kept in the presence of a senior but given to a serving trainee. When the meal is over, trainees must be satisfied with it and require nothing more. From both the rational and the practical outlook one should try never to waste a single grain of rice at mealtimes; the whole universe is completely identified with the meal. The bowls may not be struck with the chopsticks or spoon, thus causing noise, nor may the lustre of the bowls be impaired. If the bowls lose their lustre they will become unuseable as a result of dirt and grease. When water is drunk from the bowls no sound may be made with the mouth in doing so, nor may it be disgorged into the bowl or other utensils. The face and hands may not be wiped with the napkin.

In order to wash the bowls, the sleeves of the robe must be carefully arranged so that they do not touch anything; then hot or cold water must be received in the first bowl. After receiving the water, the bowl must be carefully washed with the bowl-washing stick, the bowl being turned carefully from left to right. The used water is then poured into the second bowl, and the first bowl is washed carefully again, both inside and out, with the washing stick, turning the bowl with the left hand and holding the washing stick in the right. The bowl is then held in the left hand whilst the dishcloth is unfolded with the right and spread out as if to cover the bowl. The bowl is then taken in both hands and wiped with the unfolded dishcloth, being turned from left to right in the wiping. The dishcloth is put into the bowl so that it may not be seen from the outside, and the bowl is replaced on its stand. The spoon and the chopsticks are next washed in the second bowl and wiped with the dishcloth. During this the dishcloth must remain in the first bowl to hide it from view, only a corner of it being used to wipe the spoon and chopsticks. When the spoon and chopsticks have been wiped, they must be put into the chopstick bag and placed in front of the second bowl. The second bowl is then washed in the third one; it and the bowl-washing stick are held lightly with the left hand; the third bowl is taken in the right hand and put in the place the second one occupied. The water is then transferred to the third bowl, and the second bowl is washed in the third one in the same way as the first one was. The same sequence for washing is used for the third and fourth bowls. No spoon, chopsticks or bowls may be washed in the first bowl. First the first bowl is washed and wiped, then the spoon, chopsticks, second, third and fourth bowls. All the bowls are put into the first one separately as each is washed; then the bowl-washing stick is wiped and put into the chopstick bag. The napkin may not be folded before the dirty water has been discarded. This water may not be thrown upon the floor. The Buddha said that leftover food may not be put into the water. This point must be studied carefully. When the dirty-water bowl is brought, trainees must make gasshō and empty the water into it, being careful to see that the dirty water does not soil the sleeves of the robe. Fingers may not be washed in the water nor may it be thrown away in an unclean place. The second, third and fourth bowls are put into the first one with the thumbs only, in the reverse order from when they were removed.

The first bowl is then held up with the left hand and placed in the middle of the bowl cover, the lacquered table-top being taken out from underneath it with the right hand. This table-top is then folded with both hands over the top of the first bowl and placed on top of it. The bowls are covered with the cover, the nearer end of it being put over the bowls and the far end folded towards the trainee. The napkin is folded and placed on the cover, and the chopstick bag is placed on top of the napkin. Originally the bowl-washing stick was put on top of the napkin, but now it is put into the bag. The dishcloth is put on top of the chopstick bag and the two other corners of the cover are tied together over the bowls. Both ends of this tie should be on the right, in order to tell the right way round of the bowls and to make their untying simple. When the bowls have been wrapped, the trainees make gasshō and sit quietly. The wooden block is struck once by the Mañjuśrī statue attendant. This means that the trainees may leave the meditation hall.

The trainee sitting to the left of the abbot's attendant, on the gaitan, rises from his seat, bows to the Mañjuśrī statue, goes to the west side of the wooden block on the south side of the incense bowl, bows to the block, makes gasshō, and waits for the abbot and the trainees to wrap their bowls completely. When they have all finished he hits the wooden block once, covers the mallet with the mallet cover, makes gasshō and again bows to the block. The disciplinarian then recites the following:

> The universe is as the boundless sky,
> As lotus blossoms above unclean water;
> Pure and beyond the world is the mind of the trainee;
> O Holy Buddha, we take refuge in Thee.

Abbot Eisai transmitted this traditional way of ending meals, and so we continue to do it thus.

The abbot then leaves the hall. When he leaves his chair, the attendant of the Mañjuśrī statue must immediately leave the place where he has been standing beside the wooden block and hide behind the curtain of the Mañjuśrī statue lest he should be seen by the abbot.

The trainees then rise and replace their bowls above their seats. The bowls must be held with both hands as the trainees stand up, turn to the right and place the bowls above the seat with the right hand, hanging them on the hook whilst supporting them with the left hand. The trainees then make gasshō, come back to the edge of the tan and descend slowly. They put on their slippers and bow to each other. When tea is taken in the meditation hall, behaviour is the same as above, and the method of sitting down on the tan and descending from it is always the same at all times.

The cushions are placed under the tan, and the trainees leave the hall. When the abbot has left the hall, the end of morning Zazen is announced by three strokes of the bell. If Zazen is to be continued no bell is sounded. However, if a donor asks the trainees to go to the meditation hall, they must do so even if the bell has already been rung. Thereafter the bell must be rung again to announce the end of morning Zazen. When tea is over in the afternoon and the abbot has bowed to Mañjuśrī and left the hall, the bell is struck three times to tell the trainees to leave the hall, and they then descend from the tan. They leave the hall in the same way that they entered it, as described earlier. All walking in the meditation hall must be after the manner of kinhin, half a step to each breath, as is done in the kinhin periods during Zazen.

BENDŌHŌ

How to Train in Buddhism

The Buddhas and patriarchs have only ever been able to grasp the Way of Buddhist training because of the way it shows itself in the Dharma. When sitting down or when lying down to rest, all trainees must behave in exactly the same way; most of their actions must be done in an identical manner. As long as they live, trainees must live a life of purity in their monastery; they must realise clearly that wilful acts against other trainees are valueless, being contrary to the behaviour of true Zen trainees. The correct ordering of daily life is therefore the heart of Buddhism. When by the correct ordering of our daily life we exhibit the heart of Buddhism, we are free from delusive body and mind. As this is so, the disciplined life of the trainee is the embodiment of both enlightenment and practice, pure and immaculate since before time began. It is the first appearance of the kōan. For those who follow it there is never any need to try to grasp enlightenment.

Evening Zazen commences with the sound of the evening bell. The trainees put on their kesas and go to their places in the meditation hall. The abbot does his evening Zazen in his chair facing the Mañjuśrī statue, the chief junior sits quietly facing the edge of the tan, and the other trainees do their Zazen facing the wall. The abbot's attendant or other serving trainee sits on the stool behind a screen, which is placed behind the abbot's chair so that he may attend the abbot.

The abbot enters on the right-hand side of the front entrance of the meditation hall, goes to bow to Mañjuśrī, offers incense, bows again, goes around the meditation hall in the fashion of kentan, making gasshō, returns to Mañjuśrī and bows. He then goes to his seat, bows thereto, turns round clockwise to face Mañjuśrī, bows again, sits down and pulls up the sleeves of his robe tidily, having taken off his slippers and covered his feet with his robe whilst sitting in paryanka. The attendant or serving trainee does not do kentan with the abbot but waits to the left of the front door. After the abbot has sat down, this attendant goes to his seat behind the abbot, where he bows to Mañjuśrī before sitting down. The attendant always carries the abbot's incense box. Should the abbot wish to sleep in the meditation hall, his bed must be made ready at the left-hand side of the chief junior. When the abbot awakens, he at once leaves his bed to continue his Zazen in his chair. It is customary for trainees to wear no kesa during early-morning Zazen, and that of the abbot is hung on his chair.

The drum and bell are struck at the end of evening Zazen to tell the time at which the abbot wishes to do his morning meditation, both hour and minute, and the han is struck thrice.

At the sound of the han the trainees make gasshō, remove and fold their kesas, put them in their cases and place them upon the top of their cupboards. The abbot does not remove his kesa. He leaves his chair, bows to Mañjuśrī, and leaves the hall by the right-hand side of the front entrance; his attendant and serving trainee wait for him in front of the meditation hall door; this is also the place where they stand when he enters the meditation hall. Should the abbot sleep in the meditation hall, one or two of his serving trainees must remain on the stool or form behind his chair whilst some of his five attendants sleep to the left of the Mañjuśrī statue attendant, on the gaitan where the new trainees have their sitting place. All trainees must continue to do Zazen until the abbot leaves the meditation hall. When he has gone, they quietly make their beds, set their pillows and lie down together. No one is allowed to remain sitting in Zazen by himself nor to observe those who are sleeping; nor may anyone deliberately leave his place and go to the lavatory. This is correct behaviour in the meditation hall, for the Scripture of the Three Thousand Manners says that there are five rules when sleeping: (1) The head must always point in the direction of the Buddha statue. (2) No one may observe the Buddha from a lying position. (3) The legs may not be stretched out. (4) Trainees may not face the wall or lie on their faces. (5) The knees may not be raised.

The right side, never the left, must always be towards the floor when lying down or sleeping. Heads must point towards the edge of the tan in the direction of the Mañjuśrī statue. It is forbidden to lie on the face or back with the knees up or the legs crossed. The legs may not be stretched out, the bedclothes may not be pulled down, and the body may not be stripped as is the fashion amongst unbelievers. At all times when lying down, our minds must be filled with light as brilliant as that of the heavenly beings.

The han in front of the chief junior's room is usually struck at three in the morning, as stated above; however, the exact hour depends upon the abbot's wishes. The trainees rise in silence, without making any fuss. No one is permitted to remain in bed alone on the tan; this is impolite to others. Each trainee puts his pillow in front of his own cupboard in silence for fear of disturbing his neighbouring trainees. He then remains in his own place, wearing part of his bedding as a covering and sitting on his Zazen cushion. No one is permitted to close his eyes, for should he do so he would feel sleepy. Trainees must strive to open their eyes over and over again; the morning breeze will eventually open them completely. All are far from understanding the Way of the Buddhas, and time flies as does an arrow. Should a trainee feel sleepy he must not shake himself, straighten up, yawn, sigh or disturb others; respect for others must always be the first consideration when with fellow trainees. No one may despise another. The head may not be covered with any part of the bedding; if sleepiness becomes overwhelming, the bedcover must be removed and Zazen continued in light clothes.

The correct time for washing the face and hands behind the meditation hall is when there are not too many other trainees doing so. A long towel, folded double, must be carried over the left arm with both ends hanging inside. The trainees rise and descend from the tan, leaving the meditation hall by the rear door as quietly as possible, after rolling up the bamboo screen outside it. Those who sit to the right of Mañjuśrī leave the hall by the right-hand side of the door, using their right foot to step through it. Those on the left side use their left foot and leave by the left side. Slippers may not be dragged when walking, nor may trainees walk noisily. They also may not speak to anyone they meet on the way to the washroom, nor may they chant any scripture, not even if no one else is present. The hands must not hang down whilst walking, but be kept folded. In the washroom, trainees must not dig others in the ribs with their elbows when waiting their turn to wash, but wait quietly. Having secured a place in which to wash, the trainees do so.

The correct way of washing the face is to hang the towel round the neck with both ends hanging on the chest. These ends are then brought back under the arms, crossed at the back, brought forward again to the chest, and tied securely. This is as if the sleeves were tucked beneath a sash tied under the armpits; in this way the collar and sleeves are held back from the arms and thereby protected.

All trainees then take the toothbrush and make gasshō, reciting the following:

> I take the toothbrush that all living things may profit;
> May they understand the Truth quickly and become naturally pure.

The teeth are then cleaned and the next verse recited:

> Our teeth are cleaned this morning that all living things may profit;
> Since they control the fang of delusion, let us crush delusion as this toothbrush is crushed in the mouth.

The Buddha said that we should not crush the toothbrush over more than one-third of the thicker end; in both cleaning the teeth and cleansing the tongue the Buddha's teachings must be carefully followed. The tongue should not be scraped with the toothbrush more than three times, and if the tongue bleeds, trainees must cease to scrape it. The old regulations for trainees say that the crushing of the toothbrush, the rinsing of the mouth and the scraping of the tongue are the proper way to cleanse the mouth. When others are present at this time, the mouth must be covered so that the sight of its cleaning may not disgust them. Blowing the nose and spitting must also be done discreetly. In Great Sung most temples had no washroom behind the meditation hall, but here it is to be found there.

The washbasin is placed by the water heater; hot water is ladled into it and carried to the place for washing. Water is then taken in the hands and the face carefully washed. The eyes, nostrils, ears and mouth must be washed so that they become the embodiment of the purest immaculacy according to the Buddha's Precepts. Trainees must be careful in the use of hot water so that they are not wasteful of it; water with which the mouth has been rinsed must not be disposed of in the washbasin but spat out elsewhere. The body must be bent or the head lowered whilst the face is washed; trainees may not stand upright, thereby splashing others or their basins. All dirt, grease and sweat must be washed from the face, the water being scooped up by the hands. The right hand unties the knot in the towel and the face is then wiped; however, if there is a public towel, this should be used instead. Others must not be disturbed by noise made with the basin and the ladle, nor may the throat be gargled. According to the old regulations, face washing at four in the morning is part of Buddhist training. The regulations also say that it is not permitted for trainees to spit deliberately or disturb others with noise made by mishandling the basin.

Trainees return to the meditation hall in the same way that they left it. After returning to their seats they continue to do Zazen correctly, using part of the bedding as a covering if they so wish, but no kesa is worn at this time. Trainees may not leave their seats when changing their night clothes for day clothes. To do so they must put the day robe over their head, unfasten the night robe carefully and take the arms from the sleeves, slipping it off the shoulders so that it drops to the knees like a covering. The day robe is then fastened and the night robe taken by the sleeves and folded, after which it is put inside the trainee's own cupboard; the procedure is the same when changing from day to night clothes. Nakedness is strictly forbidden on the tan; trainees may not fold clothes standing up; they may not scratch their heads or recite their rosaries, thus showing contempt for other trainees; nor may they talk to their neighbouring trainees or sit or lie in a crooked line. Trainees may not creep about on the tan when getting on or leaving it; when so doing, they must be careful not to make a rustling noise with their robes by sweeping the tan with either their sleeves or their skirts. The han in front of the chief junior's room is struck at four in the morning. No trainee may enter by the front entrance after the abbot and the chief junior have sat down. Beds may not be put away in cupboards until after the umpan has been sounded in the kitchen and the hans in front of the various buildings struck to announce the end of Zazen. At the sound of these, beds and pillows are put away, the curtain is raised, the kesa is put on, and all turn round to face each other. The serving trainee belonging to the sick-room attendant priest rolls up the bamboo screens at the front and back doors of the meditation hall, offers incense and lights the candle in front of Mañjuśrī.

The correct way to fold the top cover of the bed is to take two corners and put them together, doubling it lengthwise, and then fold it in four. It is then folded in four again crosswise, making sixteen folds altogether, and put into the trainee's cupboard, with the pillow inside it, the folds of the bedding facing the cupboard door. The trainees make gasshō, take their kesa cases and put them on top of the bedding, open them, make gasshō, turn two sides of the case downwards so as to cover the bedding to the right and left but not to the front or back.

The trainees make gasshō again, place the kesa on their heads, again make gasshō and recite the following verse:

> How great and wondrous are the clothes of enlightenment,
> Formless yet embracing every treasure;
> I wish to unfold the Buddha's teaching
> That I may help all living things.

The kesa is then unfolded and put on, and the trainees turn round to sit facing each other, folding their bedding carefully lest it should touch the seat of a neighbouring trainee. All trainees must behave prudently, never being either rough or noisy, the Law being ever with them. Trainees must respect other trainees in their every act, never at any time doing anything against them. When the bell for the end of Zazen has been rung, it is not permitted for any trainee to remake a bed and lie thereon. When breakfast is over, all trainees return to the trainees' hall, have tea or hot water, or sit quietly in their places.

The notice saying "Zazen" is hung outside the meditation hall, the trainees' hall and the chief junior's room, as well as by the abbot's room and the sickroom. The chief junior and all the other trainees put on their kesas, enter the meditation hall and go to their places, and all except the chief junior meditate facing the wall, including the trainees who live in the western half of the monastery. As previously, the abbot sits in his chair facing Mañjuśrī. No trainee may turn his head to observe others entering or leaving the hall, or for any other purpose.

If a trainee wishes to leave the hall in order to go to the lavatory, he must remove his kesa before leaving his seat, put it on top of the folded bedding and leave the tan whilst making gasshō. Such a trainee must turn round, facing the edge of the tan, put his feet over the edge and put on his slippers. The eyes must be lowered when entering or leaving the meditation hall, since no trainee may observe the backs of other trainees. When walking, the feet and body must move in such a way that their movements are combined naturally, the eyes being fixed upon the floor on a spot approximately eight feet in front of the feet. The correct length of a step when walking is the length of the trainee's own foot; the walking must be done slowly and silently so as to give the semblance of standing still; the feet may not be dragged, causing noise with the slippers, nor may trainees make a pit-pat noise with them for fear of being impolite and disturbing the minds of other trainees. All walking must be done with the hands folded, the sleeves never being allowed to hang down to the legs.

The kesa may not be folded whilst standing on the tan, nor may the ends thereof be held in the mouth; it may not be shaken, trodden on or held under the chin; it may not be touched with wet fingers, or hung beside Mañjuśrī or on the edge of the tan. When a trainee sits down whilst wearing his kesa, he must be careful to see that he does not sit upon it as well as make sure that no part of it is under his feet. It may only be put on after making gasshō; trainees must also make gasshō when they place their kesas in their cases, for this is the traditional manner and must be carefully followed.

It is strictly forbidden to leave one's seat and go out of the hall whilst wearing the kesa. When the umpan is struck in the kitchen all trainees make gasshō at the same time, this being the signal for the end of morning Zazen. If it is early-morning Zazen, the trainees put on their kesas after hearing the umpan and leave the hall, leaving their cushions on their seats since these may not be put away until lunchtime. The sickroom attendant priest tells the serving trainee to put away the notice announcing Zazen after hearing the closing bell of late-morning Zazen, for this is the only period of Zazen at which this notice is hung up. Should there be no evening Zazen, the notice which says that there will be no Zazen that evening is hung up until the evening bell is sounded. The correct way to announce Zazen is to strike the han in the morning and the bell in the evening. When hearing these, each trainee puts on his kesa, enters the meditation hall and, after sitting down, does his Zazen facing the wall. For early-morning Zazen and for evening also, the kesa is not worn when entering the meditation hall; in the evening all trainees enter the hall carrying their folded kesas over their left arms, go to their seats, take out their cushions and do Zazen, beds not yet having been made, although originally the traditional way was to make half of each trainee's bed. The folded kesa is taken from the left arm, folded in four and put on top of the bedding, after which Zazen is done. During early-morning Zazen the kesa is put on the top of the cupboard; the kesa may not be moved about as trainees wish.

Cushions must always be used during Zazen. The correct way of sitting is completely cross-legged with the right foot resting on the left thigh and the left foot resting on the right thigh. It is also permitted to sit half-cross-legged, which means that only the right foot is placed upon the left thigh.

The back of the right hand is then rested on the left leg and the left hand is placed in the right palm, the thumbs touching each other lightly. All must then sit upright, their heads in a straight line with their spines, neither leaning to right or left nor bending backwards or forwards. The ears should be in line with the shoulders and the nose with the navel. The tongue should rest lightly behind the top teeth, with lips and teeth firmly closed. The eyes must be kept naturally open, the pupils not being covered with the eyelids; the back of the neck must be in a straight line with the back. Breathe quietly through the nose, not hard or noisily; the breaths must not be too long or too short, too fast or too slow. Sitting in this steady position of both body and mind, trainees should breathe all their breath all the way out and sway from right to left seven or eight times. Thoughts must not be discriminated about: this is good or this is bad; understanding is only possible when one is beyond discriminative thought. This is vital to Zazen.

When wishing to leave the tan, trainees must do so quietly and slowly after standing up. They must not walk quickly, and their hands must be in a folded position, for they are not permitted to dangle. When walking, trainees are not permitted to look about them, but must look modestly at their feet, taking gentle steps. All trainees must perform all their actions together regularly and in a timely manner. This is the correct way to practise Buddhism.

If there is to be no evening Zazen, this fact is announced during the afternoon Zazen. The trainees put away their cushions after lunch and leave the meditation hall in order to go to the trainees' hall to rest in their places. After about two hours, which is roughly around three in the afternoon, they return to the meditation hall, take out their cushions and do Zazen, after which they leave their cushions until the time for lunch on the following day. The chief junior enters the meditation hall from the gaitan, using the left-hand side of the front door, before it is announced that there will be no evening Zazen. Prior to doing this, he sometimes strikes the han in front of his room three times. After entering, he offers incense to Mañjuśrī, goes around the meditation hall, following the edge of the tan as in kentan, and then sits down in his place. The sickroom attendant priest's trainee server goes to all the rooms in the temple to tell the other trainees that the chief junior is now in the meditation hall. If there is no evening Zazen, the han in front of the trainees' hall is struck three times. On hearing this, the trainees return to the meditation hall, put on their kesas and sit down facing each other on the tan; those who usually look at the wall put on their kesas and then turn round and face each other. The sickroom attendant's serving trainee hangs up the notice which says there will be no evening Zazen, this having been permitted by the abbot. He then rolls up the bamboo screen, re-enters the hall, bows to Mañjuśrī and goes to bow to the chief junior, making gasshō. Bowing, he says softly that the abbot has released all trainees from evening Zazen.

The chief junior acknowledges this with a silent gasshō, and the serving trainee goes to Mañjuśrī, bows, rises, makes gasshō and says in a loud voice, "Rest," which means that there will be no evening Zazen. He then leaves the hall to strike the bell three times to announce this to everyone. The trainees bow to each other, making gasshō in the same way as at meals. If the abbot is present he rises, bows to his chair, bows to Mañjuśrī and leaves the hall. The trainees leave the tan, bow to each other, get up on the tan again to make their beds, lower the bamboo screen and go to the trainees' hall. After arriving there they bow to each other and sit on their seats facing each other. If they wish, they may take supper.

An offering of hot water is respectfully made to Mañjuśrī after the chief junior has sat down, and the priest in charge of the hall offers incense. During this incense offering all trainees must make gasshō. Whilst making this offering, the priest in charge may have a kesa hanging over his left arm if the abbot has so directed, or if it is the custom of the temple.

The priest in charge then bows to Mañjuśrī, offers incense with his right hand, makes gasshō, turns right, for the incense offering was made at the censer, returns to Mañjuśrī, bows, makes gasshō, bows in the centre of the right half of the hall, makes gasshō, turns right, goes to the centre of the left half of the hall, passing in front of Mañjuśrī, bows, makes gasshō, turns right, returns to Mañjuśrī, bows, makes gasshō, makes the hot-water or tea offering, offers incense again and bows as previously.

GYAKUDOYŌJINSHU

Important Aspects of Zazen

1. NECESSITY FOR A DESIRE FOR THE WAY

Although there are many names given to that which seeks the Way, they all refer to one and the same Mind. Nagyaarajyuna said, "The universality of change, the arising and disappearing, when completely understood, is the seeing into the heart of all things, and the Mind that thus understands is the Mind that truly seeks the Way." As this is so, why is temporary dependence upon the ordinary mind of man called the Mind that seeks the Way? If one sees through the changeability of the universe, the ordinary selfish mind is not in use; that which seeks for the sake of itself is nowhere to be found.

Time flies like an arrow from a bow and this fact should make us train with all our might, using the same energy we would employ if our hair were to catch fire. We must guard against weakness of body, our effort being as that of the Buddha when raising his foot. Sounds that flatter and distract, such as the call of Kinnara and the voice of the kalavinka bird, should be thought of as no more than the sound of the evening breeze. The sight of beautiful courtesans should be regarded merely as dew touching the eyes. Once free from perceptual bondage, sound and colour, the Mind that seeks the Way is naturally in harmony with you. From ancient times there have been those who did not hear Buddhist Truth, and some have had little opportunity of hearing or reading the scriptures. Once trapped in the bonds forged by fame and gain, most people lose the life of Buddha for eternity; such a fate is to be pitied and mourned. Just to read the scriptures, thereby understanding Truth with the ordinary mind, and to transmit that which is clear and that which is hidden, is not to possess the Mind that seeks the Way if fame and gain are not forsaken.

There are those who believe that the Mind that seeks the Way is truly enlightened since there is no dependence upon fame and gain. There are those who say that the Mind that seeks the Way embraces three thousand worlds in a moment of thought as its meditation. There are those who say that the Mind that seeks the Way teaches the non-arising of any delusion. There are those who say that the Mind that seeks the Way enters straightway into the World of the Buddhas. None of these people yet know the Mind that seeks the Way and therefore they devalue it, being far from the Truth of the Buddhas. When one reflects upon the selfish mind, which concerns itself with only fame and gain, it is clear that it has no knowledge of the three thousand worlds within a thought-moment, nor is it non-delusional. Such a mind knows nothing other than delusion because of its immersion in fame and gain; it cannot be compared to the Mind that seeks the Way. Although many of the wise have used worldly methods to reach enlightenment, it is certain that they had no misunderstanding in their own minds concerning fame and gain; they did not even have an attachment to Truth, and no desire whatever for the world as most men know it.

The Mind that truly seeks the Way can be any one of those previously mentioned so long as it also clearly sees through the changeability of the universe, understanding utterly arising and disappearing. The Mind is utterly different from the mind of ordinary men. It is excellent to practise the meditations of the non-arising mind and the appearance of the three thousand worlds after you have gained the Mind that seeks the Way, but do not confuse the two by putting them in the wrong order.

Forget the selfish self for a little and allow the mind to remain natural, for this is very close to the Mind that seeks the Way. Self is the basis of the sixty-two private opinions, so when you are beginning to become full of your own opinions, just sit quietly and watch how they arise. On what are they based, both within you and outside you? Your body, hair and skin come from your parents. The seeds that came from your parents, however, are empty both from the beginning of time until the end of it. Within this there is no ego; the mind that is fettered by discrimination, knowledge and dualism of thought blinds us. After all, in the end, what is it that inhales and exhales? These two are not the self, and there is no self to which to cling. They who live in delusion cling to all things, whilst they who are enlightened are free of clinging and things. But still we measure the unreal self and grasp at worldly appearances, thus ignoring true Buddhist practice; by failing to sever the ties of the world, we are turning our backs upon the true teachings and chasing after false ones. Such mistakes must be carefully avoided.

2. THE NECESSITY OF TRAINING FOR TRUTH

When a loyal servant gives advice, its power is frequently far-reaching; when the Buddhas and patriarchs give so much as a single word, all living things will be converted. Only a wise king will take advice; only an exceptional trainee will truly hear the words of the Buddha. If the mind cannot change from one side to the other, the source of transmigration can never be severed; unless the loyal servant's advice is taken, the government of a country will show no virtue and wisdom in its policy.

3. THE NECESSITY OF CONSTANTLY PRACTISING THE WAY IN ORDER TO REALISE ENLIGHTENMENT

Most people think that one must study in order to gain wealth, but the Buddha teaches that training embraces enlightenment. As yet I have heard of no one who became wealthy without much study, nor of anyone who became enlightened without undergoing training. There are, of course, differences in training methods, differences between faith and understanding, between sudden and gradual, but enlightenment can only be realised as a result of training. Some means of study are shallow and others deep, some are interesting and others boring, but treasure is derived from much study. None of these things depend upon the ability of rulers or on just plain luck. If treasure is attainable without study, who is able to teach the way through which rulers learn to truly rule? If enlightenment can be realised without training, the teaching of the Buddhas cannot be perfected. Although you may be training in the world of delusion, it is still the world of enlightenment. If you can understand that ships and rafts are but a past dream, you will for ever leave behind the self-opinions which fettered you to the scriptures. The Buddhas do not force you; it comes out of your own efforts in the Way. When you train you are beckoning to enlightenment; your own treasure is within you, not outside. Training and enlightenment are their own reward; enlightened action leaves no sign by which it can be traced. To look back upon one's training with enlightened eyes is to see no speck of dust. To look for such a thing is the same as trying to see a white cloud at a distance of ten thousand miles. When encompassing training and enlightenment, no single speck of dust can be trodden upon; should we do so, heaven and earth would collapse, but in returning to our True Home, we are transcending the status of the Buddha.

4. THE NECESSITY OF SELFLESS TRAINING

The truth of Buddhist training has been handed on to us by our predecessors, and for this it is impossible to use the selfish mind. We can gain the Truth of Buddhism neither with mind nor without mind. It must be remembered that if the will to train and the Way of the Buddhas are not harmonised, neither body nor mind will know peace; if body and mind are not at peace, they know only discomfort.

How do we harmonise the Way of the Buddhas with training? To do so the mind must neither grasp nor reject anything; it must be completely free from the fetters of fame and gain. Buddhist training is not undergone for the sake of others, but, like the minds of most people nowadays, the minds of most Buddhist trainees are far from understanding the True Way. They do that which others praise although they know such action to be wrong; they do not follow the True Way because it is that which others heap scorn upon. This is indeed a great grief. Such behaviour is no right use of the Mind of the Buddhas. The Buddhas and the patriarchs selflessly illuminated the universe with their all-penetrating eyes, and it is our duty to copy them. Since Buddhist trainees do almost nothing for themselves, how is it possible that they should do anything for the sake of fame and gain? Only for the sake of Buddhism must one train in Buddhism. Out of their deep compassion for all living things the Buddhas do absolutely nothing either for themselves or for others, merely doing all for the sake of Buddhism, and this is the True Tradition of Buddhism. Even insects and animals cherish their young, bearing any hardship for their sake, and when later they are full-grown the parents seek no gain therefrom. Just as compassion is strong in such small creatures, even so is compassion for all living creatures strong in the Buddhas. But compassion is not the only expression of the great teachings of the Buddhas; they appear in a myriad ways throughout the universe, this being the True Spirit of Buddhism. Since we are all already the children of Buddha, we have no alternative but to follow the path of Buddhism. You, as a Buddhist trainee, must not think of training as done for your own benefit and fame, nor must you train in Buddhism for the sake of getting results or performing miracles; you must simply train in Buddhism for the sake of Buddhism, this being the True Way.

5. THE NECESSITY OF FINDING A TRUE TEACHER

A former patriarch once said, "If the mind that seeks is untrue, training will be useless." This is utterly true, and the quality of the training inevitably depends upon the quality of the teacher. The trainee is like a beautiful piece of wood which the teacher must fashion as does a skilful carpenter; even beautiful wood will show no graining unless the carpenter is an expert, but a warped piece of wood can show good results in the hands of a skilled craftsman. The truth or falsity of the teacher is in ratio to the truth or falsity of the enlightenment of his disciples: understand this clearly and become enlightened. Yet for centuries there have been no good teachers in this country. How do we know? Just look at their words. They are like people who try to measure the source of flowing water from a scooped-up handful. Throughout the centuries this country's teachers have written books, taught trainees, given lectures to both men and gods, but their words were like green, unripe fruit, for they had not reached the ultimate in training; they had not become one with true enlightenment. All that they transmitted was words, reciting names and sounds. Day in and day out they counted in the treasury of others, contributing nothing thereto of themselves. There is no doubt that this is the fault of the teachers of old, for some of them misled others into believing that enlightenment must be sought outside the mind and some taught that rebirth in other lands was the goal; herein is to be found the source of both confusion and delusion. Unless one follows the prescription on the medicine bottle, an illness may be made worse by taking medicine; it may even be the same as drinking poison. For centuries there have been no good doctors in this country who were capable of prescribing correctly and of knowing the difference between true medicine and poison; therefore it is extremely difficult to cure the sufferings and diseases of life. Since this is so, how is it possible for us to escape from the sufferings brought on by old age and death? Only the teachers are to blame for this problem; it is certainly no fault of the disciples. Why is this so? Because the teachers are leading others along the branches of the tree and ceasing to climb up the trunk to the source. They lure others into false paths before they have their own under-standing based in certainty, and fix their concentration solely upon their own selfish opinions. It is indeed terrible that teachers have no perception of their own delusions. Under these circumstances, how can disciples understand what is right and what is wrong? As yet Buddhism has not taken root in our tiny country and thus true teachers are yet to be born. If you truly want to study the very best Buddhism, you must visit the teachers in China, which is very far away, and you must think deeply upon the true road which is beyond the mind of delusion.

If a true teacher is not to be found, it is best not to study Buddhism at all. They who are called good teachers, however, are not necessarily either young or old but simple people who can make clear the true teaching and receive the seal of a genuine master. Neither learning nor knowledge is of much importance, for what characterises such teachers is their extraordinary influence over others and their own will power. They neither rely on their own selfish opinions nor cling to any obsession, for training and understanding are perfectly harmonised within them. These are the characteristics of a true teacher.

6. THE NECESSITY OF BEING AWARE DURING ZAZEN

Zazen being of grave importance, neither neglect it nor regard it lightly. There have been magnificent examples of old masters in China who cut off their arms or fingers for the sake of the Truth. Centuries ago the Buddha forsook both his home and his country, which is another sure sign of true training. However, the men of the present time say that they need only practise that which comes easily, and this is very bad; such thinking is not at all akin to true Buddhism. If you concentrate on only one thing and consider it training, then it is impossible even to lie down in peace. If one action is done with a bored or uneasy mind, then all things become boring or uneasy; I know full well that they who seek things the easy way do not look for the True Way. Shakyamuni was able to give the teaching to be found in the present world after undergoing very difficult training, and thus he is the Great Teacher; his was the source. As this is so, how can the descendants of Shakyamuni gain anything by taking it easy? The Mind that seeks the Way does not search for easy training. Should you look for an easy means of training you will probably not reach the true realisation, and you will never find the treasure house. The most excellent of the old patriarchs said that training was hard to undergo, for Buddhism is deep and immense. The great masters would never have spoken of the difficulty

of Buddhism had it been easy. By comparison with the old patriarchs, people nowadays amount to not even so much as a single
hair in a herd of nine cows. Even if they do their best, pretending it
is hard, they do not begin to attain the easy training and understanding of the patriarchs because of their lack of strength and knowledge.
What is taught as easy training and beloved by present-day man?
It is neither secular nor Buddhist, for it cannot even be compared
to the teachings of devils and evil gods, nor can it be compared to
heresy and the Two Vehicles. For the delusions of ordinary people
have deep roots, and they trap themselves in eternal transmigration
by pretending to escape from the present world. It is difficult to break
the bones and crush the marrow from outside, and to control the
mind is more difficult still; it is of even greater difficulty to undergo
true training and long austerity, whilst the greatest difficulty of all
is to harmonise the training of body and mind. Many in olden times
underwent a training which required the crushing of their bones, and
if this were valuable they should have become enlightened, but only
a handful did. They who endured austerity, in like manner, should
have become enlightened, but here again, few did. This is because
when undergoing such training, it is extremely difficult to harmonise
body and mind. However, neither a clear head nor a good knowledge
of learning is of great importance, any more than is mind, will, consciousness, thought, understanding or perception; all of them are useless; to enter the stream of Buddhism one must simply harmonise
the mind and the body. Shakyamuni said that one must turn the
stream of compassion within and give up both knowledge and its
recognition. Herein lies the full meaning of the above, for in this
neither movement nor stillness is in the ascendancy and this is true
harmony. If one could penetrate Buddhism through intelligence and
learning, certainly Jinshū Jōza could have done so. If it were difficult
to penetrate Buddhism because of low birth and class, Daikan Enō
could never have become supreme patriarch. The means by which
Buddhism is transmitted is far beyond normal intelligence and understanding; look carefully for all signs within yourself, meditate upon
yourself and train hard.

The teachings of Zen make no choice between old and young.
Jōshu did not begin to train until he was over sixty, but he was a

very fine patriarch. The priestess Teijō started her training at the age of twelve and became the finest of the priests in her monastery. It is the amount of effort made that conditions the understanding of Buddhism received, and this differs according to the training or lack thereof. Those who have spent much time in worldly or scriptural study should visit a Zen training centre; many have already done so. Bodhidharma taught the clever Eshi, known as Nangaku, whilst Daikan Enō taught Yōka Genkaku. To make the Truth clear and enter the Way, one must study with a Zen master. One must never try to bring a Zen master's teaching down to one's own level of understanding, for should you try to understand it from your own self-opinionated viewpoint, you will never understand. Before asking for the Truth from a master, you must make your body and mind pure and quieten your perceptions so that both eyes and ears perceive and hear in peace; simply listen to the teaching and do not allow it to become soiled by your own thoughts. Your body and mind must be at one with each other as water is poured from one bowl to another. If you can achieve such a state of body and mind, the Truth that the master teaches can be made one with yourself.

At the present time, the unwise memorise the scriptures and cling to what they have heard and try to equate such things with the master's teaching; they therefore only rehear their own opinions and those of others which do not at all equate with the teaching they have just received. Some are convinced that their own opinions are right and then memorise a few parts of the scriptures, calling this Buddhism. Should the teaching you hear from a Zen master go against your own opinions, he is probably a good Zen master; if there is no clash of opinions in the beginning, it is a bad sign. People who are stuck with their own opinions frequently do not know how to get rid of them and so cannot use the teaching given them. For a long time they suffer from grave confusion and must be regarded with great grief.

Presumption, discrimination, imagination, intellect, human understanding and the like have nothing to do with Buddhism when studying Zen. Too many people are like children, playing with such things from their birth. You must awaken to Buddhism right now.

Above all, you must avoid presumption and choice; reflect carefully upon this. Only the Zen masters know the gateway to the Truth; professors have no knowledge thereof.

7. THE NECESSITY FOR ZAZEN WHEN TRAINING TO BE TRULY FREE

Because of its superiority, Buddhism is sought by many people, but whilst Shakyamuni was alive, there was only one teaching and one teacher; by himself the great Shakyamuni guided all living things to complete understanding. Since Makakashyo commenced the transmission of the Truth there have been twenty-eight patriarchs in India, six in China; the patriarchs of the five schools have, without interruption, transmitted it to the present time. Since the period of Ryokai all really worthy persons have entered into Zen Buddhism, whether they were in the priesthood or of royal blood. One should love the excellence of true Buddhism rather than what passes for Buddhism. It is wrong to love the dragon as did Sekkō. In some countries east of China a web of learning rather than true Buddhism has been spread across the seas and mountains; although it spreads over the mountains, the heart of the clouds is not within it; although it spreads across the seas, the heart of the waves is destroyed thereby; fools take pleasure herein; such people are as those who treasure a fish's eye in the belief that it is a pearl, making a plaything of it. To behave thus is to treasure a pebble from Gen as if it were a jewel. There are many who are ruined by falling into the hall of the demons.

In a country where there is much bias, the Truth has difficulty in appearing because of the way it is beset by contrary winds. Although China has already taken refuge in the Truth of Buddhism, neither our country nor Korea has as yet had any real contact with it. Why? At least the Truth can be heard in Korea, but here it is not, simply because those who went to China clung to erudition. They seem to have transmitted the scriptures, but they forgot to transmit the Truth. What merit is there here? None whatsoever. Their failure was due to their lack of understanding of true training. How unfortunate it is that the body should be thus vainly employed in hard work for all its natural life.

When learning the Way, listening to the teaching of the master, training after first entering the gate, there is something you should know. In the *Ryogonkyo* it says that external things control the self and that the self controls external things; should I control external things, then I am strong and they are weak, but should the external things control me, then they are strong and I am weak; from the beginning these opposites have existed in Buddhism. Unless someone has had a true transmission, this cannot be understood; unless a true master is found, even the names of these opposites are unheard of. Those who have no knowledge of this can never study true Buddhism, for how can they ever differentiate between right and wrong? They who practise true Zen by studying the Way naturally transmit the meaning of these opposites; they make no mistakes such as are found in some teachings. It is not possible to understand the True Way without the training of Zen.

8. HOW A ZEN TRAINEE SHOULD BEHAVE

The Truth has been transmitted directly to the present time from the time of the Buddhas and patriarchs; in all the twenty-eight patriarchates in India and the six in China no thread has been added to it or speck of dust taken away from it. After the robe was given to Daikan Enō, the Truth spread from one end of the world to the other, and so the Buddha's Truth flourishes in China. Truth can never be sought, and they who once see the Way forget all knowledge and fame, for they transcend relative consciousness; Gunin was at Ōbai when Daikan Enō lost his face. Eka, the Second Patriarch, cut off his arm in front of Bodhidharma's cave, thereby gaining the marrow of Buddhism by destroying the selfish mind. Having gained the core of Buddhism he gained vital freedom, dwelling neither in body nor mind and having no attachment, stagnation or grasping. A trainee asked Jōshu if a dog had Buddha Nature, to which Jōshu replied, "Mu." How can "mu" be measured, for there is nothing to hold on to; just let go. What are body and mind? What is Zen behaviour? What are birth and death, the affairs of the world, mountains, rivers, earth, men, animals, home? If you continue thus, neither action nor non-action arises as distinct of itself, and so there is no inflexibility. Few indeed understand this, as most suffer from delusion. The Zen trainee can gain enlightenment if he reflects upon himself from the centre of his being. But it is my sincere hope that you will not take pride in gaining the True Way.

9. THE NECESSITY OF TRAINING IN ORDER TO ATTAIN THE WAY OF BUDDHISM

They who would study the Way must first find out if they are looking in the right direction. Shakyamuni, who learned to control his self, saw the morning star whilst sitting beneath the Bodhi tree, thereby becoming suddenly enlightened to the highest degree; because of this his way cannot be compared with that of the śrāvakas and pratyekabuddhas. Not only did the Buddha enlighten himself, he transmitted that enlightenment to the other Buddhas and patriarchs so that even to the present day the transmission has not been interrupted. As this is so, how can they who are enlightened help but be Buddhas?

To face the Way squarely is to know the true source of Buddhism and make clear the approach thereto, for it is beneath the feet of every living person. You find Buddhism in the very spot where you perceive the Way. The perfection of self comes with the penetration of enlightenment, but should you become proud of your enlightenment, you will only know the half thereof.

In such a frame of mind must you face the Way, but they who study the Way only do not know whether it is open or shut. Some greatly desire to perform miracles and are gravely mistaken, for they are as those who forsake their parents and escape, or give up treasure and just wander. They are as the only son of a rich father who becomes a beggar through seeking for external things; this indeed is a true picture.

To truly study the Way is to try to penetrate it, and in order to do this, one must forget even the slightest trace of enlightenment. One who would train in Buddhism must first believe in it completely, and to do so, one must believe that one has already found the Way, never having been lost, deluded, upside down, increasing, decreasing or mistaken in the first place. One must train oneself thus, believing thus, in order to make the Way clear: this is the ground for Buddhist study. By this method one may cut off the functioning of consciousness and turn one's back upon the road of learning. In such a way as herein described must trainees be guided. Only after such training can we be free of the opposites of body and mind, enlightenment and delusion.

They who believe that they are already within the Way are truly rare, but if you can truly believe it, the opening and closing of the Great Way are understood quite naturally and the root of delusion and enlightenment is seen as it is. If you try to cut off the function of conscious discrimination, you will almost see the Way.

10. THE RECEIVING OF DIRECT TEACHING

There are two ways in which to set body and mind right: one is to hear the teaching from a master, and the other is to do pure Zazen yourself. If you *hear* the teachings the conscious mind is put to work, whilst *Zazen* embraces both training and enlightenment; in order to understand the Truth, you need both. All living beings possess both body and mind, irrespective of strong or weak behaviour, for behaviour itself is variable. However, it is by means of the body and mind that we become enlightened, and this is the receiving of the teaching. There is no need to change the present body and mind; all one has to do is follow in the enlightened way of a fine Zen master, for this is the receiving of the teaching directly. To follow a Zen master is not to follow in old ways nor to create new ones; it is simply to receive the teaching.

BENDŌWA

Lecture on Training

The Buddhas have a very excellent way to understanding so that they may transmit the Truth; when transmitted from one Buddha to another, it is the embodiment of meditation which is of itself utterly joyful. Correct sitting is essential as the true gateway to entering naturally into this meditation. Every living being has a great store of Buddha Nature, but it can never be seen unless practice is undertaken, nor can it be evinced in daily life unless one becomes enlightened. If you do not cling to it your hand will be full thereof, for it transcends both all and nothing. If you speak of it your mouth will be full thereof, for its height and width are immeasurable; all Buddhas dwell therein eternally clinging to no one-sided attachment whatsoever; all living beings work therein once they have transcended one-sided attachment. That which I now teach shows all things within original enlightenment, expressing unity in action; once this is thoroughly mastered there is an end to clinging to trifles.

After the Way-seeking Mind was awakened within me I visited many Buddhist teachers throughout the country, finally meeting Myozen at Kenninji. I served him for nine years and the time passed swiftly; from him I learned much about Rinzai. Myozen was the chief disciple of Eisai and transmitted the highest Buddhism then available, none of the other disciples being able to bear any comparison with him. On visiting China I also visited Zen teachers, learning much about the five different schools of Buddhism represented there. Finally I studied under Nyojō in Tendōzan, thus completing my training. At the beginning of Shōtei I returned to Japan, since I wished to rescue all living beings by spreading the Truth; I was like a man who carried a heavy burden. It then occurred to me to give up this idea of spreading the Truth, so as to wait for a more suitable time for carrying out my purpose. I wandered in many places, sincerely trying to teach what I had learned, for there are true trainees to be found, those who truly turn their backs on fame and gain in order to search for the True Way. However, it is a great grief that they are often misled by untrue teachers, resulting in the hiding of true understanding. The trainees thus become uselessly inebriated with the madness of self and eventually drown in the delusive world. Under such circumstances, how can the true seed of wisdom give forth shoots and the opportunity to gain enlightenment be made use of?

As like a cloud or a reed I wander from place to place, I ask myself what mountain or river I will visit. Because my sympathies lie with those who seek the Way, I went to China and discovered the type of monastery there; I also received the Truth of Zen. I gathered all this, wrote down all that I saw, and leave it as a legacy to all trainees in order that they may be able to find the Truth of Buddhism. This is the very core of Zen. Shakyamuni Buddha transmitted the Truth to Makakashyo on Mount Ryoju, and from him the long line of patriarchs handed it down to Bodhidharma, who in turn went to China and transmitted the Truth to Taisō Eka.

Thus was started the eastern transmission of Zen, and it came naturally to the Sixth Patriarch, Daikan Enō, in all its original purity; thus true Buddhism was transmitted to China completely free of all trivia. The Sixth Patriarch's two great disciples, Nangaku and Seigen, transmitted the Buddha's Truth, being leaders of both men and gods; their two schools spread and the five styles of Zen emerged, being Hōgen, Igyō, Sōtō, Ummon and Rinzai; however, at the present time only Rinzai flourishes in China. The five styles differ somewhat, but they are all part of the One Truth of the Buddha Mind; from the end of the Han period until the present time, all the scriptures of the other schools were taught but no one was able to decide which of them was the best. From the time of Bodhidharma's arrival from India, however, this problem was solved and pure Buddhism could be spread; it is for us to try to do the same thing in this country. All the Buddhas and patriarchs have taught that the True Way to understanding is entered through simply sitting and meditating in a way which is of itself utterly joyful; all who have been enlightened did this because both masters and disciples transmitted this method from one to the other and thereby received the Truth in all its purity.

Question 1: It is said that Zazen is superior to other methods, but ordinary people will perhaps doubt this, saying that there are many gates to the Buddha's Way. As this is so, why do you advocate Zazen?

Answer: My answer to such persons is that Zazen is the only True Gateway to Buddhism.

Question 2: Why is Zazen the only True Gateway?

Answer: Shakyamuni, the great master, gave us this unequalled Way to understanding, and all the Buddhas of past, present and future were enlightened by means of Zazen in the same way, as were also the Indian and Chinese patriarchs. Because of this I can tell you that this is the True Gate by which man enters heaven.

Question 3: True transmission and the unequalled Way of the Buddhas, as well as following the Way of the patriarchs, are beyond ordinary comprehension. For most people the natural way to enlightenment is to read the scriptures and recite the nembutsu. Since you do nothing more than sit cross-legged, how can this mere sitting be a means of gaining enlightenment?

Answer: Since you regard the meditation and Truth of the

Buddhas as just sitting and being idle, you are looking down upon Mahāyāna Buddhism. Such a delusion is similar to that of someone who, whilst in the midst of a vast ocean, cries out for water. We are lucky indeed that we are even now sitting comfortably in the Buddha's meditation, which is of itself utterly joyful. Is not this a great blessing? How piteous it is that your eyes are closed and your mind inebriated. The World of the Buddhas is nowhere to be found in ordinary thinking or consciousness, nor can it be known through disbelief or low knowledge, for in order to enter therein, one must have true belief. However much an unbeliever may be taught, he will still have trouble in finding it. When the Buddha was preaching at Ryoju, the unbelievers were allowed to depart. In order to develop true belief in your own mind, you must study and train yourself hard; if you cannot do so you should give up for a little, at the same time regretting the fact that you are uninfluenced in your search for Truth by former good karma. Of what use is it to read the scriptures and recite the nembutsu? It is useless to imagine that the merits of Buddhism come merely from using one's tongue or voice; if you think such things embrace all of Buddhism, the Truth is a long way from you. You should only read the scriptures so as to learn that the Buddha was teaching the necessity of gradual and sudden training and that from this you can realise enlightenment; do not read them so as to make a show of wisdom with useless intellection. To try to reach the goal of Buddhism by doing thus is the same as pointing to the north and then heading south. You are putting a square peg into a round hole. So long as you are seeing words and phrases your way will remain dark; such behaviour is as useless as that of a doctor who forgets his prescriptions. Just to continually repeat the nembutsu is equally useless, for it is as a frog who croaks both day and night in some field. Yet those who suffer from the delusion of fame and gain find it extraordinarily difficult to give up nembutsu, for the fetters that bind them to such craving are deep-rooted, extending from the past right down to the present; such people are piteous to see. You need only understand this clearly: if the Truth of the Seven Buddhas is truly transmitted by both masters and disciples, it manifests itself quite plainly and is experienced completely. They who do nothing more than study the scriptures and their characters never understand this, so just stop it and thereby cure your delusions and doubts. Just follow the teachings of a true master and, through the power of Zazen, find the utterly joyful enlightenment of Buddha.

Question 4: Both the Tendai and Kegon teachings have been brought to Japan, representing the highest form of Buddhism. The Shingon school, which was transmitted from Vairocana Buddha to Vajrasattva directly, teaches that no stain exists between master and disciple, maintaining that Buddha is this very mind—that this mind becomes Buddha; it gives no indication of any necessity for long and painstaking training, teaching simply the instantaneous enlightenment of the Five Buddhas. This teaching is unparalleled in all Buddhism. Bearing these facts in mind, why do you regard Zazen as superior even to the extent of excluding all other teachings?

Answer: The accent in Buddhism must always be placed on the truth or inaccuracy of the actual training; the excellence, worthlessness, depth or shallowness of the teaching is of secondary importance. In olden times that which brought a man to Buddhism was the grass, flowers, mountains or streams; some received the Truth of the Buddha by taking dirt, stones, sand or grit in their hands. The Truth exceeds all forms, so that even a speck of dust can preach a sermon. To say this mind is Buddha is like beholding the moon's reflection in water. To say that sitting cross-legged is of itself Buddhism is the same as seeing a figure in a mirror; do not become the victim of clever word-manipulation. In advocating this training for instantaneous enlightenment, I do so because I wish to make a true being of you and so am showing you the highest way as transmitted by the Buddhas and patriarchs. So as to transmit the Buddha's Truth you must find an enlightened teacher; do not simply follow some scholar who is concerned with the characters in which the scriptures are written, for this is the same as a blind man leading blind men. It is respect for those who are enlightened that sustains the Truth which is transmitted by the Buddhas and patriarchs. When that which is worldly rejects the Zen master and the enlightened Arahants seek for the Way, the means of opening the Buddha Mind is provided, but the other teachings could not endure such means of training. All that the followers of Buddhism have to do is study the Truth; understand clearly that the highest wisdom is to be found herein, and that although we may enjoy it for eternity, we will not always be in harmony with it, simply because we are self-opinionated and desirous of material gain; these things will give us pause in the Way. Ghosts arise as a result of being self-opinionated. Take, for example, the doctrines of Dependent Origination, the twenty-five worlds, the Three Vehicles, the Five Vehicles, the Buddha and no-Buddha: all these things give rise to countless speculation, but true training requires no knowledge whatsoever of these matters. Therefore, when sitting cross-legged and allowing the Buddha Nature to manifest itself by giving up all opinions and cutting all ties, we enjoy great wisdom quite naturally, for we instantly enter into the world which lies beyond both delusion and enlightenment, wherein there is no difference between the wise and the foolish. It is impossible for anyone who clutches at words to reach this height.

Question 5: Enlightenment is to be found within the three styles of training, and the methods of meditation within the six stages of enlightenment which all Bodhisattvas study from the commencement of their training without discriminating between the clever and the stupid; perhaps this Zazen is part of such training. Why do you insist that the Truth is contained in its entirety in Zazen?

Answer: This question results from giving the name of "Zen sect" to the treasury of the Truth to be found in the unequalled teachings of Buddha, but this name was given to it in China and the east, never having even been heard of in India. When Bodhidharma stared at the wall in Shōrinji for nine years, neither the priests nor the laity there understood the Truth of the Buddha, simply regarding Bodhidharma as a teacher who insisted on the importance of sitting cross-legged; yet after him, every patriarch has devoted himself to this cross-legged sitting. Those members of the laity with no knowledge of these matters, when first seeing them, spoke of the practitioners of Zazen as members of the Zazen sect in such a nonchalant manner as to prove their complete lack of understanding of the Truth. Nowadays the prefix *za* has been dropped from the word and they who practise Zazen are called members of the Zen sect, as is clear from all the writings of the patriarchs. Do not put Zazen into the same category as that of the six stages and the three training styles. The spirit of the transmission is very clearly expressed in the life and work of the Buddha. Only to Makakashyo, on Ryoju, did the Buddha transmit the Truth, and this was seen by only a few of even the gods in heaven. Never doubt that the heavenly deities protect Buddhism for eternity; even today this is a true fact. Understand clearly that Zazen is the whole of the Buddhist way and is utterly incomparable.

Question 6: There are four main types of action. As this is so, why does Buddhism select cross-legged sitting as the only means to enlightenment?

Answer: It is not for me to analyse the Buddha's training methods for the purpose of gaining enlightenment, and neither should you. The patriarchs praised the method of sitting cross-legged and called it the comfortable way, and I myself know that of the four actions this is the most comfortable. You should understand clearly that it is not merely the training method of one or two Buddhas but of all of them.

Question 7: For those who as yet know nothing of Buddhism, enlightenment must be obtained through the means of Zazen and training, but of what use is Zazen to someone who has already clearly reached enlightenment?

Answer: I may not speak of last night's dreams or give tools to a woodcutter, but I still have something that I can teach to you. It is heretical to believe that training and enlightenment are separable, for in Buddhism the two are one and the same. Since training embraces enlightenment, the very beginning of training contains the whole of original enlightenment; as this is so, the teacher tells his disciples never to search for enlightenment outside of training since the latter mirrors enlightenment. Since training is already enlightenment, enlightenment is unending; since enlightenment is already training, there can be no beginning whatsoever to training. Both Shakyamuni and Makakashyo were used by training which was enlightenment, and Bodhidharma and Daikan Enō were moved by it in the same way; such signs of transmission are usual in Buddhism, for training is inseparable from enlightenment. Since from the very beginning, training transmits enlightenment, original enlightenment is gained naturally. Both the Buddhas and the patriarchs insisted upon the necessity of intense training in order that enlightenment might be kept pure, being identical with training itself. If you do not cling to training, your hand will be full of enlightenment; if you do not cling to enlightenment, your whole body will be filled with training. In many parts of China I saw Zen monasteries in which there were from five hundred to a thousand two hundred trainees practising Zazen both day and night in their meditation halls. Whenever I asked those Zen teachers who had been entrusted with the Truth what the Truth of Buddhism was, they all said that training and enlightenment was inseparable, and they urged their followers to continue in the path of their teachers since it was that which was taught by the Buddhas and patriarchs. They advocated Zazen for all seekers of the True Way, irrespective of whether they were advanced or just beginning, wise or foolish, and did not merely teach it to their disciples. Nangaku once said that it is untrue that there is no training and no enlightenment, but that should you cling to them, they will become sullied. Another patriarch said that anyone who sees the Way also trains it. Therefore it is essential that you train within enlightenment.

Question 8: Why did the former Japanese patriarchs, on returning from China, propagate teachings other than this one of Zen?

Answer: The former patriarchs did not propagate or transmit Zen because the time for doing so had then not yet arrived.

Question 9: Did the former patriarchs understand Zen?

Answer: Had they understood it, they would have propagated it.

Question 10: It was once said that one should not throw away delusion, for there is an easy way of becoming free of birth and death, since the spirit is eternal. This means that although the body may be condemned to birth and death, yet the spirit is immortal. Should this spirit, which has neither beginning nor end, reside within me, then it is the true original spirit; and though my body takes a physical, unmoving shape, dying here and resurrecting there, the spirit, being eternal, is unchanging from the past to the future: if one knows this, one is free of birth and death. When one knows this, birth and death vanish and the ocean of the spirit is entered. Should you become one with this ocean your virtue will be as that of Buddha. Since your body is the result of your former delusions, however, you will not be the same as the wise even should you know these facts; should you not know them, you will be doomed to eternal transmigration. Therefore, it is essential to know nothing more than the eternity of the spirit; there is no hope for you even if you sit and waste your entire life in doing so. Is not this the opinion of the Buddhas and patriarchs?

Answer: This opinion is not Buddhist, being the Srenika heresy.

This heresy teaches that there is knowledge of the spirit within our bodies and that because of this, we can differentiate between like and dislike, right and wrong, pleasure and suffering, pain and enjoyment. When the body dies, this spiritual knowledge leaves it to be reborn in another one; therefore, although it may seem to die in one place, it is reborn elsewhere and thus, never dying, is eternal. If you hold to this heresy, believing it to be Buddhism, you are as stupid as someone who treasures tiles and pebbles in the belief that they are gold. It is a shamefully foolish idea and not worthy of any serious thought. Echū gave a very grave warning about this heresy. People who believe in it think that the mind is eternal and form is passing, and they say this is equal to the training of the Buddhas; by so doing they think they have freed themselves from birth and death, but they are merely perpetuating them. Such an opinion is not only untrue but piteous; you must not listen to it. I should not say this; however, being sorry for you, I wish to cure your delusion. Buddhism teaches that body and mind are one as are spirit and form; this is understood clearly throughout both India and China. When a teaching speaks of eternity, all is eternal, so body and mind must not be separated. When a teaching speaks of cessation, all things cease, so spirit and form must not be separated. It is contrary to the Truth to say that the body dies whilst the mind lives eternally; understand clearly that life and death are Nirvāna itself, and we cannot speak of Nirvāna without life and death. You are completely wrong if you think that the wisdom of the Buddhas is free from life and death. Your mind knows and sees, comes and goes and is not eternal in any way; you must understand this completely, for Buddhism has always maintained that body and mind are one. Taking this into consideration, why should the mind be released from birth and death whilst the body is fettered by them? Should you insist that body and mind are one at one time and not at another, the teaching of the Buddha becomes unclear, and to think that birth and death should be avoided is clearly an error in Buddhism, for they are truly the means by which Buddhism is taught. In the awakening of faith in Mahāyāna Buddhism, the Buddha's treasury enfolds the causation of birth and death and does not divide reality and appearance or consider appearance and disappearance. Enlightenment is nothing other than the Buddha's treasury, being identical with and containing all things. All teachings are based upon that of the One Mind; make no mistake in this matter, for this is to understand the Buddha Mind. How is it possible to divide the Buddha Mind into mind and body, delusion and enlightenment? Already you are the child of Buddha, so do not listen to the lunatics who teach heresy.

Question 11: Must one who takes the practice of Zazen seriously keep the Precepts strictly and purify both body and mind?

Answer: The Buddhas and patriarchs have handed down the practice of strict observance of the Precepts and pure living as the rules governing Zen. Any who have not yet received the Precepts should do so at once, and those who have broken them should repent of their wrongdoing; by so doing they may become one with the wisdom of the Buddhas.

Question 12: Is there any harm in a serious student of Zazen saying Shingon mantras or practising the peaceful-illumination training of Tendai at the same time as doing Zazen?

Answer: When I was in China, the teachers from whom I learned the Truth of Buddhism said that they had never heard of any patriarch, either before or now, who had undergone such simultaneous training and then transmitted the Truth of the Buddha. One should concentrate solely on one thing if one would understand the Truth.

Question 13: Can laymen practise Zazen, or is it for priests alone?

Answer: All patriarchs who have clearly understood Buddhism have taught that there is no difference between the Zazen of a man and a woman, a rich person and a poor one.

Question 14: Since the priests have no ties, there is nothing in the way of their practising Zazen, but how can a busy layman do serious training in order to reach enlightenment?

Answer: The gates of compassion have been opened wide by the Buddhas and patriarchs out of their limitless love for all living things, whether they be men or gods. There are innumerable examples right from the beginning up to now. The state officials Tan-tsung and Sung-tsung were both extremely busy with affairs of government, yet they penetrated the Way of the Buddhas and patriarchs through the practice of Zazen; the prime minister Li and the other prime minister Fang did the same thing, at the same time acting as the emperor's counsellors. Everything depends upon the will of the person involved and has nothing whatever to do with being either a layman or a priest. If one can distinguish between excellence and mundaneness, one can believe in Buddhism naturally. A person who believes that worldly work is a hindrance to Buddhism knows only that no Buddhism exists in the world, for nothing in Buddhism can be set apart as a worldly task. The prime minister P'ing, of China, wrote the following poem after becoming one with the Way of the patriarchs:

> When not engaged in affairs of state, I practised Zazen
> To such an extent that I hardly ever slept;
> My fame as a Zen master spread throughout the world
> In spite of the fact that I am prime minister.

P'ing was very busy with official business, but his determination to train was earnest and so he became one with enlightenment. Think of your own situation in the light of the situation of these people from the past. In China even now, the emperor, ministers, soldiers and people, both men and women, are interested in the Way of the patriarchs; both warriors and scholars have the will to train themselves and many will understand the Truth; all these people's lives tell us clearly that worldly work is no hindrance whatsoever to Buddhism. Whenever true Buddhism is spread in any country, the Buddhas and heavenly deities protect it and the whole world becomes peaceful; whenever the world is peaceful, Buddhism becomes strong. Even criminals who heard the Buddha's teaching whilst he lived were enlightened, and those who hunted or chopped wood were enlightened under the patriarchs; all you have to do to realise enlightenment is hear the instructions of a true teacher.

Question 15: Is it still possible to gain enlightenment through Zazen in the present degenerate times of this evil world?

Answer: Most teachings concern themselves with the names and styles of the doctrines, but the true teaching sees no difference in the three five-hundred-year periods. Anyone who truly trains must certainly realise enlightenment, and within the correctly transmitted Truth, you may always thoroughly enjoy the rarest of treasures which is to be found within your own house. Anyone who trains knows whether or not he has reached enlightenment, in the same way that someone drinking water knows for himself whether or not it is hot or cold.

Question 16: There are those who say that one has only to understand that this mind itself is the Buddha in order to understand Buddhism, and that there is no need to recite the scriptures or undergo bodily training. If you understand that Buddhism is inherent in yourself, you are already fully enlightened and there is no need to seek for anything further from anywhere. If this is so, is there any sense in taking the trouble to practise Zazen?

Answer: This is a very grievous mistake, and even if it should be true and the sages should teach it, it is impossible for you to understand it. If you would truly study Buddhism, you must transcend all opinions of subject and object. If it is possible to be enlightened simply by knowing that the self is, in its self-nature, the Buddha, then there was no need for Shakyamuni to try so diligently to teach the Way. This fact is proved by the high standards maintained by the old teachers. Once a Zen teacher named Hōgen asked his disciple, "How long have you been in this temple?" "Three years," replied the disciple. "Since you are younger than I, why do you never question me concerning Buddhism?" asked Hōgen. "I cannot lie to you," said the disciple, "but whilst studying with my former master, I understood Buddhism." "From what words did you get your understanding?" Hōgen asked. "I asked, 'What is the true self of a trainee?' and he answered, 'The god of fire is calling for fire.'" "That is excellent," said Hōgen, "but I doubt if you understood it." "Fire belongs to the god of fire," replied the disciple, "and fire needs fire; it is the same as saying that self needs self." "You obviously did not understand it at all," said Hōgen, "for if Buddhism were thus, it could never have continued until the present time." The disciple was deeply perturbed and left the temple. However, whilst on his way home, he thought, "Hōgen has five hundred disciples and is a most excellent teacher. Since he has pointed out my mistake, there must be some value in what he says." He then returned to Hōgen's temple and, repenting his former behaviour, greeted Hōgen and asked, "What is the true self of the trainee?" Hōgen replied, "The god of fire is calling for fire." Hearing this, this disciple became completely enlightened. It is obvious that one cannot understand Buddhism simply by knowing that the self is the Buddha, for if this were Buddhism, Hōgen could never have shown the Way to his disciple as he did nor could he have given him such advice. When you first visit a teacher you should ask for the rules of training, then practise Zazen earnestly. Do not becloud your mind with use-less knowledge; only then will the unequalled Way of Buddhism bear fruit.

Question 17: Both in India and China, from the beginning of time to the present day, some Zen teachers have been enlightened by such things as the sound of stones striking bamboos, whilst the colour of plum blossoms cleared the minds of others. The great Shakyamuni was enlightened at the sight of the morning star, whilst Ananda understood the Truth through seeing a stick fall. As well as these, many Zen teachers of the five schools after the Sixth Patriarch were enlightened by only so much as a word. Did all of them practise Zazen?

Answer: From olden times down to the present day, all who were ever enlightened, either by colours or sounds, practised Zazen without Zazen and became instantaneously enlightened.

Question 18: The men of India and China had integrity and, culture being universal, were able to understand Buddhism when they were taught. However, from early times men in our country have been wanting in fine intellect, and so it has been difficult for the Truth to take root. This is indeed unfortunate and is caused by the barbarianism amongst us. There is also the fact that the priests here are inferior to the laymen of other countries. Everyone in Japan, being foolish and narrow-minded, clings tightly to worldly rank and is hungry only for things that are superficial. Is it possible that such people can reach enlightenment quickly just by practising Zazen?

Answer: All this is as you say, for the people here have neither knowledge nor integrity, and even if they should see the Truth, they change its sweetness to poison. They look for fame and gain and have difficulty in freeing themselves from clinging. However, in order to become enlightened, it is not possible to rely upon the worldly knowledge of either men or gods. Whilst the Buddha lived there were numerous stupid and crazy persons who worked for en-lightenment by various means and later found the True Way to free themselves from delusion as a result of true faith. One female trainee, who waited with a cooked meal for a foolish old priest, was enlightened simply by observing his silent sitting. None of these enlightenments depended on knowledge, scholarship, characters or sayings; every one of them points to the necessity of being helped by true faith in Buddhism. Buddhism has spread to various countries during the last two thousand years, and it appeals to other people besides the cultured, clever and rich, for Truth, with its inherent power for good, spreads naturally throughout the world when it is given the chance. Anyone who trains with true faith will be enlightened equally with everybody else, without differentiation between the clever and the stupid. Do not think that because Japan is a country of low culture and uneducated people it is unready for Buddhism; all beings have an abundance of the seed of Truth, but few people know this fact. They do not train with true faith, for they have no adequate recognition of Buddhist Truth and no experience in applying it.

Perhaps these questions and answers may seem unnecessary; however, I have tried to help those with poor eyes to see blossoms where none were before. As yet the core of Zazen has not been transmitted in Japan, and those who wish to know it are thereby made unhappy. So, when in China, I collected all that I saw and heard, wrote down what the masters taught, and with all this, wish to help those who are in search of training. I also want to teach the rules and ceremonies to be found in the temples, but have no time to do so, for they cannot be described in simplified form. Buddhism came from the west to Japan around the time of the emperors Kinmei and Yomei, although we are far from India, and its coming was indeed fortunate for us. However, as a result of names, forms, objects and relationships, many knots are created and the way of training is lost.

From now on I will take my simple robe and bowl and dwell amongst the reed-clothed rocks. Whilst I sit and train here, true Zen Buddhism, which transcends even the Buddha, appears naturally and thus the end of training is brought to fulfilment. This is the teaching of the Buddha and the method bequeathed by Makakashyo. The rules for Zazen are to be found in the *Fukanzazengi*, which I wrote during the Karoku period. In order to propagate Buddhism in any country, one must obtain the permission of the ruler thereof, but many kings, ministers and generals appeared as a result of the Buddha's transmission on Mount Ryoju, and these were grateful for the Buddha's guidance as well as being mindful of the spirit which has always pervaded Buddhism since the beginning. Wherever the teachings have been spread is the Buddha's own country, so there is no sense whatever in carefully choosing some special place, time or condition when propagating them. It is wrong to think that today is just the beginning. And so I have made and left this record for those True Seekers of the Way, the True Trainees, who wander from place to place in search of the Truth.

SHUSHŌGI

What is Truly Meant by Training and Enlightenment

1. INTRODUCTION

The most important question for all Buddhists is how to understand birth and death completely. Should you be able to find the Buddha within birth and death, they both vanish; all you have to do is realise that birth and death, as such, should not be avoided and they will cease to exist, for if you can understand that birth and death are Nirvāna itself, there is not only no necessity to avoid them but also nothing to search for that is called Nirvāna. To understand this breaks the chains that bind one to birth and death; therefore this problem, which is the greatest in all Buddhism, must be completely understood.

It is very difficult to be born as a human being and equally difficult to find Buddhism. However, because of the good karma that we have accumulated, we have received the exceptional gift of a human body and are able to hear the Truths of Buddhism; we therefore have the greatest possibility of a full life within the limits of birth and death. It would be criminal to waste such an opportunity by leaving this weak life of ours exposed to changeableness.

Changeableness offers no permanent succour. On what weeds by the roadside will the dew of our life fall? At this very minute this body is not my own. Life, which is controlled by time, never ceases even for an instant; youth vanishes for ever once it is gone. It is impossible to bring back the past when one suddenly comes face to face with changeableness, and it is impossible to look for assistance from kings, statesmen, relatives, servants, wife or children, let alone wealth and treasure. The kingdom of death must be entered by oneself alone, with nothing for company but one's own good and bad karma.

Avoid the company of those who are deluded and ignorant with regard to the Truth of karmic consequence, the three states of existence, and good and evil. It is obvious that the law of cause and effect is not answerable to my personal will, for without fail, evil is vanquished and good prevails; if it were not so, Buddhism would never have appeared and Bodhidharma would never have come from the west.

There are three periods into which the karmic consequences of good and evil fall: one is the consequence experienced in this present world, the second is consequence experienced in the next world, and the third is consequence experienced in the world after the next one. One must understand this very clearly before undertaking any training in the Way of the Buddhas and patriarchs; otherwise, mistakes will be made by many and they will fall into heresy; in addition to this, their lives will become evil and their suffering will be prolonged.

None of us have more than one body during this lifetime; therefore it is indeed tragic to lead a life of evil as a result of heresy, for it is impossible to escape from karmic consequence if we do evil on the assumption that if an act is not recognised by us as evil, no bad karma can accrue to us.

2. FREEDOM IS GAINED BY CONTRITION

Because of their limitless compassion the Buddhas and patriarchs have flung wide the gates of compassion to both gods and men, and although karmic consequence for evil acts is inevitable at some time during the three periods, contrition makes it easier to bear by bringing freedom and immaculacy. As this is so, let us be utterly contrite before the Buddhas.

Contrition before the Buddhas brings purification and salvation, true conviction and earnest endeavour. Once aroused, true conviction changes all beings in addition to ourselves, with benefits extending to everything, including that which is animate and that which is inanimate.

Here is the way to make an act of perfect contrition: "May all the Buddhas and patriarchs, who have become enlightened, have compassion upon us, free us from the obstacle of suffering which we have inherited from our past existence, and lead us in such a way that we may share the merit that fills the universe, for they, in the past, were as we are now, and we will be as they in the future. All the evil committed by me is caused by beginningless greed, hate and delusion. All the evil is committed by our body, speech and mind. I now confess everything wholeheartedly." By this act of contrition we open the way for the Buddhas and patriarchs to help us naturally. Bearing this in mind, we should sit up straight in the presence of the Buddha and repeat this act of contrition, thereby cutting the roots of our evildoing.

3. RECEIVING THE PRECEPTS

After this act of contrition we should make an act of deep respect to the Three Treasures of Buddha, Dharma and Sangha, for they deserve our offerings and respect in whatever life we may be drifting. The Buddhas and patriarchs transmitted respect for the Buddha, Dharma and Sangha from India to China.

If they who are unfortunate and lacking in virtue are unable to hear of these Three Treasures, how is it possible for them to take refuge therein? One must not go for refuge to mountain spirits and ghosts, nor must one worship in places of heresy, for such things are contrary to the Truth. One must instead take refuge quickly in the Buddha, Dharma and Sangha, for therein is to be found utter enlightenment as well as freedom from suffering.

A pure heart is necessary if one would take refuge in the Three Treasures. At any time, whether during the Buddha's lifetime or after his demise, we should repeat the following with bowed heads, making gasshō: "I take refuge in the Buddha, I take refuge in the Dharma, I take refuge in the Sangha." We take refuge in the Buddha since he is our True Teacher; we take refuge in the Dharma since it is the medicine for all suffering; we take refuge in the Sangha since its members are wise and compassionate. If we would follow the Buddhist teachings we must honour the Three Treasures; this foundation is absolutely essential before receiving the Precepts.

The merit of the Three Treasures bears fruit whenever a trainee and the Buddha are one. Whoever experiences this communion will invariably take refuge in the Three Treasures, irrespective of whether he is a god, a demon or an animal. As one goes from one stage of existence to another the merit increases, leading eventually to the most perfect enlightenment. The Buddha himself gave certification to the great merit of the Three Treasures because of their extreme value and unbelievable profundity. It is essential that all living things shall take refuge therein.

The Three Pure Collective Precepts must be accepted after the Three Treasures. These are: Cease from evil. Do only good. Do good for others. The following Ten Precepts should be accepted next: (1) Do not kill. (2) Do not steal. (3) Do not covet. (4) Do not say that which is untrue. (5) Do not sell the wine of delusion. (6) Do not speak against others. (7) Do not be proud of yourself and devalue others. (8) Do not be mean in giving either Dharma or wealth. (9) Do not be angry. (10) Do not debase the Three Treasures.

All the Buddhas have received and carefully preserved the Three Treasures, the Three Pure Collective Precepts and the Ten Precepts.

If you accept these Precepts wholeheartedly, the highest enlightenment will be yours, and this is the undestroyable Buddhahood which was understood, and is understood, in the past, present and future. Is it possible that any truly wise person would refuse the opportunity to attain to such heights? The Buddha has clearly pointed out to all living beings that whenever these Precepts are truly accepted, Buddhahood is reached, every person who accepts them becoming the True Child of Buddha.

Within these Precepts dwell the Buddhas, enfolding all things within their unparallelled wisdom. There is no distinction between subject and object for any who dwell herein. All things, earth, trees, wooden posts, bricks, stones become Buddhas once this refuge is taken. From these Precepts come forth such a wind and fire that all are driven into enlightenment when the flames are fanned by the Buddha's influence. This is the merit of non-action and non-seeking; the awakening to True Wisdom.

4. AWAKENING TO THE MIND OF THE BODHISATTVA

When one awakens to True Wisdom, it means that one is willing to save all living things before one has actually saved oneself. Whether a being is a layman, priest, god or man, enjoying pleasure or suffering pain, he should awaken this desire as quickly as possible.

However humble a person may appear to be, if this desire has been awakened, he is already the teacher of all mankind. A little girl of seven, even, may be the teacher of the four classes of Buddhists and the mother of True Compassion to all living things. One of the greatest teachings of Buddhism is its insistence upon complete equality of the sexes.

However much one may drift in the six worlds and the Four Existences, even they become a means for realising the desire for Buddhahood once it has been awakened. However much time we may have wasted up to now, there is still time to awaken this desire. Although our own merit for Buddhahood may be full ripe, it is our bounden duty to use all this merit for the purpose of enlightening every living thing. At all times there have been those who put their own Buddhahood second to the necessity of working for the good of all other living things.

The Four Wisdoms, charity, tenderness, benevolence and sympathy, are the means we have of helping others, and represent the Bodhisattva's aspirations. Charity is the opposite of covetousness; we make offerings although we ourselves get nothing at all. There is no need to be concerned about how small the gift may be so long as it brings true results, for even if it is only a single phrase or verse of teaching, it may be a seed to bring forth good fruit both now and hereafter.

Similarly the offering of only one coin or a blade of grass can cause the arising of good, for the teaching itself is the true treasure and the true treasure is the very teaching. We must never desire any reward but always share everything we have with others. It is an act of charity to build a ferry or a bridge, and all forms of industry are charity if they benefit others.

To behold all beings with the eye of compassion and to speak kindly to them is the meaning of tenderness. If one would understand tenderness, one must speak to others whilst thinking that one loves all living things as if they were one's own children. When we praise those who exhibit virtue and feel sorry for those who do not, our enemies become our friends and they who are our friends have their friendship strengthened. This is all through the power of tenderness. Whenever one speaks kindly to another, his face brightens and his heart is warmed; if a kind word be spoken in his absence, the impression will be a deep one. Tenderness can have a revolutionary impact upon the mind of man.

If one creates wise ways of helping beings, whether they be in high places or lowly stations, one exhibits benevolence. No reward was sought by those who rescued the helpless tortoise and the sick sparrow, these acts being utterly benevolent. The stupid believe that they will lose something if they give help to others, but this is completely untrue, for benevolence helps everyone, including oneself, being a law of the universe.

If one can identify oneself with that which is not oneself, one can understand the true meaning of sympathy. Take, for example, the fact that the Buddha appeared in the human world in the form of a human being; sympathy does not distinguish between oneself and others. There are times when the self is infinite and times when this is true of others. Sympathy is as the sea in that it never refuses water from whatever source it may come; all waters may gather and form only one sea.

O you seekers of enlightenment, meditate deeply upon these teachings and do not make light of them. Give respect and reverence to their merit which brings blessing to all living things; help all beings cross over to the other shore.

5. PUTTING THE TEACHINGS INTO PRACTICE AND SHOWING GRATITUDE

The Buddha Mind should be thus simply awakened in all living things within this world, for their desire to be born herein has been fulfilled. As this is so, why should they not be grateful to Shakyamuni Buddha?

If the Truth had not spread through the entire world, it would have been impossible for us to have found it, even should we have been willing to give our very lives for it. We should think deeply upon this. How fortunate have we been to be born now when it is possible to see the Truth! Remember the Buddha's words: "When you meet a Zen master who teaches the Truth, do not consider his caste, his appearance, shortcomings or behaviour. Bow before him out of respect for his great wisdom and do nothing whatsoever to worry him."

Because of consideration for others on the part of the Buddhas and patriarchs, we are enabled to see the Buddha even now and hear his teachings. Had the Buddhas and patriarchs not truly transmitted the Truth, it could never have been heard at this particular time. Even so much as a short phrase or section of the teaching should be deeply appreciated. What alternative have we but to be utterly grateful for the great compassion exhibited in this highest of all teachings, which is the very Treasury-Eye of the True Teaching? The sick sparrow never forgot the kindness shown to it and rewarded it with the ring belonging to the three great ministers, and the unfortunate tortoise remembered too, showing its gratitude with the seal of Yōfu. If even animals can show gratitude, surely man can do the same?

You need no further teachings than these in order to show gratitude, and you must show it truly, in the only real way, in your daily life; our daily life should be spent constantly in selfless activity with no waste of time whatsoever.

Time flies quicker than an arrow and life passes with greater transience than dew. However skilful you may be, how can you ever recall a single day of the past? Should you live for a hundred years just wasting your time, every day and month will be filled with sorrow; should you drift as the slave of your senses for a hundred years and yet live truly for only so much as a single day, you will in that one day not only live a hundred years of life but also save a hundred years of your future life. The life of this one day, today, is absolutely vital life; your body is deeply significant. Both your life and your body deserve love and respect, for it is by their agency that Truth is practised and the Buddha's power exhibited. The seed of all Buddhist activity and of all Buddhahood is the true practice of Preceptual Truth.

All the Buddhas are within the one Buddha Shakyamuni, and all the Buddhas of past, present and future become Shakyamuni Buddha when they reach Buddhahood. This very mind is itself the Buddha, and should you awaken to a complete understanding thereof, your gratitude to the Buddhas will know no bounds.

SHŌJI

Life and Death

There are no life and death when the Buddha is within them; when there is no Buddha within life and death, we are not deluded by them. These sayings are those of two great Zen teachers, Gassan and Tōzan respectively, and they must be considered very seriously as well as clearly understood by all who wish to become free from birth and death. Should a man seek the Buddha outside life and death, he is as one who turns his cart to the north whilst heading for Esshū, or as one who tries to see the North Star whilst looking southwards. By so doing, that which is the cause of life and death will be increased and the way to freedom lost sight of.

Should it be possible for us to understand that life and death are, of themselves, nothing more than Nirvāna, there is obviously no need either to try to escape from life and death or to search for Nirvāna, and for the first time, freedom from life and death becomes possible. Do not make the mistake of believing that a change takes place between life and death, for life is simply one position in time already possessing both before and after. Therefore Buddhism says that life as we know it is not life. Likewise death also is simply one position of time with a before and an after; therefore death itself is not death. When called life, there is only life; when called death, there is only death; if life comes, it is life; if death comes, it is death. There is no reason whatsoever for a being to be controlled by either, nor should hope be put in them. This very life and death *is* the Buddha's own life, and should you try to escape from them, you will lose the life of the Buddha in escaping therefrom. Should you do this, all you will be doing is clutching at the apparition of Buddha, but if you neither refuse nor search for this life, you will enter immediately into the Buddha Mind.

Do not, under any circumstances, try to understand this intellectually or give it expression in words. If you allow your concern for and attachment to body and mind to fall away naturally, you will precipitate yourself into the realm of Buddha. When the Buddha does all, and you follow this doing effortlessly and without worrying about it, you gain freedom from suffering and yourself become Buddha.

Since this is so, what is there to hinder you within your own mind? The way to Buddhahood is easy. They who do not perpetrate evil, they who do not try to grasp at life and death but work for the good of all living things with utter compassion, giving respect to those older and loving understanding to those younger than themselves, who do not reject, search for, think on or worry about anything, have the name of Buddha. You must look for nothing more.

ŪJI

Existence, Time

It was Yakusan who said the following: "To stand upon a mountain peak is existence, time; to descend to the depth of the ocean is existence, time; Kanzeon Bosatsu is existence, time; a Buddha who is eight or ten feet tall is existence, time; the staff and the hossu are existence, time; the post and the lantern are existence, time; your next-door neighbour and yourself are existence, time; the whole earth and the limitless sky are existence, time." This existence, time, means simply that time itself is existence and all existence itself is time. The golden body of the Buddha is time. Since all is time, time is expressed in all things and they become, as it were, its ornamentation. It is therefore imperative that we study the twelve hours now in front of us. The body of Kanzeon Bosatsu is exhibited through the aegis of time, and this body permeates the present twelve hours. Although we have not yet measured this twelve hours, yet we still call it twelve hours; it is because the passing of time leaves behind the signs of its passage that we do not doubt its existence, even though we do not understand it. Since the average man is not in the habit of profound thought, he doubts all things of which he has no full understanding; because of this his future doubts are out of harmony with his present ones, but even doubt itself is only a part of time.

Outside this doubting self no world exists, for the world actually is this very self. All things in this world must be regarded as time, and all things are in the same unhindered relationship one with the other as in each moment of time. Because of this, the longing for enlightenment arises naturally as a result of time, and as a result of mind, time arises also; in addition to this, training and enlightenment also arise, and so, from this, it is clearly seen that the self itself is time.

Since this is true, it is important for us to learn that upon this earth many things appear and many forms of grass exist, and that each thing that appears and each form of grass is in no way separate from the whole earth. It is after reaching this viewpoint that we can commence training, for having reached this point in our journey, but one thing appears and one form of grass remains. Sometimes that which appears is recognised, and again not always; there are times when the grass is recognised, and again not always. Because there is only time of this description, "ūji" is all of time, existence, and every single form of grass and everything that appears is also time, existence; all existences and all worlds are present in each and every moment. Just think: is there any existence or world that is apart from time?

The average person, with no knowledge of Buddhism, thinks as follows when he hears the word "ūji,": "There was a time when Buddha was active as Kanzeon Bosatsu, and there was a time when he was eight or ten feet tall when crossing the rivers and climbing the mountains; we too have passed over these rivers and mountains and now dwell in this lordly mansion; mountains, rivers, heaven, earth and I are separate." However, time is far more than this, for when these mountains and rivers are passed over, not only I myself am present but so also is time. As I am now here, time and I are one, for should time not include coming and departing, the eternal now is the very moment when the mountain is climbed. Should time include coming and departing, then I am the eternal now and this too is "ūji." The time at which the mountain is climbed and the river crossed engulfs the time when I am within my lordly mansion; the time when I am within my lordly mansion is the time at which I cross the river and climb the mountain.

The three heads and eight arms of Kanzeon Bosatsu are the time of yesterday, whilst the time of being a Buddha eight or ten feet tall is that of today. Yet what we say are yesterday and today are one and the same thing, in the same way as, when looking at mountains, we see many peaks with only one glance. Time itself never flows, for the Kanzeon Bosatsu of yesterday passes on as our existence, time; it appears to be elsewhere, but it is actually here and now. The Buddha who is eight or ten feet tall, the one of today, passes on as our existence, time, seeming again to be elsewhere but actually being here and now. As this is true, both the pine and the bamboo are time. Time does far more than merely fly away; there is much more to it than that. If all you can understand is that time flies, you cannot understand "ūji," for by such understanding, what you have realised is something that is passing away.

In the end you will realise that all existences are joined together and are themselves time; my own personal time; the chief trait of "ūji" is continuity, going from today to tomorrow and from today to yesterday, from yesterday to today, from today to today and from tomorrow to tomorrow. Since continuity is one of time's chief characteristics, neither past time nor present time accumulates. Since there is no accumulation, Seigen, Ōbaku, Kōsei and Sekitō are all time. Since self and other are time, training and enlightenment are time also, as are the entering of mud and water. Although some say that the disinterested relationship of the views of the average person is what that person sees, they are wrong, for the Truth simply puts the average person into passing causal relationships. Since we learn that time and existence are not the Truth, we think that the golden body of the Buddha is not ours and we try to free ourselves from this very fact of being the golden body of the Buddha. However, even in this dire strait we are still "ūji," as are also those who are not yet enlightened.

The hours of twelve and one follow each other in order in the world as we know it, and are made clear by the ascending and descending of seemingly fixed time. The hours of six and eight are time, as are also all living things and Buddhas. The heavenly deities enlighten the world as does Kanzeon Bosatsu, through their three heads and eight arms; Buddhas do the same thing by means of their ten-foot-high golden bodies. If one can transcend motion and rest, the world has been fully entered; the signs of becoming a True Buddha are shown whilst searching, attaining, in enlightenment and in Nirvāna, and these are all existence, time. There is absolutely nothing more than the careful studying of time as existence. However, since delusion is delusion, existence, time which is not properly studied is the study of only half of existence, time; even a body that is incorrectly seen is existence, time, and should you do nothing to remedy the mistake, enfolding both the before and after thereof, it is still existence, time. To work without restraint in one's own environment is existence, time. Do not waste time believing all this to be trivial, and at the same time, do not spend hours intellectualising about it. It is believed by most that time passes; in actual fact, it stays where it is. This idea of passing may be called time, but it is an incorrect idea, for since one only sees it as passing, one cannot understand that it stays just where it is. How is it possible for persons holding this view to find freedom? Who is able to give expression to this freedom, even supposing that he could understand fully that time stays where it is? But even should you be able to give expression to your understanding after many years, you will still be unaware of your original face, for should you think of existence, time in the usual way, both wisdom and enlightenment become merely things that appear in the arising and departing of time.

Free of all craving, existence, time manifests itself, sometimes here and sometimes there; the kings of heaven and their servants are not apart from the arising of existence, time, and all beings, whether on land or in the sea, come forth therefrom. Existence, time gives rise to all things whether they be good or evil, and their arising is the very process of time, nothing whatsoever being apart therefrom. It is wrong to think that continuity goes from east to west in the manner of a storm. Words are neither unmoving nor standing still, and this is an example of continuity. Spring, too, is the same as this, for therein certain events take place which are spoken of as continuity; if you can understand that nothing exists outside this continuity, you can understand that spring is always spring. Understand that continuity is perfected in springtime as the actual continuity of spring. The average person thinks that continuity is a passing through many worlds and lives, but this opinion is clearly the result of inadequate training.

When advised by Sekitō, Yakusan visited Basō and said, "I have studied almost all the teachings of the Three Vehicles. Why did the patriarch come from the west?" "There are times when I make the

Buddha raise his eyebrows and blink," replied Basō, "and there are times when I do not do so. There are times when it is good for him to do these things and times when it is not. What do you think?" Yakusan was immediately enlightened and said, "When I was in Sekitō's temple I was like a mosquito that was trying to bite a bull made of iron." Basō was trying to say something rather different from what most others say, for the raising of the eyebrows *is* the mountain and the ocean. Since the mountain and the ocean are the raising of the eyebrows, you must truly see the real mountain in its actual form if you would perform this act, and if you want to understand the meaning of the blink, the ocean must truly appear before your eyes. The opposites are familiar to each other; action and non-action are one. That which is not good is not necessarily of no use, for it is all existence, time; if this were not so, there would be neither ocean nor mountain. It is impossible to say that time does not exist, for the mountain and the ocean are in the absolute present. Should time decay, so will the mountain and the ocean; if it does not do so, then neither will they. Because of this both eyes and picked flowers appear, and this is existence, time; if it were not so, then all the foregoing is not so.

Shuzan's disciple Sekken Kisei once said to the trainees, "There are times when the will is adequate but words are not; there are times when words are adequate and the will is not; there are times when both words and will are adequate and times when neither is so." Both will and words are existence, time; adequacy and inadequacy are existence, time. When it is adequate it is unfinished; when it is inadequate it is already completed; will is a donkey and words are a horse; words mean horse and will means donkey; existence, time is as this. They travel fastest who are not there, since arrival is hindered by arrival but quite definitely not hindered whilst on the journey. The journey is hindered by non-arrival but not hindered by arrival. It is by means of the will that we understand the will; it is by means of words that we understand words. By being hindered we understand hindrance, and hindrance is hindered by hindrance: this too is existence, time. Other things may use hindrance, but no hindrance whatsoever can use other things. People meet me; they meet each other; myself meets me and exit meets exit; these things could not be if existence, time was not shared by all. The kōan in daily life is will; words are its key; adequacy is oneness; inadequacy is duality; and each of these, will, words, adequacy and inadequacy, is itself existence, time. This must be both understood and experienced.

These things have been said many times by the Zen teachers of old, but it is necessary for me to repeat them. Both will and words that go only halfway are existence, time; those that do not even reach halfway are existence, time. In such a way as this should study be undertaken. To make the Buddha raise his eyebrows and blink is half of existence, time; to make the Buddha raise his eyebrows and blink is all of existence, time; not to do so is half of existence, time; not to do so is all of existence, time. Both to study and experience this and not to study and experience this are existence, time.

GENJOKŌAN

The Problem of Everyday Life

Delusion, enlightenment, training, life, death, Buddhas and all living things are in existence when there is Buddhism; none of these exist when all is within the Truth; since the Way of the Buddha transcends unity and duality, all these things exist; whilst we adore flowers they wither; weeds grow strong whilst we long for their destruction. When we wish to teach and enlighten all things by ourselves, we are deluded; when all things teach and enlighten us, we are enlightened. To enlighten delusion is to become Buddha; most living things are deluded within enlightenment. Some are enlightened within enlightenment; others deluded within delusion. There is no need to know that one is identical with Buddha when Buddha is truly Buddha, for a truly enlightened Buddha expresses his Buddhahood in his daily life. To observe objects and voices with complete awareness of body and mind is very different from seeing a reflection in a mirror or the moon reflected in water; even if you see one side of something, the other will still be in shadow.

When one studies Buddhism one studies oneself; when one studies oneself one forgets oneself; when one forgets oneself one is enlightened by everything, and this very enlightenment breaks the bonds of clinging to both body and mind, not only for oneself but for all beings as well. If the enlightenment is true, it wipes out even clinging to enlightenment, and therefore it is imperative that we return to, and live in, the world of ordinary men. When a man first sees the Truth he automatically transcends the boundaries of truth; once the Truth has been awakened within a man, he is simultaneously his own original face. It is normal for a man, whilst sailing and observing the shore, to think that the shore is moving instead of the boat, but should he look carefully, he will find that it is the boat which is doing the actual moving. In the same way as this, it is because man observes everything from a mistaken viewpoint of his body and mind that he comes to the conclusion that they are eternal; however, should he learn to observe them correctly as a result of penetrating Truth, he will discover that no form attaches itself substantially to anything. The wood that is burnt upon a fire becomes ashes; it does not again become wood; you must not think that wood comes first and ashes afterwards. You must clearly understand that a piece of burning wood has both a before and an after; however, in spite of the fact that it has before and after, it is cut off therefrom. Ashes, however, have before and after. In the same way that wood does not again become wood after becoming ashes, so, in the very same way, man is not reborn again as man after dying. Therefore, it is correct for Buddhism to say that life does not become death. It is equally true to say that death does not become life, and the Buddha himself constantly preached this. These two views are called non-life and non-death. The two, life and death, are simply positions in time as are spring and winter; winter no more becomes spring than spring becomes summer. The moon reflected in water is the same as the enlightenment that a man can reach; the moon is not wetted by the water and the water does not become disturbed. However much light the moon may radiate, its reflection can still be seen in a puddle; in the same way, the full moon and the limitless sky may be seen reflected in a single dewdrop suspended from a grass-blade. Man is not restrained by enlightenment and the moon is not restrained by the water; man puts nothing in the way of enlightenment and the dewdrop puts nothing in the way of either the moon or the limitless sky; in addition to this, the deeper the moon's reflection, the higher the moon. The length of time of the reflection is in ratio to the depth of the water and the fullness of the moon.

When a man has an incomplete knowledge of the Truth he feels that he already knows enough, but when he has understood the Truth fully he feels sure that something is lacking. If you can see no land or mountains when sailing, the ocean appears rounded, but it is neither round nor square, being in possession of a myriad characteristics. Some people regard it as a palace and others as a form of ornamentation. It is only for a very short time that it appears round, owing to the distance we are able to see; this distance is constantly changing; we must view all things bearing this in mind. There are many things within the world of enlightenment, but the Zen trainee can only see as far as his present understanding permits him. If one would know the Truth, it is essential to know that the ocean and the mountains have many other attributes in addition to being square or circular, and that there are many other worlds in addition to this. Our immediate surroundings are of no account. It is essential to know that the ocean is contained within a single drop of water and that the Truth is manifesting itself eternally on the very spot on which we are now standing.

The ocean is limitless no matter how far fish may swim therein; the sky is limitless no matter how far a bird may fly therein. From the very beginning of all things, both the fish and the birds have been one with the ocean and the sky. Understand clearly that when a great need appears, a great use appears also; when there is small need, there is small use; it is obvious, then, that full use is made of all things at all times according to the necessity thereof. When birds are out of unity with the sky, or fish out of unity with the ocean, they die, for the life of fish is the ocean and the life of birds is the sky. It is equally true that the life of the sky is the birds and the life of the ocean is the fish; birds are life and fish are life. It is easily possible to find many examples of this idea. In spite of the facts of training and enlightenment and variations in the length of a man's life span, all ways of living are the very personification of Truth. However, should a fish try to go beyond the limitations of the ocean or a bird beyond the limitations of the sky, there will be no resting place for either.

Should you touch the Truth your every action will be vital and express the Way naturally, for your every action will be fully understood and digested Truth performed in the ordinary daily activities of an ordinary man. This Truth can never be understood as a result of conceptual duality such as big and small, or subject and object; the Way of Truth exists from the very beginning and makes no special appearance now, which is just as it should be. It is because the Way of Truth is as stated above that, after taking up one thing, you understand that one thing, and after finishing a practice, you understand that practice; and this is the way in which Buddhism itself is practised. It is not possible for us to know clearly when we are giving deep expression to the Way of Truth, since it is an action which arises simultaneously and synonymously with Buddhist study.

It is wrong to believe that one is fully aware of being enlightened, as personal knowledge, even after enlightenment. That which is intuitive cannot necessarily be given easy expression and definite form even though enlightenment is already ours. One summer day a Zen teacher sat fanning himself when a monk asked, "Since the nature of wind is stationary and universally present, why do you use a fan?" The teacher replied, "Although you know its nature to be stationary, you do not know why it is universally present." "Why is it universally present?" asked the monk. For answer the teacher merely continued fanning himself, and the monk bowed. The true way of transmission and enlightenment which is the result of real experience is the same as this. One who thinks that fanning is not needed simply because wind is stationary by nature, and requires no fan since it can be sensed, understands nothing of its nature and its eternal presence. It is because it is eternally, always here that the wind of Buddhism makes the earth golden and the rivers run with ghee.

TENZOKYOKAN

Instructions to the Chief Cook

From its inception Zen Buddhism has had six chief offices, called the Chīji in Japanese, and the priests who hold them, as the Buddha's sons, are jointly in charge of all the affairs of the temple. Among these is the office of tenzo, that of chief cook, and this post is always held by a senior priest.

None but the finest priests, fully awakened to and eager for Buddhahood, have up to now been trusted with the office of tenzo, for unless there is an earnest desire for Buddhahood, however great an effort the priest holding this office may make, he will not be successful therein. The Zen Temple Regulations state that the desire for Buddhahood must for ever be kept active within the mind of the tenzo priest, and he must, at various times, devise such dishes as will create great pleasure for the monks who partake of them. Excellent priests such as Tōzan have held this office; it is important to understand that the tenzo priest is utterly different from a royal cook or waiter.

I often asked questions of the senior priests when I was undergoing my training in China, and all of them were very kind in telling me what they knew of the duties of a cook, saying that they who were entrusted with this office were the very cream of Buddhism as it has been handed down to us from the enlightened Buddhas and patriarchs. If we would understand the duties of a cook we must study the Zen Temple Regulations thoroughly, listening to the explanations given by seniors in the minutest detail.

Every twenty-four hours, after lunch, the cook has a consultation with the treasurer and assistant director concerning the food to be used for the following breakfast and lunch: how much rice and the quantity and type of vegetables. Once the food has been prepared, it must be cared for in the same way as we care for our own eyesight. It was said by one Zen teacher that the common property of the temple must be accorded the same care as that accorded our own eyes. This food must be dealt with as if it were for the royal table; exactly the same care must be given to all food, whether raw or cooked.

After the above-mentioned consultation, another is held in the temple kitchen for the purpose of deciding which vegetables shall be eaten, which tastes relished, and what gruel made. The Zen Temple Regulations state clearly that when food is prepared the cook must consult with all the officers, that is, the treasurer, assistant director, guestmaster, disciplinarian, cooks and general maintenance personnel, as to what tastes shall be relished at breakfast and lunch and the number of vegetables to be used. When these matters have been decided, the menu for the day is written upon the boards which are hung in front of the abbot's room and the trainees' hall. Thereafter the following morning's breakfast gruel is cooked.

When rice and vegetables are being examined and washed, it is imperative that the cook be both single-minded yet practical, ensuring that the work is done to the very best of his ability and without allowing contempt for any foodstuff to arise in his mind. He must be diligent in all his work without discriminating against one thing as opposed to another. Although he dwells within the ocean of merit he must never waste so much as one drop of that ocean's water, even though he may have his hut upon the very summit of the mountain of good works. However minute may be the merit of anything he does, he must never forget to accumulate that merit even if it seems to him infinitesimally small and therefore not worth bothering about.

The Zen Temple Regulations say that unless the cook has carefully arranged the six kinds of tastes to be relished and cooked with a gentle, pure heart, bearing in mind utter respect for the food, he has not fulfilled his duty as cook to his brother trainees. Therefore he must be very careful in all things—for example, removing sand from rice—and in so doing he will cook naturally with a gentle and pure heart, as well as properly arranging the six kinds of tastes.

Seppō, when holding the office of cook under Tōzan, was once washing rice when Tōzan came into the kitchen. "Is there rice or sand left when you have finished the washing?" asked Tōzan. "I wash away both at the same time," replied Seppō. "If you do that, what will the trainees eat?" asked Tōzan. At this question Seppō turned over the rice bin. "One day you will be enlightened," said Tōzan, "but it will be under someone other than me." By such methods as this the old and excellent teachers trained their disciples when in the office of cook, and we of the present day must never be lazy should we ever be appointed thereto. The cook must seek for Buddhahood with as much zeal when cooking as men of the present time apply to their work when stripped to the waist. It is imperative that we ourselves look carefully at both rice and sand and make certain that we never mix them. The Zen Temple Regulations say that the cook must personally examine all food carefully and ensure its cleanliness; therefore the water with which the rice is washed must not be idly thrown away. In the old days a straining bag was used for the purpose of ensuring that no rice was ever left in the water. Rice must also be protected against rats and the curious after being put into the pot.

The following day's breakfast vegetables are prepared first and thereafter the rice and soup for lunch. The dining table, rice box and all necessary tableware must be washed and kept carefully clean in a convenient place ready for use. Whether chopsticks, ladles or other articles, they must all be made ready in the same single-minded way as the food and handled just as gently.

The following day's lunch rice is then prepared after all rice weevils, green peas, bran, dust, sand and grit have been removed from it. The Scripture for the God of Fire is always recited if rice and vegetables are mixed, the recitation being done by a junior trainee.

After this, all vegetables, liquids and other raw foods are made ready; that which has been provided for the temple officers must be cooked with the same care as that shown to ordinary food, irrespective of quantity or quality. The chief cook must never be concerned about the unappetising appearance of food, nor must he complain about it. He must be so single-minded in his own training that no resting place can ever be found between him and the actual food, the two being identical with each other.

The following day's breakfast must be completely prepared before midnight and cooked after that hour has struck. The following morning, when breakfast is over, the pot must be cleaned and the lunch rice steamed together with the soup. Every grain of rice must be washed carefully in the scullery by the chief cook personally; he must never leave until the washing is done, and he must on no account throw away even a single grain. When the washing has been completed, as well as the soaking, the rice is put into the pot and steamed over the fire. It was said by one old priest that the pot in which the rice is cooked must be thought of as our own head; the water in which the rice is washed must be regarded as our own life. In summer all rice must be put in a rice chest before being put upon the dining table.

The vegetables and soup must be cooked as soon as the chief cook begins the cooking of the rice, and here again the chief cook himself must handle the work. He occasionally gives orders for the necessary utensils to be prepared by a serving trainee, servant or stoker. In olden times, however, only the chief cook was allowed to handle the cooking, although in recent times there have been some serving trainees with the title of rice cook or meal supervisor, being in charge specifically of rice and gruel, and also that of accountant, who were allowed to assist in the actual cooking in the larger temples.

The chief cook must not eye the food superficially or with a discriminatory mind; his soul must be so free that the Buddha Land appears within a blade of grass whenever he and others behold it, and he must be capable of giving a great sermon even on the very heart of a particle of dust. He must not be contemptuous when making poor-quality soup, nor should he be overjoyed when he makes it with milk. If he is unattached to the last-mentioned, he will not hate the first. There must be no laziness in him however unappetising the food may be; should the food he beholds be of good quality, his training must become all the deeper so that he may avoid attachment thereto. His speech in the presence of all men must be the same, unchanging in mode, for should he change it he is not a true seeker after Buddhahood. He must be polite in all he does and strenuous in perfecting his efforts at cooking, for these actions will lead him in the path of purity and care once trodden by the excellent priests of old. I myself long to be thus. How is it possible to be so single-minded at all times? It is true that once a very fine old chief cook made a poor soup for only three small coins, but a true chief cook must be able to make a fine soup for exactly the same price. Most modern chief cooks would find this very difficult, for there is as big a difference between ancient and modern as there is between heaven and earth. It is extremely difficult for a modern chief cook to be as those of olden times, but if he strives with all his might and is gentle when cooking, he will go even further than they did. People of the present day seem to be completely unaware of this fact, primarily because they give free rein to their own pettiness, discrimination and feeling to such an extent that they are like wild horses prancing or wild monkeys swinging about from one tree to another. Should one meditate deeply upon oneself, discarding pettiness, discrimination and feeling, the oneness of self and others will be realised. Therefore, if one is moved by things and people, one is also able to move them. It is absolutely essential that the pure actions of the chief cook shall come forth from his realisation of unity with all things and beings; having no prejudices himself, he must be able to see clearly into the minds and hearts of others. He must be so kaleidoscopic that from only a stalk of cabbage, he seems to produce a sixteen-foot-long body of the Buddha. Even in this present day and age it is possible for him to develop a kaleidoscopic nature to such a degree that he helps all living things thereby.

All food, after being cooked, must be put away in a safe and suitable place. Thereafter, when the chief cook hears the drums or gongs, he must go to do his Zazen in the meditation hall and listen to the words of the abbot both morning and evening along with everyone else. On returning to his room, he must shut his eyes and think quietly of the number for whom he must make food, not forgetting the seniors in their private rooms, the sick members of the community in the infirmary, the aged members of the community, those who are absent, guest monks in the guesthouse and any other guests that may be present. Should he be in any doubt as to the number within the temple, he must ask the disciplinarian and other officers as well as the chief junior. When he is certain of the number, he should remember that to whosoever eats a grain of rice with True Mind another grain should be given, for this grain can be divided into two, three, four or more grains. Even only half a grain is sometimes as good as one or two, and two halves, once they come together, become one. Should one grain be divided into ten sections and nine be given away, how many grains are left? When these same come together again, how many are there left? He who eats this grain with True Mind sees Isan and tames the pale-blue cow: the pale-blue cow also consumes Isan. It is important that the chief cook think carefully about himself to see if he has fully understood the importance of a kaleidoscopic character. If he has done so, he must teach all people according as he is able, making great efforts for religion every day.

If someone offers money for food for the community, the chief cook must discuss the matter with the other officers; this is the traditional way of making all decisions concerning the distribution of offerings to the community. Under no circumstances may the chief cook encroach upon the duties of others.

After the rice and soup have been prepared, they are put upon the dining table. The chief cook burns incense after putting on his kesa. He then spreads his mat and bows nine times towards the meditation hall before sending food to the dining hall. Always he must be diligent in preparing breakfast and lunch every day, under no circumstances being idle. By being conscientious in all his work he will naturally awaken the seed of Buddhahood within himself, for should he meditate deeply, he will find that such action leads to ultimate bliss.

Although Buddhism was brought to Japan a long time ago, I have never yet read anything written by any Zen teacher concerning the correct way of cooking, nor is it written anywhere that the chief cook must bow to the meditation hall before sending food to table. It is because people know nothing of the True Mind revealed within the correct meaning of the community's food and their cooking methods that it is said such food is just the same as that of mere birds and animals. This is a great shame. Let us examine the reason why it is so.

When I was staying in Tendōzan the name of the chief cook was Lu. After lunch one day, when on my way to another part of the temple which was reached by means of the eastern corridor, I saw him busily drying mushrooms in front of the Butsuden, wearing no hat and using a bamboo stick. The sun was scorching both his head and the pavement, but he continued to work hard, perspiring greatly. Feeling concern for the pain he was obviously enduring at so great an age, for his back was bent as taut as a bow, I said to him, "How old are you?" His big eyebrows were as white as the feathers of a crane. "I am sixty-eight," he replied. "Why do you not give such work to the junior trainees or servants?" I asked. "They are not me," he replied. "I know that you are very sincere, but the sun is now blazing hot. Why work so hard at such a time?" I asked. "What other time is there than now?" he replied. The conversation went no further than this, but as I continued on my way along the corridor, I suddenly understood intuitively why the position of chief cook is so very important.

During May of the sixteenth year of Kia-ting I was on board ship speaking with the captain when an old priest of about sixty came aboard to buy mushrooms. We took tea together, and I learned that he was the chief cook of a large temple. "I am from Shi-shu," he said, "and am sixty-one years old. I left home forty years ago. In almost all the temples where I have lived, the life of the community was pure and truly religious. Early last year I was in Ku-yung and had the opportunity of staying in Ayuwan, but did not make use of it at that time. Luckily, however, I was later appointed chief cook there at the end of the summer. Tomorrow being the fifth of May, I must make an offering of food to the entire community, but there was nothing suitable in the temple. I originally wanted to give them vegetables and noodles but had no mushrooms, so I have come here." "When did you leave Ayuwan-shan?" I asked. "After lunch," he replied. "Did you have to come far?" I asked. "About thirty-four or thirty-five ri," was his answer. "When will you return?" "As soon as I have the mushrooms." "I am so glad we were able to meet and talk. I would like to offer you something," I said. "I am afraid that is impossible, for should I stay longer, who will do tomorrow's cooking?" he replied. "Surely in a temple as big as Ayuwan-shan someone else is capable of cooking food? I cannot believe that the absence of one chief cook could cause trouble." "Although I am old I, as the chief cook, am in charge of cooking. Since this is the training of my old age, how is it possible for me to give such duties to others? It must also be remembered that I did not get permission to stay out for the night," was his reply. "Surely it would be better for you to do Zazen or study kōans," I said. "Whatever is the use of working so hard merely at the duties of a chief cook?" He laughed heartily at my comment, saying, "My good foreigner, you have no idea of the true meaning of Buddhist training, nor of its character." Feeling greatly ashamed and somewhat surprised at this comment, I said, "What are they?" "Remain still and quiet in the very depths of your own question and their meaning will manifest itself," he replied. I was unable to understand him, and realising this, he said, "If you cannot understand me I suggest you come to Ayuwan-shan; then we can talk of these matters." He then rose to leave, saying, "It grows dark; I must get home quickly. I have no time for idle chatter."

He came to see me the following July when I was in Tendōzan and told me, "I am going to resign as chief cook after this summer and go home. By accident I heard from a fellow trainee that you were here and I was anxious to see you." I was overjoyed to see him, and in the course of discussing many things, we touched upon the matters we had spoken of on the ship. "If someone wishes to understand the true character of Buddhist training," he said, "its original meaning must be thoroughly realised. If one undergoes Buddhist training, he must understand the true meaning of that training." "What is this true character?" I asked. "One, two, three, four, five," he answered. "What is the discipline of Buddhism?" I asked. "The whole universe manifests itself quite naturally," he answered. I will not make mention of the other things of which we spoke, but primarily because of him, I was able to understand to a considerable extent what the character and discipline of Buddhism are. When I spoke of these matters to my late teacher, Myozen, he happily agreed with my opinions. Some time later I read the following verse by Setchō in the Monastic Precepts:

> One, seven, three, five,
> Nothing may be depended upon by any universe;
> Night comes and the moon floods the water with light;
> Within the dragon's jaws I find many exquisite jewels.

This verse said exactly the same thing as had the chief cook the year before; I know that he was a True Seeker of Buddhahood.

In the beginning my characters were one, two, three, four and five, and now they include six, seven, eight, nine and ten. It is essential that we trainees study the true character of Buddhism wholeheartedly without attachment to any opposite, for only then will the unity of Zen be understood in characters; should we do otherwise, innumerable varieties of Zen will ruin us to such an extent that we shall be unable to cook food for the community properly.

All chief cooks were diligent in their work, and within this fact we can find the original meaning of Buddhist training and its true character, for it is the very marrow of rightly transmitted Buddhism.

The Zen Temple Regulations state that breakfast and lunch must be most carefully prepared, bearing in mind the necessity for a sufficient supply of food at both. This is true not only of breakfast and lunch but of all food and drink, as well as of clothing, medicine and bedclothes. The Buddha gave twenty years of his life for our benefit; so great is the light which he radiates that it is too great for us to appreciate fully. Because of this the chief cook must have no thought other than service to the community, having no concern for lack of wealth. Should he be completely unattached to the results of the work which he does, eternal bliss will be his; I believe that the same attitude of mind as that of the chief cook towards the community should also be adopted by the abbot thereof.

The best way of handling food is for whoever is doing so to possess a sincere and appreciative opinion of it, irrespective of its quality. Because of the sincerity of mind with which a woman offered the Buddha a bowl of milk, it was foretold that she would become a pratyekabuddha in the following life. Because King Asoka, as his last good action, offered the half of a fruit to the priests attending him on his deathbed, he was free from all suffering at the moment of death. From this it may be seen that small acts of charity, made in a devotional spirit, are beneficial not only in the present but in the future also. However minute may be the offerings we make to Buddha, they must be given in the spirit of true religion and sincerity; such deeds are the right action of all men.

The chief cook must never consider rich cream milk a superior food to soup or vegetables when choosing ingredients; whenever such a choice is involved, it must be made with a mind free from defilement and in utter sincerity. Once a priest has entered the vast ocean of Buddhism he sees no difference at all between rich cream milk and coarse soup or vegetables, for then everything is identical with the ocean of Buddhism. It goes without saying that no chief cook sees any difference whatsoever between such things once he has truly awakened the seed of Buddhahood. It was once said by a great teacher that priests do not differentiate between various foods just as a fire does not differentiate between various sorts of firewood. If we are sincere when cooking, even the coarsest food can help us to exhibit the seed of Buddhahood. Never make light of such things; however minute in quantity or coarse in quality food may be, they who would lead both men and gods must be able to save all living things thereby.

Priests vary in age, being old or young; some have great merit whilst others have none; the chief cook must understand this quite clearly in its entirety. It is impossible for him to know what the future may hold and even more impossible for him to know the future of others; it would be thoroughly wicked of him to judge others by his own standards. All members of the priesthood are the Treasure of Buddhism, whether senior or junior, clever or stupid.

That which was wrong yesterday may be correct today; it is impossible to separate the sacred from the secular. The Zen Temple Regulations say that whether priests are holy or unholy they all have the potential of embracing and enfolding the universe. One must be entirely free from moral discrimination. Strenuous training, of itself, is the True Way. Although Buddhism may be right before your eyes, you will be very far from the Truth should you make so much as one false step in the direction of moral discrimination. The true meaning of morality has been shown by the masters of old in their strenuous efforts to practise Buddhism. Because of this, all future chief cooks must be very active when holding their office. There is no deception in the Zen Temple Regulations of Hyakujō.

When staying in Kenninji on my return to Japan, I was greatly surprised to find that the chief cook was completely unaware of the true way of preparing food. It was indeed unfortunate that he had no opportunity of learning from the great chief cooks of other temples, for he spent much of his time in idleness, which is highly detrimental to Buddhism. He never personally took charge of the cooking or preparing of either breakfast or lunch, leaving all his work, whether important or otherwise, to a coarse servant who knew nothing, and cared less, about the correct way of cooking food. He never went to see if the man was doing anything correctly, and yet saw no shame in visiting a woman who lived nearby. His only other occupations seemed to be gossipping with others and reciting scriptures in his room. He did nothing more, for he never went near the kitchen however long he had been absent from it, nor would he buy any new utensils or consider the number of tastes to be relished in the food. Obviously he did not consider that cooking was the work of Buddha. He had no notion of the fact that food could only be served after he had offered incense and bowed to the meditation hall. It is indeed a shame that he had no idea of how to lead his juniors during meals. Since he did not possess the Way-seeking Mind, he had never been a True Seeker of Buddhahood; he was as one who returns from a mountain or ocean of treasures empty-handed. Even though he had not awakened to Buddhahood he could still have behaved correctly as a chief cook once given the chance to see a true teacher, one who was truly awakened to Buddhahood. Since he neither awakened the seed of Buddhahood nor bothered to cook, what use was he?

The term of office of any officer in a Chinese temple is one year. When special offerings are made by members of the laity, as sometimes happens at mealtimes, these priests have special duties. They must always make special efforts in their work for the benefit of both themselves and others, as well as raise the standard of perfection of their own training by adhering strictly to the temple regulations and trying to reach the standards set by the old masters through copying their methods. If we compare this with the behaviour of the chief cook described above, we find that he thought of his training with as little interest as if it belonged to someone else, whilst those who followed the code of conduct outlined above considered the training of others with as much care as if it were their own. There is an old poem which says:

> Although he has already spent two-thirds of his life
> He has not yet purified his mind;
> Being solely interested in fame and gain
> He fails to heed the warning of my words.

It is clear from this that without true teachers, we would be engulfed in fame and gain. The chief cook I spoke of is like the stupid rich man's son spoken of in the Lotus Scripture, who on receiving a fortune bequeathed to him, ran away from home and threw it away as if it were nothing worth; it is a terrible situation for a chief cook.

When I think of the old chief cooks, I realise that all were worthy of their posts. All were enlightened when performing their duties as chief cooks, and Tōzan showed the Buddha to the entire community in three pounds of flax. There is nothing of greater value than enlightenment, and no time more precious than now.

Let us now consider some examples of those who truly sought enlightenment. Because a child once handed its treasure of a handful of sand to Buddha, he later became King Asoka. Shakyamuni Buddha once told King Udayana that after his death whoever should make a statue of Buddha would be handsome or beautiful from one generation to another, no matter how many times he might be born; in addition to this, such a person would be born in heaven after death. Obviously both the office and the name of chief cook will remain exactly as they are. Since the actions of the old chief cooks have come down to us, these priests can, if we truly train ourselves, be seen again in us.

Three attitudes of mind must be cultivated by all temple officers, in addition to that of the chief cook. These are gratitude, love and generosity. The mind of ecstasy expresses gratitude. If we were to dwell in heaven, our joy would be so excessive that there would be no time for us to either train or awaken the seed of Buddahood within us, and we would never prepare food for the Three Treasures. There is nothing of greater value of excellence than the Three Treasures; they far surpass the greatest deity in heaven in both value and excellence, as well as equally surpassing the highest upon earth. The Zen Temple Regulations say that priests have far greater excellence than any other beings, for their body and mind are pure and wholly free from earthly clinging. How wonderful it is that we are fortunate enough to have been born human and so can become chief cooks with the honour of preparing pure food for the superlative Three Treasures. Than this there is no greater delight. Had we been born in one of the evil worlds such as hell, the world of the hungry ghosts, that of animals, that of asuras, or any of the other eight in which it is very hard to hear Buddhist Truth, it would not be possible for us personally to make pure food for the Three Treasures together with the great priesthood, for both body and mind would be subject to suffering. We are fortunate that in this life we have the opportunity to offer pure food to the Three Treasures. How lucky we are! How blessed is this body! For all eternity there will be no greater opportunity than that offered to us now; its merit is undefilable. When we serve our fellow trainees purely, hundreds and thousands of lives are enfolded in one single day's or hour's work which will bear fruit for many lives to come. To grasp Truth thus clearly is to express gratitude. Even were we the highest in all the world, such rank would be as useless as a bubble if we did not make pure food for the Three Treasures.

The mind of our parents expresses love, and we must love the Three Treasures in the same way as our parents love us. However poor a person may be, it is frequently possible to see the love he expresses towards his children. Yet who is capable of understanding the extent of his loving mind other than he himself? All men, whether rich or poor, long for their children to grow strong and big, protecting them with unsparing devotion against inclement weather; this is the greatest of all sincerity. No one who does not possess this mind can understand it. A chief cook must love water and rice in the same way that parents love their children. The Buddha gave us twenty years of his life because he wanted to teach us parental love by his example, not because he was eager for fame and gain.

A generous mind is one that is as firm as a rock and as limitless as the ocean, completely lacking in discrimination. One who possesses such a mind makes no difference between base metal and gold; he is not bewitched by beautiful voices or ugly-sounding ones, nor is he concerned at the changes of the seasons. We must make our own personal understanding of this mind clear by writing it down, fully comprehending it and learning it in everything we do in our ordinary life.

Without a mind as above described, a former chief cook could not have taught his wicked and frivolous trainee, nor could Daii have shown his understanding to his master by blowing three times on a dead fire or Tōzan exhibited the Buddha in three pounds of flax. You should understand from this that all the old teachers exhibited this mind in their everyday actions. Even now they are showing us clearly the true meaning and importance of training, thus leading us to emancipation. The wide highway to enlightenment is our own training. Whosoever we are, abbot, officer or any other trainee, we must all keep the three kinds of mind constantly in our thoughts.

川

The Teachings of
Keizan Zenji

INTRODUCTION TO THE TRANSLATIONS

KEIZAN ZENJI was born in Fukui Prefecture in 1267 and entered Eiheiji, under Koun Ejō, at the age of twelve; thereafter he studied under Tetsū Gikai of the same temple. Much of his life was spent in establishing temples in different parts of Japan, until he became chief abbot of Daijōji in Ishikawa Prefecture, where he spent ten years teaching. In 1321, at the request of Jōken-risshi, he became chief abbot of Shōgakuji; he renamed this temple Shōgaku-zan Sōjiji. Sōjiji, which was made an Imperial Prayer Temple under Emperor Gō-Daigo (1318–1339), became one of the two head temples of the Sōtō Zen Church of Japan, ranking as equal with Eiheiji, and Keizan Zenji became the greatest of the Sōtō Zen patriarchs next to Dōgen Zenji. The sacred picture of the Sōtō Zen Church shows Shakyamuni Buddha at the top, in the centre, with Dōgen Zenji on his right hand just below him, and Keizan Zenji on his left. Dōgen is regarded as the father of Sōtō Zen and Keizan as its mother.

Before Keizan's advent Sōtō Zen had been confined to a few small monasteries, none of which were to be found in Kyoto, the spiritual centre of Japan at that time. As a result of Keizan's genius, Sōtō not only flourished but became the largest of all the Buddhist sects, eventually rivalling the Shin Church in later centuries.

Keizan Zenji's writings, unlike Dōgen's, are highly intuitive. Whereas Dōgen was somewhat like a puritanical father, constantly exhorting his children to the utmost sincerity in their meditation, Keizan, as will be seen from the following translations, was an intuitive genius who knew better than anyone else the temper of the times and how that temper could be exploited for the furtherance of Sōtō Zen.

Keizan's works include the *Denkoroku* and the *Sankon Zazen Setsu*, as well as the majority if not the entirety of the ceremonies at present used in the Sōtō Zen Church. From the point of view of understanding Buddhism, however, his most important work by far is the *Denkoroku*, or *Book of the Transmission*. This consists of fifty-two chapters, each one describing the particular kōan, and its solution, of each of the patriarchs from the time of—and including— Shakyamuni Buddha to the time of Dōgen. The chapters are very short and succinct. Each commences with a description of the actual moment of solving the kōan, together with the kōan itself. Then follows a short history of the patriarch, usually with an anecdote concerning either his miraculous birth or some miraculous happening during his lifetime which has somehow crept into history and become part of Buddhist legend. The most valuable part of each chapter is the explanation of the circumstances and frame of mind required for solving the particular kōan concerned, giving careful attention to the fact that all of the kōans and the methods of solving them are identical, although the outward appearances in each case may be different, and that the individual kōan is but a facet of the eternal kōan, which is universal. To better this end, Keizan finishes off each chapter with a short poem, appropriate to the facet of the eternal kōan under discussion, in which a thread can be seen running from chapter to chapter that binds them into one magnificent spiritual work of art. In the *Denkoroku* Keizan's poetic and intuitive genius is to be seen in all its full flowering. It would be impossible for anyone reading it with a sincere desire to learn to know Zen not to come away with at least a small but quite genuine understanding of what Zen is all about. This is what makes the translation of this work absolutely essential, now that so many books have appeared on the market which purport to be about Zen teaching. Only the first fifteen chapters are included here, but these should be sufficient to whet the appetite of all those who truly desire to know Zen, and may induce some other scholar to continue the work that Reverend Yogo and I have begun.

The *Sankon Zazen Setsu* is a short work describing the three types of mind that result in the three types of meditation practice. It was many years before this manuscript was unearthed, and apart from one very poor translation it has never before, as far as I know, appeared in the English language.

The *Kyojūkaimon*, and the ceremonies in Book IV, are essential if one would understand the moral training and the scope of Sōtō Zen teaching. Each ceremony was designed not only to embody the teachings of Shakyamuni Buddha but also to explain them and show their use in everyday life, as well as to indicate the attitude of mind which leads beyond ceremonial as a form and turns it into meditation.

By no means all of the Sōtō ceremonies are included in Book IV; only the essential ones. Many ceremonies were created simply as an alternative form of meditation in monasteries where, in the fourteenth century, there was little else to do than till the land. In order to bring home to the trainees of the time that all activity, of whatever form, was actually meditation if done with the correct mind, Keizan Zenji worked on perfecting the ceremonies; but he achieved far more than merely teaching his trainees that all life's activities are one. Through the magnificence of these ceremonies he was also able to reach the poorer classes, who, having very little beauty in their lives, could nevertheless come to the temple and see something beautiful. Many of them were able to sublimate what they saw and go beyond it, making every activity of their lives a meditation practice in the same way as the trainees.

I have kept all these translations as literal as possible without actually using bad English. Unlike Dōgen, whose works require considerable editing, Keizan seems to have had a good idea of form and style in writing. Dōgen's works contain many afterthoughts which pop up in all the wrong places; Keizan's writings are artistically whole. With the centuries various traditions have grown up around some of the ceremonies, and slight discrepancies will be seen between them as they are performed in some temples today and as they were originally written—between what Dōgen wrote concerning the way to take meals, for example, and the actual mealtime ceremonial as described in Book IV. It would be impossible to say if the method of taking meals was ever used exactly as Dōgen describes it. Eiheiji makes this claim, but it is not true. After studying the ceremonies as they were originally and as they are now performed in many temples, I have come to the conclusion that the exact copying of outward form is not nearly as essential as the understanding of the internal spirit. Therefore, my fellow translators and I have gone boldly ahead with translating the ceremonies according to the traditions prevalent in Sōjiji. The reader, should he visit Japan, should not become concerned if the ceremonies he witnesses are not exactly as shown here, or for that matter, if the ones shown here are different from those now performed in Sōjiji under its new abbot; Chisan Kōhō Zenji had his way and his successors have theirs. Abbots are as if gods in their own right, with unlimited power even with regard to ceremonial. If this is borne in mind, misunderstandings will not create problems.

It would be neither advisable nor practical to translate the ceremonies of Jūkai and Kessei exactly as performed in Sōjiji. This is simply because most American and British temples are extremely small, and priests and others might be discouraged from performing these ceremonies if they felt it was essential to have an enormous temple with many halls and a host of assistants. Basically only three persons are needed for any of these ceremonies, with the exception possibly of Hossen, though even this is often performed in Japan with only the master, his chief junior and one or two others present. Again, it is not the actual form that is essential so much as its internal spirit, though this does not mean that one can be slapdash about ceremonial performance. Understand clearly that the body expresses the mind; keep the spirit of the tradition without being bound thereby. This was the intention of Keizan Zenji; it is also mine and that of my fellow translators.

The historical details of the lives of Shakyamuni Buddha and the patriarchs are not accurate as presented by Keizan Zenji in the *Denkoroku*. This work must be read as a work of intuitive art and not as historical fact; historians please take note.

Denkoroku

THE BOOK OF THE TRANSMISSION

Chapter I

SHAKYAMUNI BUDDHA

When Shakyamuni saw the morning star and was enlightened, he said, "I *was* enlightened instantaneously with the universe."

Shakyamuni Buddha belonged to the Nisshu race, which is known in India as the Race of the Sun. At nineteen years of age he escaped from his castle at midnight and fled to Mount Dandokusen, where he cut his hair. He then practised asceticism for six years. For six years he sat still in one place, with spiders' webs upon his brow and birds' nests in his hair. Reeds grew between his legs and around him, but he sat still for six years.

As the morning star rose on December eighth, he understood spiritual enlightenment and for the first time spoke the words quoted above. He was thirty years of age.

After that, for forty-nine years, he was never alone. There was never a day when he was not lecturing to his disciples, nor was there a day when he had no begging bowl and robe. He lectured to as many as three hundred and sixty groups.

The last time he transmitted the Truth was to Makakashyo, and this transmission has continued to the present time. Indeed, all over India, China and Japan the Training for Truth has come down to this day.

His sayings, actions and behaviour are the rule of his disciples. Even though he had the thirty-two marks of a Buddha, the good aspects and the eighty appearances, he had the form of an old monk. His form was no different from our own. Therefore, after him, in the three ages of Shō, Zō and Matsu, everyone who yearns for him takes the same form as he; they take the Lord's way of life and do not set themselves up as better than he. Since Shakyamuni Buddha's time, every Buddha and every ancestor has continued to transmit the Truth constantly. This fact is clear.

Although the various illustrations, facts and words which were pointed out and lectured on to the three hundred and sixty groups of people for forty-nine years were different, none were outside this Truth. The so-called "I" is not Shakyamuni Buddha. He is born out of this "I." Not only he but also the whole world and animate things are outside it. When Shakyamuni Buddha *is* enlightened, the whole world and animate things are enlightened at the same time, just as the main rope has every branch rope connected with it. Not only the whole world and animate things are enlightened, but all Buddhas in the Triple Universe apprehend the Truth.

Although this is so, Shakyamuni Buddha is not conscious of being enlightened. Do not look for Shakyamuni Buddha outside the whole world, the ground and animate things. Everything in the universe is within Shakyamuni's eyes. You too are standing within them. Not only are you within them, they are you. Further, Shakyamuni's eyes become a globule of your flesh, and all is within all, unruled by anything. Therefore, do not think that Shakyamuni's eyes are Shakyamuni's eyes and that you are you, constantly, unchangeable. You *are* Shakyamuni's eyes. Shakyamuni is all of you. As this is so, what is the principle of enlightenment?

I ask of you this question:

Is Shakyamuni enlightened with you, or are you enlightened with Shakyamuni?

If it is said that you are enlightened with Shakyamuni or Shakyamuni is enlightened with you, then it is not Shakyamuni's enlightenment; this cannot be the principle of enlightenment. If you want to understand the principle of enlightenment in detail, throw away Shakyamuni and you at the same time and know they are "I." The "I" and "with" in Shakyamuni's first utterance *is* the whole world, universe and animate things; this "I" is not the *old* Shakyamuni.

Study in detail, think fully, and understand "I" and "with." Even if you can understand "I" and you cannot realise "with," you cannot understand fully; you see with only one eye.

But "I" and "with" are not one and two. Your skin, flesh, bones and marrow are all "with." The Lord of the House is "I." After all, if you want to know the eternal Lord of the House, you must not think of it as the whole world and animate things.

Although the Lord of the House is represented in spring, summer, autumn and winter, and although mountains, rivers and the ground are different in time, the Lord is represented fully in the world in the raising of the eyebrows and winking of the eyes of old Shakya-muni.

The Lord neither discards everything worldly nor does not discard it. The Reverend Hōgen said, "There is no need to speak," and the Reverend Jizō said, "*What* is called everything?" Therefore, practise in detail, realise fully, and understand the enlightenment of Shakyamuni and that of yourself. Understand this kōan fully. Speak from your own heart without borrowing the words of the ancestors and your contemporaries. The answer should be shown to me at our next meeting.

Do you want to hear my humble words?

> The branch of an old plum tree grows straight;
> Its thorns spread with time.

Chapter II

THE FIRST ANCESTOR, MAKAKASHYO SONJA

Then Sesson Shakyamuni, the most respectable person in this whole world, took a flower and winked. Makakashyo smiled. Shakyamuni said that the Truth was within him, and transmitted Makakashyo.

Makakashyo Sonja, the respectable, belonged to the Brahman race. His Indian name was Kashapa, which means "Light-Drinker."

When he was born the room was filled with golden light, and the light entered his mouth. Because of this he was called the Light-Drinker. His body was golden and had thirty of the good aspects. Only the cupola on the top of his head and the white hair curling to the right on his brow were missing.

He met Sesson Shakyamuni for the first time before Tashi Tower, that is, the Tower of Many Sons. Sesson said, "Welcome, monk," and immediately Makakashyo's hair and beard fell out and a kesa was placed upon his body.

Having received the Transmission of the Truth, Makakashyo practised the Twelve Zuda, or the ways by which we can control worldly desire and let the mind of Truth show itself. He never passed a day idly or in vain.

But so haggard was his shape and so coarse were his clothes that everyone wondered what he was.

Therefore, whenever Shakyamuni Sesson lectured, he gave half his seat to Makakashyo to sit upon. From that time he was always the highest senior.

He was thus at all times, not only at the lecture meetings of Shakyamuni but also at the ones of the past Buddhas. You should know he was an excellent Buddha. Do not let him be among the shōmon who are beneath the Bodhisattvas.

At the meeting on Mount Ryoju, before eighty thousand people, Shakyamuni took a flower and winked. Most people cannot realise the meaning of this and are silent. Only Makakashyo smiled. Shakyamuni said, "I have the Right Law; the excellent Nirvāna, Mind, the round and clear Law which has no aspect. Now I have transmitted it to great Makakashyo." The so-called "taking of a flower" has come down to this time, being transmitted from one ancestor to another. Those who are not transmitted cannot understand it, nor can the teachers of scriptures and logic. I *know* they have no understanding that is real. As this is so, this is not the kōan at the Ryōzen meeting but the one at the Tashi Tower. It is wrong to say that this is the kōan at the Ryōzen meeting, as it does in the *Dentōroku* and *Futoroku*. When Buddhism was transmitted for the first time, there was the ceremony described above.

Leave the "taking of a flower" as it is. You should understand Shakyamuni's wink clearly. There is no difference between your ordinary wink and Shakyamuni's. Further, there is no difference between your talking and smiling and Makakashyo's talking and smiling.

But if you do not really understand what raised its brow and winked, you are thinking that there is a difference between Shakyamuni and Makakashyo in India and that you are in a restricted body. The flower is beclouding your eyes, like vapour from the summer sun, from the far past to the limitless future. If you can really catch the Lord, Makakashyo will live in you. Did you know that when Shakyamuni raised his brow and winked, he had disappeared? Further, did you know that when Makakashyo smiled, he had been enlightened? Then is this fact not universal? In the same way as this, the Truth has been transmitted to us. Therefore, we can name it neither Makakashyo nor Shakyamuni.

There is nothing to give or to be given. This is called the Right Law. By taking a flower Shakyamuni showed that Truth *is* eternal, and by smiling he pointed out that it *is* endless. Because of this, in seeing each other face to face, the Life of the Truth has come down from master to disciple to this time.

So, having perfect wisdom without worldly knowledge, and cutting off his consciousness, Makakashyo entered Mount Keisoku, where he *is* waiting for Miroku. Therefore, Makakashyo is not dead.

If you can really understand and practise the Truth, not only Makakashyo is eternal but Shakyamuni is eternal too. Therefore the Truth, which *is* being transmitted from the far past when no one *is* born, is spreading constantly all over the past and the future.

Do not yearn for two thousand years ago. At the present time, if you practise the Truth wholeheartedly, Makakashyo will not enter Mount Keisoku; he can come here. Therefore the warm flesh of Shakyamuni is now and always here, and the smiling of Makakashyo is now and always new. If you can find this spiritual place, you can accept the Truth directly from Makakashyo and Makakashyo will accept it from you. Not only can the Very Truth pass through to you from the Seven Buddhas, but you can be the ancestor of the Seven Buddhas. The Very Truth is now here, eternally, beyond all ages. Therefore *Shakyamuni* accepted *Makakashyo's* transmission and is now in Tosotsuten. *You* are now at the Ryozen meeting and unchangeable. Do you not know the poem:

> Constantly I am at the Ryozen meeting throughout the universe.
> Even should there be a great fire my heart is always safe and calm and filled with angels.

India, China, Japan and the whole world must be included in the Ryozen meeting. The Truth of the Lord comes to us unchanged. Since this is so, this meeting must be the Ryozen meeting and the Ryozen meeting must be this one. Only when you concentrate your mind will Buddhas appear. Because of your ignorance about "yourself," Shakyamuni died long ago. You are the children of Buddha; why do you kill Buddha?

Therefore, if you are in a hurry to practise the Truth, soon you can meet Buddha. In daily life Shakyamuni *is* walking, stopping, sitting, lying down, talking and seeing *in you*, and is *not apart from you*, even for a moment.

If you cannot see him all through your life, you must be an undutiful being. Already you *are* the children of Buddha, but if you are undutiful a thousand Buddhas cannot help you.

Today do you want to hear my humble words?

> Did you not know that at the edge of a deep valley there is an
> excellent pine tree
> Growing up straight in spite of the many years of cold?

Chapter III

THE SECOND ANCESTOR, ANANDA SONJA

Ananda asked Makakashyo, "My dear senior, what did Shakyamuni transmit to you other than his kesa of gold brocade?" Makakashyo called, "Ananda." Ananda replied, "Yes?" Makakashyo said, "Chop down the flagpole." Ananda was enlightened.

Ananda Sonja was born in Osha Castle; he belonged to the Kshatriya race. His father was King Kokubon, a cousin of Shakyamuni. He was named Ananda, which means "Joy." He was born on the same night that Shakyamuni was enlightened. He had classical features, and no one in the sixteen neighbouring countries could be compared with him for looks. Everyone who saw him was pleased. Because of this he was so named.

He was the cleverest and the most learned among the disciples of Shakyamuni, and because of this he passed twenty years as Buddha's servant. There was not one of the Buddha's lectures at which he did not act as interpreter; there was not one of the Buddha's ways that he did not learn.

At the same time that Shakyamuni transmitted the Truth to Makakashyo he ordered Ananda to help him. Ananda therefore obeyed Makakashyo for a further twenty years. There was no Truth in him that had not been transmitted.

Here is the proof that the Truth of our ancestors is different from the Truth of others. Ananda was already the cleverest and the most erudite among the disciples; there were many spiritual prizes that Buddha had awarded him. But still he did not hold the Truth and was not enlightened.

When Makakashyo was going to collect the doctrines that had been left by Buddha at Hipparakutsu, Ananda was not permitted to go to the meeting because he was not enlightened. Then Ananda obtained Arahant rank, and Makakashyo said, "You have obtained Arahant rank. You can enter by sorcery." Changing his body to a small one, Ananda entered Hipparakutsu. All the disciples said, "Ananda was the servant of Buddha and is the cleverest and most erudite among us. There are no sayings that have not been transmitted to him in the same way as the water from one cup is poured into another. We hope that Ananda will repeat the sayings of Buddha again."

Then Ananda, who had been ordered by Buddha himself to help Makakashyo, agreed to Makakashyo's request, worshipped at the feet of the disciples and stood on the lecture platform. He repeated all the lectures of Buddha with the following as an opening: "Thus have I heard, once the Lord lived in . . ." Makakashyo asked many of the disciples if there were any mistakes, but they replied that there were none. Ananda's words were no different from the Buddha's. They who said this were the great Arahants who had the Three Wisdoms and the six sorceries; there was nothing they had not heard from Buddha. They all said, "We are wondering if the Lord has come back again or if these are the lectures of Ananda. The waters of the Sea of Buddhism have flowed into Ananda." Through Ananda's efforts the sayings of Buddha were able to be handed down to us.

I know well that the Real Truth is not in the clever and the erudite, nor is it in those who gain worldly rank. This is the proof. Ananda followed Makakashyo for twenty years and was enlightened in the way described earlier. He was born on the same night that the Lord was enlightened. He did not hear the *Kegon Sūtra* and other sūtras, but he could repeat the sayings of Buddha because of kaku-sammai [capacity given by a Buddha]. However, like us, he could not enter the Truth of our ancestors.

Ananda had had the wish for the Truth when he was with Shakyamuni under Kūō Buddha, but he liked erudition and because of this was not enlightened. Shakyamuni Buddha concentrated his mind and so was enlightened. I know well that erudition disturbs enlightenment: this is the proof. Therefore the following saying is in the *Kegon Sūtra:* "A poor man who counts another's treasure cannot have his own. Erudition is like this." If you wish to understand the Truth really, you should not like erudition. Concentrate your mind hard.

Ananda was always thinking that there must be something other than the kesa of gold brocade. Therefore one day he asked, "My dear senior, what did Shakyamuni transmit to you other than the kesa of gold brocade?" Knowing the time was right, Makakashyo called, "Ananda." Ananda replied, "Yes?" Makakashyo said at once, "Chop down the flagpole by the gate." By the tone of his voice Ananda was enlightened, and the clothes of Buddha came and hung themselves on his body. The kesa of gold brocade is the very one transmitted from the time of the Seven Buddhas.

> *Commentary.* There are three theories about this kesa. The first is that Shakyamuni wore it in the interior of his mother's womb. The second is that it was offered by Jōgōten [the world]. The third is that a hunter offered it, and there are several kinds of Buddha's kesa other than this. The kesa conveyed from Bodhidharma to Sōkei is made of kutsujun cloth

and is blue-black in colour. In China this kesa was lined with blue cloth, and it is preserved in the tower of Daikan Enō Zenji, being an important national treasure. In the *Chidoron* it is said that Shakyamuni wore a coarse kesa. It is the brocade kesa mentioned above that, in one of the sūtras, is said to have been offered to Buddha by his aunt and woven by her personally. These are a few among several kesas. The miracle of the kesa can be found in many sūtras. Once Bashyashita Sonja got into trouble with an evil king who took the kesa and threw it into the fire. The kesa shone, radiating five-coloured light, and after the fire had been extinguished it was still safe. This kesa was believed to have been Buddha's, and will later be given to Miroku.

The Truth was not transmitted to both Makakashyo and Ananda; only Makakashyo had the Lord's permission. Ananda held the Truth after spending twenty years as a servant. We should know, therefore, that there is something other than the sūtras. However, at the present time most people think that the Truth and the sūtras are one. If both are one, Ananda could be called the first ancestor, for he was the Arahant who had the Three Wisdoms and the six sorceries. Is there anyone who can understand the meaning of the sūtras better than Ananda? If there is such a person, we can allow that the Truth and the meaning of the sūtras are one. If we simply say both are one, why did Ananda spend twenty years as a servant and become enlightened by the chopping down of the flag-pole? We should know the meaning of the sūtras and doctrines as different from the Truth of our ancestors. We are not saying that Buddha is not true Buddha. Although Ananda was the Lord's servant he could not have the Truth transmitted to him, for he had not the true understanding of the Real Mind of Buddha.

The Truth cannot be gained by erudition. Although a person is clever and has sharp ears and can understand every (Chinese) character in the sūtras and doctrines, he is counting another's treasure if he cannot understand their real meaning. It is not because there is no meaning in the sūtras and doctrines; it is because Ananda had not been enlightened. Therefore, in Japan they understand the meaning of the sūtras by words and so they cannot understand fully. Of course, the Truth should be thought of sincerely. If Ananda as the disciple of Buddha could understand the sūtras and doctrines of the Lord, who is unable to follow? However, after spending many years as the servant of Makakashyo and being enlightened, he repeated the sūtras and doctrines. We should know this. If you want to become one with the Truth, as one fire combines with another fire, throw away selfish opinions, old emotions, arrogance and obstinacy, and learn the True Mind of the Lord with the naive mind of a child.

Generally, most people think that there is nothing more than the kesa of gold brocade. But they should know that after being the servant of Makakashyo, Ananda obtained something else. Knowing the time had come, Makakashyo called, "Ananda." Ananda replied, "Yes?" It was as if an echo replied to a voice and one fire sprang up between two stones.

Then, although Makakashyo called "Ananda," he was not calling Ananda. Although Ananda replied "Yes," he was not replying to Makakashyo's call. "Chopping down the flagpole" means the following: In India, when the disciples of Buddha and others wanted to argue, they set up a pole on each side of the place of debate. When either side was defeated, they chopped down their pole. If they lost, they rang no bells and beat no drums. In this case both Makakashyo and Ananda set up their poles on either side. If Ananda wins, Makakashyo is beaten: if (any)one wins, the other is beaten. But in this case it is not so. Makakashyo is one flagpole and Ananda is another. If we are thinking they are flagpoles, the Truth does not manifest itself. When the flagpole is chopped down, it manifests itself. Makakashyo said, "Chop down the flagpole." Ananda was enlightened because he understood the Truth that *is* existing from master to disciple. After enlightenment Makakashyo was chopped down too, and so were nature and everything else. Therefore the clothes of Buddha descended onto Ananda's head naturally. But do not stay with the flesh of Ananda; do not stay with cleanness. Furthermore, we should know the echo. There is only this point; many Buddhas came here in turn, many ancestors pointed for ages.

Mind is being transmitted with mind. Others cannot know it. Although both Makakashyo and Ananda are the representations of the Truth, we should not *make* them the Truth. You yourself are

the manifestation of Truth. If you can realise Truth you disappear at once. As this is so, we should not look for it outside ourselves.
Do you want to hear my humble words?

> The wistaria has withered and the trees have fallen down. The water in the valley has increased and from the stones fire has gushed forth.

Chapter IV

THE THIRD ANCESTOR, SHŌNAWASHYU SONJA

Shōnawashyu asked Ananda, "What is the *no-birth* of all things?" Ananda pointed to the corner of Shōnawashyu's kesa. Shōnawashyu asked again, "What is the fundamental nature (character) of the Truth of the Buddhas?" Ananda pulled the corner of Shōnawashyu's kesa. Shōnawashyu was enlightened.

Shōnawashyu came from Matora. In India he was named Shodaka, which means "Natural Clothes," because he was born with clothes on. These clothes were warm in winter and cool in summer. Further, when he became a monk, his worldly clothes instantaneously became the kesa. The same thing happened to the girl trainee Rengeshiki during the Lord's lifetime. In Shōnawashyu's previous life he had been a merchant and had offered a hundred blankets to a hundred Buddhas. Since that time he had been born with natural clothes on. The middle existence is the time after a person's death when he has not yet been born into the next existence. At this time he has no clothes on his body. However, Shōnawashyu was wearing clothes during the middle existence. The name Shōnawashyu is also the name of a plant, kushishu. [The interpreter's commentary says that *ku* means "nine," *shi* means "branch," and *shu* means "excellence."] Kushishu is a kind of grass, and people believe that when a saint is born it grows in virgin soil. When Shōnawashyu was born this grass grew, and he was named after it. He spent six years in his mother's womb. Long ago Shakyamuni Buddha pointed to a forest and said to Ananda, "I call this forest Uruda. A hundred years after my death a saint, whose name is Shōnawashyu, will appear and roll the Wheel of Truth."

At the end of a hundred years Shōnawashyu was born. He received the transmission of the Truth from Ananda and stayed in the forest of Uruda. He rolled the Wheel of Truth and the fire-dragon surrendered to him. For this very purpose the fire-dragon offered this forest to the Buddha, and the prophecy of the Lord was fulfilled.

Shōnawashyu was the saint of the Snow Mountain. Between Ananda and himself there was this. No one had ever asked, "What is the no-birth of all things?" Only Shōnawashyu asked it. All people have the same nature but no one knew or asked about it. Why is it called "no-birth" nature? All things appear therefrom, but there is nothing that can produce it. Therefore it is called "no-birth." Everything is no-birth. A mountain is not a mountain and water is not water. Because of this Ananda pointed to the corner of Shōnawashyu's kesa. The word "kesa" is Indian. Kesas have "broken" or "no-birth" colour. From Buddhas above to ants below and even horseflies, all creatures and their circumstances are rūpa (take form or shape). They are seen as they are from a one-sided viewpoint. In another sense, however, they do not belong to the world that can be seen. Therefore there are no worlds that are to be thrown away and no Truth that is to be caught. Thus Shōnawashyu understood. But Shōnawashyu asked again, "What is the fundamental nature of Buddha's Truth?" Although this nature is clear from the limitless past, we are misled if we do not realise it. Therefore, in order to be clear as to the place from whence Buddhas come, Shōnawashyu asked his question again. So that he should know the Truth, everyone called and the Truth answered; all knocked and the Truth appeared. Ananda pulled the corner of Shōnawashyu's kesa to let him know, and Shōnawashyu was enlightened.

Although the foregoing is clear from the limitless past, we cannot understand that we are the very source of Buddhas if we do not experience it at least once. Therefore Buddhas appear in turn and ancestors explain for generations.

Although there is no Truth which is to be accepted from others and to be given to others, we should understand it as exactly as we know our noses by touching them.

We must *really* understand the Truth by *really* studying Zen. After understanding it, we must take the test of our understanding from the most excellent person we can find. If we do not do so, we are still astray.

We must understand from this the importance of making every minute count. We should not have naturalistic feelings and put our own opinions first. Further, we should not think that the Way of the Buddhas and the ancestors is for special people and seekers and that we are not suitable for it. This opinion is the most useless of all useless opinions. None of the ancestors were born without parents and all had feelings of filial love, honour and good (well-being). However, when once they had studied Zen, they were all enlightened. Because of this there were plenty of wise and excellent people all over India, China and Japan, although they lived in different ages, that is to say, in Shō, Zō and Matsu.

Therefore we should know that we are the very persons who have the capacity for understanding the Truth, for we have the same body and heart as the ancients. We have the same body and heart as Makakashyo and Ananda. Why are we different from the ancients? Because we do not study the Truth sincerely; we let the body go on, oblivious to the passing of time, and do not know the Real Self. In order to let us know this fact, Ananda took Makakashyo as his master and then taught Shōnawashyu, and the Way of Truth was transmitted from master to disciple. Thus the Truth now is no different from the Truth during the Lord's lifetime. We should not complain that we were not born in the Lord's country and did not meet him.

You have gathered together at this meeting because you sowed good seeds and came in contact with prajñā in ancient times. You rank with Makakashyo and talk familiarly with Ananda. Although one is master and the other disciple, they are the same Buddha. Do not be muddled by the thought of old and new. Do not remain with the thought of forms. Do not waste time either by day or night. Study in detail. Become one with the ancients and accept the approval of the master now.

So that you may make sense of the meaning of this, I will tell you my humble words.

Although there is limitless water gushing from the high rocks,
Washing out the stones and scattering the clouds,
Watering the snows and crushing the flowers,
Yet is there an immaculate veil (cloth) above the dirt.

Chapter V

THE FOURTH ANCESTOR, UBAKIKUTA SONJA

Ubakikuta served Shōnawashyu Sonja for three years, and at the
end of that time shaved his head and became a monk. Shōnawashyu
asked him, "Are you a monk of body or a monk of mind?" Ubakikuta
answered, "I am a monk of body." Shōnawashyu said, "The excellent Law of Buddha has nothing to do with either mind or body."
Ubakikuta was enlightened.

Ubakikuta hailed from the country of Dali and belonged to the
Suda race. He was taught from the age of fifteen, became a monk
at seventeen and was enlightened at twenty-two. He then went to
Matsala to teach others. Because there were many people who were
ordained by him, devils were afraid of him. Every time he ordained
someone he put a numbered piece of bamboo, the length of four
fingers, into a stone room. The size of this room was eighteen chū
in length and twenty chū in width [a *chū* is roughly equivalent to a
foot], and the room was filled with them. He was cremated with
these bamboo sticks because there were so many people ordained during (his) the Lord's lifetime.

Although people called him the Buddha who had no good aspects,
the devils feared him and were angry. When he was sitting they
wanted to disturb him, but he knew what was happening. One devil
came and offered him a necklace. Ubakikuta, wanting to conquer
him, stood up, took the dead bodies of a man, a dog and a snake,
and changed them into a necklace. He then said sweetly to the devil,
"You gave me a wonderful necklace. I have one too for you."

The devil was pleased at this and accepted the necklace with out-stretched neck. At once it changed back into three bad-smelling dead bodies which were rotting and had maggots wriggling in them. The devil disliked this necklace greatly and was much worried, but al-though he did his best, he could not throw it away, destroy it or re-move it. First he went up to the six heavens and told the lords thereof; then he went to Bonten and asked to be released from the necklace. The lords told him that the power of the Disciple of the Ten Forces [that is, Buddha] was most excellent and that their powers were very poor, and therefore they could not help him. The devil then said, "What ought I to do?" and Bonten answered, "You should be converted by Ubakikuta Sonja. If you are, he will remove the necklace." Then Bonten showed him a poem:

If someone falls on the ground
He can stand up again,
But if he wants to stand above the ground
He cannot do so.

All the lords said, "You should ask the Disciple of Buddha to remove the necklace."

Accepting this teaching, the devil came down from Bonten and worshipped at the feet of Ubakikuta, confessing himself to be in the wrong.

Ubakikuta said, "Now will you continue to disturb the Lord's Truth?" The devil replied, "Upon my word, I will be converted to the Truth and cease from my wickedness."

Ubakikuta said, "If so, you should say with your own lips, 'I am converted to the Three Treasures.'" The devil recited the words three times, and the necklace was removed. Thus Ubakikuta showed the authority of the Truth in the same way as during the Lord's life-time. When Ubakikuta shaved his head at the age of seventeen, Shōnawashyu asked him, "Are you a monk of body or a monk of mind?"

There are two kinds of monks; monks of body and monks of mind. The so-called monk of body severs family ties, lives away from home, shaves his head, changes the colour of his clothes, has no servants, becomes a trainee and seeks for the Truth throughout his life. There-fore he wastes no time and has no desire. He is pleased with neither life nor death. His mind is as pure as the moon in autumn and his eyes as clear as an immaculate mirror. He does not look for the real self but seeks only the Truth. Because of this he stays neither in delusion nor enlightenment, and so he is a *real* man. This is a monk of body.

The so-called monk of mind does not shave his head and change the colour of his clothes. Although he lives among his family and attends to worldly affairs, he is as pure as a lotus untouched by dirt, or as a jewel that accepts no dust. Even if he has a family as a result of karma relation, he thinks of it only as dust and has no love for or concern with it. As the moon in the sky or a bowl rolling on a tray, he has leisure in a crowd. He goes beyond limitation on reaching limitation, knowing that worldly desire is a disease to be discarded and that it is wrong to look for the Truth. He knows that Nirvāna, birth and death are illusions in the sky and has no concern with the Truth and delusion. This is a monk of mind.

Therefore Shōnawashyu asked his question. If Ubakikuta is a monk outside these two kinds, he is not a real monk; because of this the question was so framed. Ubakikuta answered, "I am a monk of body." It was obvious that he was not a monk of mind, nature or anything else but a monk of body. He could reach this understanding naturally and knew it, and with this he was completely satisfied. He got this far without looking and so understood that everything he could not understand was as it was. Therefore he said he was a monk of body.

But the excellent Truth of Buddha should not be understood as above, as Shōnawashyu pointed out. Buddha should not be a monk of body or a monk of mind and be seen as a material or mental existence.

He was beyond both the holy and the unholy and conquered both body and mind. He was like the sky, with neither inside nor outside, and like the sea-water, with neither an obverse nor a reverse. Although he taught many doctrines, he only pointed out this one true fact. We should not say that he was Buddha because he was the most excellent person in the world. Buddha should not be spoken of as non-coming and non-going. Nor should we speak of existence before parents were born and before the world existed. The Truth of Buddha is beyond both birth and no-birth and is outside the argument of mind and no-mind. It is like the water within vessels and the emptiness of the sky. We cannot catch it with our hands and we cannot see its mark. Therefore Ubakikuta does not exist, and Shōnawashyu does not appear. We cannot understand this Truth from their actions and movements.

Although there are neither "he" and "I" nor "good" and "bad" between them, they sound like an echo and seem like the endless sky. If one does not experience the Truth with his own body, the Truth may become delusion. When this was pointed out Ubakikuta was enlightened. It was like thunder in a clear sky or a great fire on the ground.

When the thunder beat on Ubakikuta's ears, he lost his previous life. Fire burned the Law of Buddha and the teachings of the ancestors to ashes. These ashes became Ubakikuta, and they were as hard as stones and as black as lacquer. Ubakikuta threw away the dirty surface of others and took many disciples. (In vain he threw bamboos into a room and counted emptiness, then burned emptiness and left the mark in emptiness.)

Now I, a disciple in Daijō Temple, want to look for the mark beyond the clouds and to write my words in emptiness. Do you want to hear?

> The house is broken; the man has disappeared.
> There is neither inside nor outside
> So where can body and mind hide themselves?

Chapter VI

THE FIFTH ANCESTOR, DAITAKA SONJA

The Fifth Ancestor, Daitaka, said, "A monk has no self, and because of it he has no selfish thing; therefore his mind is beyond changeability: this is called constant Truth. Buddhas are thus. Neither their minds nor their bodies have aspects." Ubakikuta said, "You should understand fully from your own experience." Daitaka understood completely.

Daitaka was from Makada. When he was born his father dreamed that the golden sun shone from his house upon the world. There was a great hill decorated with many jewels, and from a fountain at the top of it much water gushed forth.

When Daitaka met Ubakikuta, he told him about this. Ubakikuta said, "I am the hill; the fountain means that your wisdom can make the Truth endless. The shining of the sun from your father's house means your entering my way. This shining shows that your wisdom is most excellent." Daitaka was named "Perfumed Elephant" before becoming a monk, and then his name was changed to its present form. In India he was called Daitaka, which means "Understander of the Truth."

After Daitaka heard his master's teaching, he sang a poem:

> Lofty mountain of Seven Treasures
> From whence constantly gush out the plentiful waters of
>   wisdom;
> Changing into the real taste of Truth,
> It does the best for everyone.

Ubakikuta sang a poem also:

> My Law has been transmitted to you;
> You should manifest your great wisdom.
> As the sun shining from a house
> So should you shine all over the world.

From that time Daitaka followed Ubakikuta and wished to become a monk.

Ubakikuta said, "You wish to become a monk. Do you wish to be a monk of body or of mind?" Daitaka replied, "I have come here to become a monk. It is neither of body nor of mind." Ubakikuta said, "Who can be a monk other than in body and mind?" Then he spoke the words quoted above and Daitaka was enlightened.

The real monk should manifest the real self without self or selfish things. Therefore we must not argue about body and mind. The real self, without self and selfish things, should be called the Real Way. We should not understand the Real Way from the viewpoint of birth and death, Buddha and Sattva, the four elements and the five skandhas, the Three Worlds and the six lokas. There is no form in mind. Although we have senses and understanding, real mind is beyond them. One who understands thus should still be called one who understands intellectually.

Although Daitaka understood, Ubakikuta said again, "Understand the Truth fully." This saying is like the seal of a king on trade goods. If the king guarantees by the use of his seal that these goods are not poisonous, of doubtful quality or commonplace, everyone can use them. In such a way the disciple is guaranteed by his master. Although there are neither disciplines that one can undergo nor ways that one cannot understand fully, yet one should be really enlightened. If not, one becomes a person who understands intellectually and cannot understand the Truth completely. Such a one is always being disturbed by the thought of the existence of both Buddha and Teaching. Further, he cannot be released from either his own or others' bondage. Therefore, although there is neither a (Chinese) character in the Lord's lectures which one does not remember nor a teaching in the three dhyānas or the five dhyānas which one does not keep, still one cannot be permitted to be a real monk. Even if one can lecture on many sūtras, make Buddha appear in this place, shake the earth and make flowers fall from the sky, still one's position is only that of a lecturer to monks (one ranks with lecturers). One is not a real monk.

We must not understand the Truth thus: The whole world comes from the mind; everything exists as it is; everything has the Buddha Nature; in any case, everything is void. The opinion "everything is void" is equal to the wrong opinion that everything is empty. We are apt to have a constant self in ourselves if we hold the opinion that "everything has the Buddha Nature." The opinion that "everything exists as it is" has some sharp edges. The first opinion, "The whole world comes from the mind," seems somewhat sensible. If you want to look for the Truth, you must not seek for it in the myriad sūtras. Should you do so, you are like the man who ran away from his father [an illustration from the Lotus Sūtra]. We must open the door of our own treasure and then we can have the Holy Doctrine as our own. If you do not understand this the Buddhas and ancestors will become your enemy. I pray you do not hear the saying, "What devil let you become a monk? What demon let you wander among teachers?" Both when you can and when you cannot teach, you should be beaten to death. Because of this one does not become a monk for either body or mind or both. It was this that Daitaka understood. Yet he was not a real monk. When Ubakikuta pointed the Way again, he was enlightened.

Study hard and in detail. Do not understand the True Meaning through the meaning of words. Throw away heaven, earth, the holy, the mean, subject and object.

Wherever you go you should be disturbed by nothing, completely free. Make a hole in emptiness; make waves on the barren earth. You should be in contact with the Face of the Buddha and realise the Truth fully. *It* (Truth) is like the gourd-vine twining round the gourd, like jewels shining brilliantly. Do you want to hear my humble words?

> The True Wisdom should be caught exactly;
> Limpen [a Chinese] has still a secret which cannot be
>   explained.
> Do not understand a constant self within the senses.

Chapter VII

THE SIXTH ANCESTOR, MISHAKA SONJA

The Fifth Ancestor, Daitaka, told the following teaching of the Lord to Mishaka: "If one practises a supernatural art, or studies Theravāda, one will be bound by *rope*. One should know oneself. If one turns away from Theravāda and enters the great sea which is Mahāyāna, one can realise no-birth." Mishaka was enlightened.

Mishaka came from the centre of India. He was the head genius of eight thousand genii. One day he worshipped Daitaka with them, saying, "In olden times I was born in Bonten, as you were, and I studied supernatural art with the genius Ashida whilst you practised dhyāna, following the disciple of Buddha. Since then our ways have been separate and six kalpas have passed." Daitaka said, "We spent a long time in separation, and it is true what you say. Now you should give up the wrong way and be converted to the right one." Mishaka said, "Long ago the genius Ashida made a prophecy that after six kalpas I would meet a classmate and be enlightened, thus reaching Arahantship. Now we meet. Is it not destiny? Please let me be released." Then Daitaka made him a monk, and he accepted the Precepts. Unfortunately, the eight thousand genii were proud of themselves, so Daitaka manifested a great sorcery causing the genii to have a longing for salvation, and all became monks at the same time. When the eight thousand genii became eight thousand monks, Daitaka gave them the teaching quoted above.

Even if one could lengthen one's life and have magic powers through supernatural arts, the term of eighty thousand kalpas from the past is still only eighty thousand kalpas to the future. Such arts have no power either after or before this term. Even if one could be born in the heaven of no-thought, lengthen one's life and have no concrete body as a result of practising no-thought samādhi, or not-no-thought samādhi, one would still be in delusion; one could not meet Buddha and realise the Truth. When the power of karma is ended, one has to enter constant hell. Therefore one is bound by rope and cannot be released.

Although one who has studied Theravāda can apprehend the first stage of enlightenment, the second, third, fourth and *alone* enlightenments, such a one still practises within body and mind, and learns within delusion and enlightenment. In the first enlightenment one can become a first-mind Bodhisattva after eighty thousand kalpas. In the second, one can do so after sixty thousand kalpas. In the third, one can do it after forty thousand kalpas, and one in the alone enlightenment can become a first-mind Bodhisattva after a thousand kalpas. Although good seeds will grow according to their nature, wandering karma is still not cut off but held by ropes. One is not really released. Although one is entirely transparent after cutting off the eighty-eight opinions and unlimited delusion, one still looks for something. This is not real Buddhahood. Both to want to return to the fundamental and to look for enlightenment are as this.

Therefore, you! Do not desire to look for anything. You may go the wrong way, and that leads only to emptiness. Do not stay beyond unlimited kalpas; otherwise you are like the dead in which the soul remains. Do not desire to apprehend real nature and remain, like floating flowers, in wrong understanding.

You are still like the saint who cuts through no-wisdom and apprehends the Middle Way. Do not make clouds in a clear sky. Do not injure a healthy body. You are like a poor son wandering about in foreign countries or a poor man becoming intoxicated with the dark. Meditate sincerely. Is there before-birth or after-death? Are there the past, the future and the present? Everything is always *as thus* from birth to death. But if one is not in real contact with this condition, one is muddled by the senses and their objects and cannot understand the real self. One should not neglect one's daily life. We do not know from where our bodies, minds and everything else come; therefore we should give up all vain desire to look uselessly for the Truth. Buddhas appear troublesomely; ancestors teach in detail. Although Buddhas and ancestors are kind to us, we say we do not know or we do not understand because we are disturbed by our selfish opinions. We are neither in real darkness nor in real contact with Truth. We understand vainly the right or the wrong only in our thoughts.

You!

One calls and one replies.

One points and one appears.

The above means "neither thinking nor sense": *this* is your Real Lord. The Lord has neither face nor aspects; the Lord moves always and unceasingly. Our senses make the Lord manifest. Our actions are termed bodily. The four elements, five skandhas, eighty-four thousand pores and three hundred and sixty bones gather together and make a body. This is like brilliant jewels and a sounding voice. Changing—birth and death—has nothing to do with the Real Lord. This changing has no beginning and no end. For example, waves on the sea leave no mark after subsiding, yet they do not disappear. They go on without going to a different place. And still the form of the sea has big and small waves. Your mind is like this; it moves always without ceasing. The Lord manifests himself as skin, flesh, bones and marrow, and uses himself as the four elements and the five skandhas. Further, he manifests himself as peach blossoms and green bamboos, and as the apprehension of the Truth and enlightenment. The Lord works in different voices and forms, seeing and hearing, clothing and eating, words and actions. The Lord is separate, but does not belong to differentiation. The Lord manifests himself in differentiation, but does not stop in forms. For example, a genius exhibits many supernatural arts or many figures in dreams. Although many forms appear in a mirror, the mirror is one. If one does not know this fact, merely learning Theravāda and practising supernatural arts, one cannot be permanently released (from suffering). No one binds you, so there is no need to be released. There is no delusion and no enlightenment; we are apart from being bound. Is not this no-birth? Is not this a great sea? Where are the brooks? Every place belongs to the Sea of the Law (Truth). Brooks, falls and rivers are works of the very sea. There are neither brooks to be thrown away nor the sea to be picked up. Thus, Mishaka threw away every detail and changed his old opinions. He became a monk instead of a genius, but his old karma relation may still work upon him.

You!

If you study hard and sincerely, you can be in real contact with the Truth. For example, as one meets an intimate friend, and as self nods at itself, you can swim always in the sea of this Real Nature, and there is no time when you are apart from it. Hear the saying of Ba, the great master:

> Every Sattva is always in the Real Nature;
> Wears clothes and eats food in it, talks and works.
> These (things) *are* the Real Nature.

But, hearing this, do not understand that all Sattvas are in the Real Nature. The Real Nature and every Sattva are as the water and the waves. There is no difference. Do you want to hear my humble words?

> There is clearness in autumn waters ranging to the sky.
> There is a most excellent vision of the moon on a spring night.

Most houses need to be clean and pure, but even a thousand sweepings cannot clear the dust away completely.

Chapter VIII

THE SEVENTH ANCESTOR, BASHUMITSU SONJA

The Seventh Ancestor, Bashumitsu Sonja, put a vessel of wine in front of Mishaka Sonja, then stood and worshipped him. Mishaka asked, "Is this vessel mine or yours?" Bashumitsu thought about it. Mishaka said, "If this belongs to me, this is your Real Nature. If it belongs to you, the Law in me should be transmitted to you." Bashumitsu heard this teaching and realised the true meaning of no-birth.

Bashumitsu came from the northern part of India; he belonged to the Harada race. He wandered about the streets with a vessel of wine in his hand, singing and chanting. People said he was mad. No one knew his name. When Mishaka went to the northern part of India he saw a golden cloud over a fence. Mishaka said to his pupils, "This cloud is the mark of a sincere seeker. There must be an excellent person (here) who can accept the Truth and become my disciple." As soon as Mishaka said these words, Bashumitsu appeared and asked Mishaka, "Do you know what I am carrying?" Mishaka replied, "That is an unclean vessel; it is apart from immaculacy." Bashumitsu put the vessel in front of Mishaka, and they exchanged the questions and answers quoted above. Suddenly the vessel disappeared. Mishaka said, "Tell me your name." Bashumitsu answered in verse:

> From the unlimited past to the time
> When I was born in this country
> My family name *is* Harada and I am called Bashumitsu.

Mishaka said, "My master said, 'Once when the Lord was in the northern part of India, he told Ananda that three hundred years after his death there would be a saint whose family name was Harada and who would be called Bashumitsu.' He then said that Bashumitsu would be the Seventh Ancestor. The Lord made this prophecy for you. You should become a monk."

On hearing these words Bashumitsu said to Mishaka, "In olden times there was one who studied dhyāna and offered a beautiful seat covering to a Buddha. He made a prophecy to me that you would become an ancestor in the age of Shakyamuni." He then became the Seventh Ancestor.

Before he went to Mishaka, Bashumitsu always had a vessel of wine with him and never threw it away. He thought it most excellent. He wanted it in the morning as well as in the evening, using it freely. Indeed, his very life *was* the vessel! Therefore, his first question was, "Do you know what I am carrying?"

Even if one understands that mind is the Very Truth or that body is the Very Truth, such understanding is clouded. If it is clouded, It will be defeated by clarity. Even such understanding as future, past and present is clouded. Further, *what* is called the past? *What* is called present? *What* is called beginning? *What* is called end? Such understanding will be shattered by clarity. Bashumitsu realised this and so put down the vessel of wine. This was the proof that he was converted by Mishaka. Therefore Mishaka asked, "Is this my vessel or is it yours?" The Very Truth is not in such understanding as the past and the present, or in going and coming. It is not me; it is not you. The Truth is apart from both. Because of this Mishaka taught: "If this belongs to me, this is your Real Nature. (The vessel therefore is not Mishaka's.) If this belongs to you, you should be transmitted by my Law (Dharma). (The vessel is not Bashumitsu's either.)" The vessel belongs neither to me nor to you, so the vessel is not a vessel. For this reason the vessel disappeared. Now, it is very difficult to know the true meaning of this. Even if one could reach a state inaccessible to many Buddhas and ancestors in spite of their power, still one would be as a clouded vessel. Surely this could be overcome by immaculacy? But real immaculacy does not insist on immaculacy; therefore the vessel does not do so. The disciple is in real contact with his master because there is no disturbance between them. My Law (Truth) should be transmitted to you because it is your Real Nature. There are neither things one can give to others nor things others can give. When we understand this, we can no longer speak of master and disciple. Therefore, the disciple stands upon his master's head and the master stands beneath the disciple's feet. There is neither duality nor separation. Because of this the vessel cannot be called a vessel; therefore it disappeared. This is the fact of transmission between the two (Mishaka and Bashumitsu).

Now if one can realise such a thing as this, body and mind are not the same as before (such realisation).

One cannot say, "This has nothing to do with the present, past, birth, going and coming—this has no skin, flesh, bones and marrow."

This is the complete clarity itself. *It* has no surface, no reverse, no inside and no outside.

Do you want to hear my humble words?

> Just as the bell rings according to the way it is struck,
> So there is no need to want any empty vessel at all.

Chapter IX

THE EIGHTH ANCESTOR, BUTSUDANANDAI SONJA

When the Eighth Ancestor, Butsudanandai, met the Seventh Ancestor, Bashumitsu, he said, "Now, I want to argue with you."

Bashumitsu replied, "You! Argument is not the Real Truth. The Real Truth cannot be proved by argument. If we want to argue about something, it will not be an argument about the Real Truth." Butsudanandai understood that what Bashumitsu said was more excellent than his own theory, and realised the reason for no-birth.

Butsudanandai came from Kalana. His family name was Gotama, and he had a fleshy projection on the top of his head; he was very clever at argument. Bashumitsu went to Kamala to spread the doctrine of Buddhism.

Butsudanandai stood in front of Bashumitsu's seat and said, "I am Butsudanandai. I want to argue with you." Bashumitsu replied, "If you want to argue, you cannot know the Truth. The Real Truth has nothing to do with argument."

Indeed, the Real Truth cannot be explained by argument, and real argument has no shadow of Truth. If there is an argument or a truth that can be taken notice of, in the real sense, then it is neither the Real Truth nor a real argument. Because of this, Bashumitsu said that if one *wanted* to argue one could not explain the Real Truth.

Therefore there are neither things to be called Truth nor argument. Furthermore, the Lord did not have two kinds of words. Because of this, one who can hear the Lord's words truly can see the Lord's body; one who can see the Lord's body can understand the Lord's tongue.

Although one may explain that the mind and the object are undivided (not two), this explanation is not a real argument. Even though one may explain that there is no change, one is not stating the Truth. Should one explain that there are neither words to explain with nor reasons to be manifested, still the Truth will not appear. Even though one explains that the Real Nature is true and the Mind right, that both the light and the world disappear, that both the light and the world do not disappear, that sometimes we are the host and sometimes the guest, the same and the one, yet no explanation is the real argument.

Although Monju said, "No words, no explaining," this saying cannot be real (true). Although Yuima sat on his seat and said nothing, his silence cannot be an argument about the Truth. Thus both Monju and Yuima were wrong. Sharihotsu, who was exceptionally clever, and Mokkenren, who was possessed of occult powers, were both unable to understand this Truth even in their dreams, just as a blind man can see nothing.

The Lord said, "Shōmon and Engaku [the two lower ranks in Theravāda] cannot understand the Buddha Nature even in dreams."

Even Bodhisattvas in the ten jū [the ten ranks in the last and highest class] made mistakes in distinguishing between water and cranes from afar.

Although they could understand, after thinking for a long time, that these were cranes, still they were not sure. They could not understand clearly the Buddha Nature from the explanation of the Lord, and they said, with pleasure, "It is because we have been muddled by no-self that we have been unable to understand the eternal rolling of birth and death from ages past. Even if one can forget what one sees and hears, both with body and mind, and is beyond enlightenment, delusion, cloud and clarity, one cannot understand the Truth even in dreams."

Do not seek for it (Truth) in the void; do not look for it in form. Still more, do not seek for it in Buddhas and ancestors.

You!

Everyone has passed through birth and death many times and, from long ago to the present time, has had mind and body endlessly. One may think of birth and death, coming and going, as floating delusion, but such thoughts should be laughed at. Is there anything being born, or dying, or coming, or going? What can be said to be the real existence of a person? What can be said to be floating delusion? Therefore one must not understand the Truth as real or as delusive. If one does, such understanding is all wrong. Study in detail. Do not fall into a thought-void. Although one realises the Truth as clarity, as clear water, or as the sky without dust, one cannot understand really.

The priest Tōzan, who followed Isan and Ungan, could do everything instantaneously, could lecture with his whole body, but there was something missing in him. So Ungan said to him, "In order to understand the Truth, study in detail." Tōzan then left Ungan and went elsewhere. Suddenly he was enlightened and uttered the following verse:

> Truly, I should not seek for the Truth from others!
> For then it will be far from me;
> Now I am going alone.
> Everywhere I am able to meet *Him*;
> *He* is *me* now;
> I am not *Him*.
> When we understand this
> We are instantaneously with the Truth.

He became the core of the Sōtō sect in China. Before (his enlightenment) he could not only understand the full reason why every part of his body lectured, he could also understand that a naked pillar [round pillar in a temple] and a garden lantern lecture too; and everything, in every place, lectures throughout the three ages [past, present and future], yet still he was lacking in full understanding.

It is very strange that one can understand the Truth by intellection, understand a mind as a Buddha and a body as a Buddha, but not understand what Buddhism is, and think vaguely that the Truth is simply that blossoms come out in spring and leaves fall in autumn.

If Buddhism is thus, why did Shakyamuni appear and Bodhidharma come to China? There were no Buddhas and no ancestors from Shakyamuni to this time who were not enlightened.

If one insists that what one gets from words and sentences is right and the Truth itself, there will be no Buddha and no ancestor. Therefore give up this type of understanding; study this one important point, and you will be able to become a Buddha. One who is not enlightened cannot be called real. Do not stay in clarity or in the void.

The priest Sensu said, "The place where one can stay eternally is unmarked. Do not stay eternally in this unmarked place. After following the priest Yakusan for thirty years I understood only this one thing. Clarity is not the place to stay in eternally.

"Do not stay in such a place, for there is no operation of the senses and no object to it." So said he.

Still more, there is no time when it is present or past, there is nothing which is enlightenment or delusion. If one is enlightened in this way there is no wall, no disturbance; one is free completely. Study in detail. Do not think hastily. Do you want to hear my humble words?

> The sayings of Subhūti and of Vimalakīrti are not complete;
> Mangalama and Śāriputra are like the blind;
> If one wants to understand the meaning of this truly,
> Salt is suitable for all food.

Chapter X

THE NINTH ANCESTOR, FUDAMITTA SONJA

The Ninth Ancestor, Fudamitta, heard the following words from Butsudanandai: "Your words are more in tune with your Mind than are those of your parents. Your behaviour is in contact with the Truth; the minds of Buddhas are thus. If you seek outside yourself for a Buddha who has aspects, that which you will find will be other than the True one. If you want to know your True Mind, you should neither be in contact with your mind nor apart from it."

Fudamitta came from Daigya. His family name was Bishara. When Butsudanandai went to Bishara's house, which was the castle of Daigya, he saw a white light rising therefrom and said to his followers, "There is a real saint here. His mouth has spoken no words because he is a real Buddhist of the Mahāyāna, and his feet have never walked upon the ground for he knows that if they do they will get dirty. Perhaps he will become my heir."

Soon the master of the house came out and, worshipping Butsudanandai, asked, "What do you need?" Butsudanandai replied, "I need a servant." The other said, "I have a son who is fifty years old. He has spoken no words and has never walked upon the ground." Butsudanandai said, "If he is thus, he will be my real disciple." Hearing Butsudanandai's words, Fudamitta stood up and worshipped him. He then asked Butsudanandai the following in verse:

> Even my parents are not in tune with me;
> What is in tune with me?
> Even the teaching of Buddhas is not real for me;
> What *is* real for me?

Butsudanandai replied with the words quoted above.

Hearing these excellent words Fudamitta took seven steps. Butsudanandai said, "When this man followed the Lord, he earnestly made his prayers. Until now he has spoken no words and has never walked upon the ground because he believed it to be very difficult to cast off his filial ties."

Indeed, our parents are not the most in tune with us, and the teaching of the Buddhas is not the most real thing for me. Therefore, if we want to understand that which is most in tune with us, we should not compare it to our parents. Also, if we want to realise the Real Truth, we should not learn it from Buddhas. The reason is that we can see, hear and work without the assistance of others. We are thus. Buddhas are thus also. We study from Buddhas and Buddhas study from us; this relationship, however, does not seem so familiar. Can it be the Truth? Fudamitta spent fifty years without speaking a word or walking on the ground for this reason. Indeed, Fudamitta was the very person who should belong to Mahāyāna. He should not remain among worldly persons. He said his parents were not in tune with him, and his saying is similar to his mind. He said the teaching of Buddha was not the Real Truth and he did not walk on the ground. This was his behaviour, and he was in contact with the Truth. If he wanted a Buddha who had aspects outside himself, his behaviour was wrong. Because of this true monks have transmitted the Truth. At transmission they represented the Truth without words, pointed out the Truth directly and understood their own True Nature. In order to let one understand this direct pointing, and let the Truth pass simply, they use no special means. They simply allow one to cut off one's delusion by sitting and permitting mould to grow up around the mouth. This does not mean that they dislike words and value silence. In order to let one know that one's mind is thus, they teach thus. Our True Nature is like clean water and like the sky. Further, it is clarity itself and, staying in peace, has no disturbance. There is nothing to manifest outside our minds, and there is nothing dirty in these minds. We cannot compare them to other jewels. We should not compare the light of these minds to the light of the sun or the moon. We should not compare them to the light of shining jewels. Do you not see that the light of our minds is as a thousand suns shining in the sky? One who does not understand completely is seeking for the Truth outside himself. One who understands completely does not seek the Truth even inside himself. Reflect quietly. Do not think that inside is in tune and outside unharmonious. The Truth is the same at all times; however, do not be selfish. Every ancestor met the next honestly, and only thus do they meet. There is no other reason for their meeting, and we should know this from the foregoing.

Butsudanandai did not say that the Truth could be understood through training, enlightenment or study; he said, "Your Mind is in tune with you, and you yourself are the Truth itself." Further, Butsudanandai suggested that we should not seek to become Buddha either with or without aspects. Therefore we can understand that there is nothing with which we ought to be in contact or from which we ought to be apart. The Truth is beyond contact and separation. Even though It can be explained by the word "body," it cannot be separated from anything; even though *It* can be explained by the word "mind," it cannot be in contact with it. Even if you understand the Truth in this way, do not seek for the mind outside the body. Body and mind belong to change, but change is not the working of mind and body. Many Buddhas hold the Truth thus at all times and are always enlightened; all ancestors hold the Truth thus and are always appearing in the countries of India, China, Japan and elsewhere. Therefore you too should hold the Truth thus and not work outside it. These things are eternal. The twelve aspects of life are explained by Shakyamuni and are the rolling of the Wheel of Truth. Wandering from one loka to another is the manifestation of Truth in Mahāyāna.

Life in the four lives is the True Life. Even if one explains the Truth as animate or inanimate, this explanation is the same as saying that our eyes have two different names, "me" and "manko." [Both words mean "eyes" in Japanese.] Although one explains the Truth as a living thing, it is only a different name for mind and will. Do not let the mind be excellent and the will non-excellent. Can we despise our "me" and respect our "manko"? There are neither senses nor their objects. Therefore everyone is the Truth itself. There is nothing outside Mind. Do you want to hear my humble words?

> Do not think we can explain
> True Nature with words and silence.
> Can the senses and their objects
> Make True Nature dusty?

Chapter XI

THE TENTH ANCESTOR, BARISHIBA SONJA

The Tenth Ancestor, Barishiba, followed Fudamitta for three years, and during that time never slept. One day Fudamitta explained the meaning of no-birth after reciting sūtras, and Barishiba was instantaneously enlightened.

Barishiba was born in central India and his name was Nansho, meaning "Difficult Birth." At his birth his father dreamed of a white elephant with a beautiful saddle upon its back. There was a brilliant jewel on this saddle which shone in all directions.

When Fudamitta went to central India, there lived a rich man there named Kōgai, who came to Fudamitta with his son and, after worshipping him, said, "This son was in his mother's womb for sixty years, and because of this he was named 'Difficult Birth.' When a genius met him he said that he was not ordinary and would become a real monk. Now we have met you I will let him become a monk." Fudamitta then shaved the son's head and ordained him.

Barishiba spent sixty years in his mother's womb and lived eighty years after his birth: therefore he was very old. When he wanted to become a monk, people warned him that as he was old and therefore not strong, it would be useless for him to enter the monks' circle. They told him there were two kinds of monks, one studying Zen and the other reciting sūtras, and that he could not manage either. When he heard this he vowed to himself that when he became a monk, he would not lie down until he could realise the Truth. So he studied Zen and recited sūtras in the daytime and sat in Zazen during the night, never sleeping. When he first became a monk, a portentous light fell upon his seat and he could feel that the bones of Shakyamuni Buddha were close to him. From then on he worked very hard without tiring for three years, and was able to realise the Truth. This realisation came when he heard Fudamitta reciting sūtras and explaining the meaning of no-birth. However, only those scriptures were recited that are real Mahāyāna, such as the *Ryogikyo*, for such scriptures have full meaning. These sūtras do not say that we need to get rid of delusion. The *Ryogikyo* not only explains doctrine, it explains actual things. Merely to explain the doctrine that all is one and all things have Buddha Nature is not good enough. Buddhas have a mind that penetrates the Truth. They study and train themselves so as to realise the Truth. There are five degrees such as human, angel, shōmon [unsui], engaku [those who have been transmitted] and Bodhisattva; the length of time of training; the names of places such as Jōdō, the place of immaculacy; these things the *Ryogikyo* explains fully. We should know that real sūtras make such explanations. Even if one realises the full meaning of one verse or one doctrine, he cannot be allowed to be an ancestor unless he realises the whole Truth. We should work hard, forgetting tiredness; have excellent wills; train ourselves strictly; study everything in detail day and night; realise the true wish of the Buddhas and what we are; and understand both the doctrine and actual things. Only thus can we become ancestors.

In recent years the way of the ancestors has been forgotten and there is no real training. Most monks think they are good enough if they understand just one verse or one doctrine. They are self-opinionated. Be careful of this. The Truth is like mountains: the farther we climb the higher they become. Virtue is like the sea: the farther we swim the deeper it becomes. When we fathom the sea's depth and climb to the top of the mountain, we become the real children of Buddha. Treat both your bodies and your minds with care. Everyone *is* the vessel of the Truth. Every day is a good day.

Understanding and ignorance come from training and from the failure to train. The Truth has no preference for any person or any time. Barishiba was a hundred and forty years old, very aged, but he realised the Truth because of his excellent will, forgetting all tiredness. He became the servant of his master for three years and never slept. Nowadays the old are often lazy. Think of the saints of ancient times. Do not think that when you work hard in hot or cold weather you will die. Do not think that you are unsuccessful. If you think positively you can become excellent; everyone who can think thus is an ancestor. Barishiba recited sūtras, but this does not mean that he recited them with his mouth only or opened the book only with his hands. We should know what the work in the house of the Buddha is; we should neither be controlled by delusion nor plant any seeds that can become a cause for greed, anger or delusion. Every place is itself a sūtra, and so we can acquire wisdom in all places and at all times. In this sense we can recite sūtras in all places and at any time. When we live thus we depend upon nothing and we realise the true meaning of no-birth. We do not know whence we come or where we go; born here, die there, always appearing and disappearing. Therefore birth is not birth and death is not death.

As a seeker for Truth, do not think of birth and death. We should know that our knowledge and our bodies are the Truth itself. We can make light radiate from our eyes so that all may see its glory. We can radiate light from our ears so that all may hear the sounds of Buddha. We can radiate light from our hands and make both others and ourselves happy. Thus we can walk with the glorious light for ever under our feet.

Now I will give you my humble words. Listen!

> How many sūtras do we recite?
> We die here and are born there.
> All is different
> And all is one.

Chapter XII

THE ELEVENTH ANCESTOR, FUNAYASHYA SONJA

The Eleventh Ancestor, Funayashya, stood in front of Barishiba Sonja, making gasshō, and Barishiba asked him, "From where have you come?"

"My mind is not going anywhere," Funayashya answered.

Barishiba asked him, "Where do you stay?"

"My mind stays nowhere," Funayashya replied.

"Then are you floating?" asked Barishiba.

"Every Buddha is as I am," answered Funayashya.

"You are not Buddha," said Barishiba. "To call something Buddha is wrong."

On hearing this saying, Funayashya trained himself for twenty-one days and realised no-self.

Then he told Barishiba, "It is wrong to call something Buddha and to call you Sonja."

Barishiba allowed him to transmit the Truth.

Funayashya came from Kashikoku; his family name was Gautama. His father's name was Hōshin. When Barishiba Sonja came to Kashikoku he rested under a tree, and pointing at the ground, said to the people, "When this ground becomes golden a saint will appear."

At that moment the ground turned golden and someone called Funayashya, the son of a rich man, appeared. The conversation quoted above took place, and Barishiba recited the following verse:

> This ground turned golden;
> I have known for some time that a saint would come.
> You, Funayashya, are to become Buddha
> So you should sit under the Bodhi tree
> As did Shakyamuni Buddha, and realise the Truth.

Funayashya replied with the following verse:

> You sit on the golden ground,
> Teaching and radiating light,
> Thus allowing me to enter samādhi.

Barishiba knew his (secret) wish and ordained him, giving him the Precepts.

Funayashya was a saint from the beginning, and so he said that his mind was beyond going and staying and that the Buddhas were alike, but still he felt himself to be in dualism. He thought that both his mind and the Buddha Mind were beyond going and staying. Then Barishiba took the most important things he had away from him, as if allowing a farmer's cow to take food from the hungry. Even a person who realises the Truth is still imperfect, and so Barishiba told him that there should be no Buddha. Because of this he said, "You are not Buddha." This cannot be realised with reasoning and cannot be understood without form. Therefore the Truth cannot be understood with the Wisdom of the Buddhas nor can it be understood with our ordinary knowledge. So Funayashya, after hearing this comment, trained himself for twenty-one days.

Finally he touched the Truth and forgot his individual mind, going beyond Buddhas. This is called no-birth. He realised what Truth *is* and spoke it: "To call something Buddha or Sonja is wrong."

The way of the ancestors cannot be understood with either reasoning or the mind. We cannot call the Dharma and the One Mind of the world the deepest Truth. We cannot understand it as eternity, immaculacy or emptiness. Therefore, when many saints came to this stage, they changed their minds, opened the gate to the Truth and ceased to be self-opinionated. Funayashya was a saint from the beginning; therefore, when he came, the ground turned golden and there was something about him which frightened others, but he trained himself for twenty-one days and understood the Truth.

So you, the disciple, must study much more deeply. I want you to hear my humble verse.

> The Mind is neither Buddha nor you;
> Coming and going are in this.

Chapter XIII

THE TWELFTH ANCESTOR, ANABOTEI MEMYŌ SONJA

The Twelfth Ancestor, Anabotei Memyō Sonja, asked Funayashya, "What is Buddha?"

"You want to know that! It is Buddha itself that does not know," replied Funayashya.

"I do not know Buddha, so how can I know that I am Buddha?" asked Anabotei.

"You do not know Buddha, so how can you know that you are not Buddha?" said Funayashya.

"This argument is like a saw," said Anabotei.

"No, it is like a tree. What do you mean when you say it is like a saw?" replied Funayashya.

"We are standing straight up (like a saw's teeth) in a line. What is the meaning of the tree?" asked Anabotei.

"You have been cut down by me," replied Funayashya.

Anabotei understood the Truth.

Anabotei came from Harana and was named Kōshō, being excellent in many virtues. Desire can be made a virtue; non-desire can also be made a virtue: therefore he was named Kōshō. He went to Funayashya and asked the first question: "What is Buddha?" Funayashya replied, "You want to know Buddha. It is Buddha itself that does not know." This is the first question to be asked by someone entering Buddhism. The Buddhas in the three generations and all the ancestors were trying to understand Buddha. If a person does not study what Buddhism is, he walks in the wrong direction. Therefore we cannot make a Buddha from forms, nor can we make one from thirty-two good aspects or eighty marks. Because of this Anabotei asked the first question and Funayashya gave the first answer: "You want to know what Buddha is. The Buddha is the very person who is asking the question"—that is, Anabotei himself. There is no difference in a person when he knows he is Buddha and when he does not. There is nothing special between before and after. Buddha was the same in ancient times as now. Sometimes he has thirty-two good aspects and eighty marks, and these show what a Buddha is supposed to look like. Sometimes Buddha has three heads and eight arms; sometimes he lives in heaven and suffers from the five discomforts; sometimes he appears in the form of a human being and suffers from the eight miseries; sometimes he has the aspects of animals, and sometimes he is in hell. He is always in the Three Worlds with the same mind and behaves in his own world of Mind, but with different aspects. Therefore no one knows what is being born or what is dying. No one can give him a definite form; no one can give him a definite name, and no one can ever realise fully what he is. Most people misunderstand this, and when they say they know what a Buddha is they just do not know. When they say they know that Buddha cannot be known and recognised, they know the True Buddha. If the true meaning of the conversation above is thus, why did Funayashya need to say such things? All people go from darkness to darkness and do not behave as Buddhas; therefore Funayashya said that Buddha is the very person who does not know Buddha. Anabotei did not understand this and showed his misunderstanding by saying, "If we do not know what Buddha is, how can we show our Buddha Nature?" Funayashya replied, "If we do not know what Buddha is, how can we show anything other than Buddha Nature? We must not look for the Buddha Nature outside ourselves; therefore the person who does not know what Buddha is, is the Buddha itself. How can we say it is not so?" "This is chop-logic," said Anabotei. "No," said Funayashya, "this logic is like wood. What is the meaning of 'chop-logic?'" "You and I are standing in the same line," replied Anabotei; "what is the meaning of the logic of wood?" Funayashya said, "I know you completely." Anabotei suddenly understood the Truth.

Indeed, you and I have the same Buddha Nature. There is no difference between you and me and our hands are full thereof. You and I can never be more than we are. You and I borrow nothing from others. Within this the master and disciple stand in the same line like the teeth of a saw. Funayashya said that the meaning of "wood" was that no one can know about anything when in darkness (concerning it). In the dark there is nothing to be taken away or added. The head of a wooden stick has no mind but functions as a head. This is the meaning of "wood."

But Anabotei could not well understand what his master meant, and Funayashya replied with compassion, "What is the meaning of 'saw'?" Anabotei said, "You and I are in the same line," and then asked his master, "What is the meaning of 'wood'?" Funayashya put his hand on Anabotei's shoulder and said, "You are known completely to me." Thus the way between master and disciple was opened and they became of One Mind. They could walk both in dreams and in heaven, so Funayashya said, "You are known to me." Thus Anabotei was enlightened completely and became the Twelfth Ancestor.

Funayashya said, "This great one was the king of Bishari. In this country there is a group of people who wear no clothes. The king turned himself into many silkworms so that they could have clothes. At a later date he was born in central India and the group cried with great feeling. Because of this he was named Anabotei, which means "Crying Horse" (the group were like a horse in being without clothes). Shakyamuni Buddha said that about six hundred years after his death there would be a wise person called Anabotei Memyō, in Harana, who would persuade others (to the Truth). This was fore-told by Shakyamuni Buddha, and so Funayashya transmitted the Truth to Anabotei Memyō.

Thinking that we are Buddha because we do not know we are Buddha, and that the Truth is transmitted without being known, does not mean that we should not think that we are Buddha because we do not know what it is. Although we do not know what Buddha is, we should enquire deeply concerning it at the time before our parents are conceived. With the knowledge that we have after we are born, we cannot know it. We cannot understand what face Buddhas, ancestors, human beings or devils have. The Truth is changing or not changing, is empty or not empty, is beyond within and without, beyond absolute and non-absolute; it is indeed our true existence. Within this Truth the average person and the saint, all things, subject and object, appear and disappear as the waves of the sea, and nothing is added. We call things Buddhas or devils, but they are the facets of one thing. When we call something Buddha we are wrong; when we call it devil we are wrong. When we teach the Truth to others, everything finds the Real Way. Therefore we perform true actions as if in a dream. The ways of teaching and the sorceries of India have come down to the present. If we train ourselves well and accept everything, being beyond birth and death, we are true monks. Now I want to tell you my humble verse.

> The peach tree does not know that its blossoms are red
> But it leads Rei-un to the Truth.

Chapter XIV

THE THIRTEENTH ANCESTOR, KABIMORA SONJA

One day, when Anabotei Sonja explained about the Sea of Buddha Nature, saying, "Mountains, rivers and the earth are all made thereof, the Three Wisdoms and the six extraordinary senses also," Kabimora Sonja realised the Truth.

Kabimora was born in Kashikoku in India. Before he learned Buddhism he had about three thousand disciples and knew various doctrines. Once when Anabotei Memyō Sonja was giving a good lecture in that country, an old man collapsed in front of him. Anabotei Sonja told the audience that this was not an ordinary person and must have an excellent appearance; then the old man suddenly disappeared and a golden one manifested itself from the bosom of the earth and changed into a woman. She pointed at Anabotei, saying in verse:

> I worship you, the great one;
> You should accept the prediction of Shakyamuni Buddha.
> Please spread the Truth throughout this world.

She then disappeared. Anabotei Sonja said, "There is a devil who wants to fight with me." Soon a storm arose and Anabotei Sonja said, "This is proof that the devil has come. I will get rid of it." He pointed to the sky, and a big golden dragon appeared which showed its power by shaking the mountains. Anabotei Sonja sat still and the devil disappeared.

After seven days there appeared a small worm, like a large Shōmei. Anabotei Sonja took it from beneath his seat and showed it to the audience, saying, "This is what the devil has changed into. It wants to steal my Dharma." Anabotei Sonja freed it from his finger, but it could not move. He told it that if it were converted to the Three Treasures of the Dharma, it would have the extraordinary senses. The devil then appeared as he truly was, bowed to Anabotei Sonja and confessed. Anabotei Sonja said, "What are you? How many followers do you have?" The devil replied, "My name is Kabimora. I have three thousand followers." Anabotei Sonja said, "Why do you change so often?" The devil replied, "It is a very easy thing for me to change the great sea into something else." Anabotei Sonja said, "Can you change the Sea of the Truth into something else?" The devil said, "What is the Sea of the Truth? I have never heard of such a thing." Anabotei Sonja explained it to him, saying, "Mountains, rivers and the earth are all made of it; the Three Wisdoms and the six extraordinary senses come out therefrom." Kabimora realised the Truth.

From the time when an old man collapsed until the time when a small worm appeared, the devil changed often. It was a small thing for it to change a great sea into a mountain and a mountain into a great sea, but since it did not even know the name of the Sea of the Truth, how could it change that? Though he did not know what changed into a mountain and other things, Anabotei Memyō Sonja explained that they were the Sea of the Truth, and that the Three Wisdoms and six extraordinary senses came out of it.

There are many samādhis, such as the following: shuryogon-zammai, the samādhi which exterminates all delusions; tengentsu,
wherein one is all-seeing; tennitsu, wherein one has supernatural
hearing; and many others. These have neither beginning nor end.
This world is full of them; in fact, it is them themselves. When
mountains, rivers and the earth are made, the samādhi changes into
the earth, water, fire and wind, grass, wood, skin, flesh, bones and
all parts of our bodies. There is nothing outside it; there is nothing
to be abandoned. Birth and death continue and both are within
samādhi. There is endless sight and sound. Even the wisdom of
Buddhas cannot understand these things. All are part of the constant
movement of the Sea of Truth. Therefore everything in the world
is endless; it is not a problem of comparison. When we see our
bodies we see our minds. When we know the mind we know the
body. Body and mind are not two separate things. Form and matter
are not different. Even though one is in another world than that of
humans, still one is in samādhi, only one does not know it and doubts
both oneself and others. If someone does not know that everything
is in samādhi, he cannot understand the fundamental Truth. Therefore the power of the devil was destroyed. It abandoned selfishness
and came to Anabotei Memyō Sonja, ceased to fight with him and
manifested his light. Even when you understand your own True
Nature, do not stay in the realm of the senses. The senses are still
facets of the Buddha, however; so are the fence, wall and stones.
The True Nature is beyond seeing, hearing, touching, movement
and stillness. When the Sea of the Truth is established, movement
and stillness arise; skin, flesh and bones appear with time. Think of
the true meaning of this; it appears as senses and sights, but not
for others. We can make sound by beating the sky, and when the
sky is changed into many things, they have various forms. We should
not think that the sky has no form and no voice. Also, when we
realise that there is nothing to be called emptiness or existence, this
is not such an existence that it is visible or invisible. There is nothing
separate. What is "other"? What is "I"? It is as if in the sky there
is nothing and in the sea there is water. This is true at all times,
past and present. When it is visible, there is nothing to be added to
it. When it is invisible, there is nothing to be hidden. Our bodies
are made up of many facets. Beyond existence there is something

which we call One Mind. Therefore, when you want to be enlightened, do not look for it outside yourself. When the Truth manifests
itself, others call it human beings and animals. Seppō said, "If we
want to understand, we should realise that we are like an excellent
mirror. When foreigners come, they appear in it; when our own
relations come, they appear in it." Therefore there is no beginning
and no end. Mountains, rivers and the earth come from this. The
Three Wisdoms and six supernatural powers come from this. There
is nothing outside our minds. Please listen to my humble verse.

> Even if great waves rise up to heaven
> The pure water does not change at all.

Chapter XV

THE FOURTEENTH ANCESTOR, NAGYAARAJYUNA

When the Thirteenth Ancestor went to the king of the dragons he
was given a Nyoi jewel. Nagyaarajyuna asked him, "Since this jewel
is the most excellent thing in all the world, has it aspects or not?"
Kabimora replied, "You know only of aspects. You do not realise
that this jewel is beyond them, nor do you know that this is not
a jewel." Nagyaarajyuna realised the Truth deeply.

Nagyaarajyuna Sonja came from the western part of India. He was
named Ryunnyo or Ryushō. The Thirteenth Ancestor went to the
western part of India after he was enlightened. There a prince named
Unjizai invited the Thirteenth Ancestor to his palace, where he
offered him many gifts. He told the prince, "There is a teaching of
Shakyamuni Buddha that says no monk can be near to a king,
nobles and the powerful." The prince said, "There is a great hill
behind my castle. On it there is a stone hall. Would you like to
meditate there?" The Thirteenth Ancestor said, "Yes." He went to
the hill, and on the way to the stone hall, he saw a large python
but took no notice of it. However, it came and encircled his body,

and he then gave it the Three Treasures. After hearing them, the python left him. When he arrived at the stone hall, an old man in poor clothes came out and made gasshō. Kabimora Sonja said to him, "Where do you live?" He replied, "When I was a monk, I liked to live alone in a peaceful forest or on a mountain. Someone who wanted to learn from me came often, but I found this very troublesome and got angry with him. For this I was reborn as a python and spent a thousand years in this stone hall. Fortunately I met you and heard the Three Treasures. Now I want to thank you for them."

Kabimora Sonja asked him, "What people are there on this hill?" He replied, "About ten ri from here there is a great one who teaches five hundred big dragons. I also listen to him." Kabimora Sonja went to Nagyaarajyuna, who came out to welcome him, saying, "This place is deep in the mountains and lonely. There are many dragons and pythons. Why has the great monk come?" Kabimora Sonja replied, "I am not great. I have just come to see a wise man." Nagyaarajyuna thought silently about whether the Thirteenth Ancestor was a great monk or not and if he had the transmission from Shakyamuni Buddha. Kabimora Sonja said, "You are thinking within you concerning me. I know well what you are thinking. Just become a monk. You do not need to worry if I am great." After hearing this comment, Nagyaarajyuna apologised and became a monk, and the five hundred dragons accepted the Precepts. After that he followed the Thirteenth Ancestor for four years. When the latter went to the king of the dragons and was given the Nyoi jewel, Nagyaarajyuna asked him, "Is this the most excellent jewel in the world or not?" as well as other questions. He was enlightened thereby and became the Fourteenth Ancestor.

Nagyaarajyuna had learned from several religions. He had also learned sorcery. He used to go to the palace below the sea to see the Sūtras of the Seven Buddhas. Seeing the titles, he understood the contents and used to teach them to the five hundred dragons. The so-called Manda Ryū-ō and Butsudanda Ryū-ō are called Bodhisattvas. They keep many sūtras in a safe place, for they were asked to do so by the ancient Buddhas. When the teachings and sūtras of Shakyamuni Buddha cease to be useful for others, they will be put in the palace beneath the sea. Although Nagyaarajyuna had such great power that he could talk with the great king of the dragons, still he was not a real monk. All he did was learn other religions.

From the time he belonged to the Thirteenth Ancestor he was enlightened truly, but people thought he was not only the Fourteenth Ancestor but the founder of many sects of Buddhism. The Shingon sect made him its true founder, as did also Tendai. The sorcerers and weavers made him their founder too. Many people learned many things from him. After he became the Fourteenth Ancestor he took no notice of them, but they still thought he was their founder. They were like animals and devils which cannot recognise the difference between jewels and stones. Only Kanadaiba could be given his Truth. He took no notice of others. Even though he had had five hundred excellent people when Kabimora Sonja came to him, he nevertheless went out, bowed and wished to test him. But Kabimora Sonja did not show his true mind. Nagyaarajyuna was thinking silently about whether he was a true monk. Kabimora Sonja said, "Become a monk. Why do you need to wonder whether I am a saint or not?" Nagyaarajyuna apologised and followed him.

Nagyaarajyuna said, "This jewel is the most excellent in the world. Has it any aspects?" Since he possessed dual thought, he could not understand the Truth. Kabimora Sonja's reply was, "Even though this jewel is the most excellent in all the world, when we speak of Truth everything is beyond aspects. This is just a jewel. A jewel that is in the hair of a wrestler, a jewel that is in the middle of the forehead of a worldly noble, a jewel of the king of the dragons and that in the pocket of a drunkard may or may not have aspects, but they are all worldly jewels and not within the Truth. However, no one knows these jewels are not jewels. You must study carefully. You have to go into these things minutely. The whole body is the jewel of the teaching. You must know that the whole ten worlds are this one bright jewel. For example, although Truth is as a jewel of the world, it does not come from outside but appears in one's own heart. If you are ill and hold this jewel, the illness will be cured. If you have this jewel when you are afraid, the anguish will be swept away. Divine appearances are also traceable to this jewel. Amongst the seven jewels of the king of the Tomoe there is a wonderful jewel from which all rare jewels are born. It is infinite.

In the world of men there are victor and vanquished—distinctions. The jewel in the world of humans can also be called a grain of rice. This is, then, a jewel stone. This, compared with the heavenly, is as something manufactured or produced which is thereafter called a jewel. The Buddha's bones and the Dharma become *the* Jewel. It brings everything and also becomes a grain of rice. It rescues living beings. Sometimes it appears as the Buddha Body, sometimes as a grain of rice; it manifests all Dharma. It manifests as one; it manifests as one's own heart. It becomes a body of five shaku [in height]; it becomes a body with three heads; it becomes all things in the universe. Like the monks of old, you must not search for tranquillity, by retiring to forests and mountains. This is truly not the Way. It is a mistake. You must take the arm of all who still hesitate and come and go together with them. To secrete yourself in forests, mountains and valleys and do Zazen alone is to be one who trains without any purpose; such a one walks the wrong road and does not know the Truth. In all things he is self first. Daibaijō Zenji sat in the pine-smoke and Isan Daien Zenji sat under clouds in the fog with the tigers and the wolves. One should not laugh because the ancients took this road and became true masters. We must do the same. If we do not train with purity we will for ever be waiting for an opportunity to do so. We must know this. Daibai received Basō's certification as well as Isan's and Hyakujō's. The old masters like Inzan and Rasan did not live alone. Having gained merit once, their names remain for future generations. Such persons have clear vision. To live in mountains and valleys and never go where one should is one-sided; such a person is the personification of training that is done only out of desire for one's own moral perfection.

If the eye is not pure and clean, and yet one trains oneself alone, one becomes only a shōmon and not a seed of Buddha. One who is a seed of Buddha does not cut himself off from the seeds of Buddha. One who keeps with others trains and realises the self, deepens himself and follows the former patriarchs. Two former patriarchs said that their disciples could not sit alone; they had to train and work with others. No one must sit apart from his fellow trainees. One who does not take this principle to heart will never be a leaf of the five gates. Enō Zenji said, "The ancients went to the mountains and their best food was rice. They forgot about the human world for ten or twenty years. Thus they could realise eternal gratitude." Ōryūnan said, "We preserve the Way for ourselves. Some go to mountains and forests, and they do not draw monks into the shūryo. No teacher of this generation likes to live alone." They are weaker than the men of old; they are only in the shūryo. They must do training as the ancients did. If they prefer solitude because of some lack of understanding and a monk should come, their behaviour could cause resentment. To behave thus is to have no understanding. You must break with attachment to body and mind. You must not live alone and apart. You must not be like Nagyaarajyuna in the mountains, even though he was lecturing, since he was only speaking about his own learning. Only through deeds of charity when living together with others can Buddha's Right Law be heard. If one trains without preference for solitude, and makes progress in training, one will extract the very source of the Dharma and become the mouth of Buddha. Do you want to hear my humble words?

One ray of light does not cause blindness;
The Nyoi radiates brilliantly in all directions.

Kyojūkaimon
GIVING AND RECEIVING THE TEACHING OF THE PRECEPTS

THE GREAT PRECEPTS of the Buddhas are kept carefully by the Buddhas. Buddhas give them to Buddhas, ancestors give them to ancestors. The Transmission of the Precepts is beyond the three existences of past, present and future; enlightenment ranges from time eternal and is even now. Shakyamuni Buddha, our Lord, transmitted the Precepts to Makakashyo, and he transmitted them to Ananda. Thus the Precepts have been transmitted to me in the eighty-fifth generation. Now I am going to give them to you in order to show my gratitude for the Compassion of the Buddhas and thus make them the eyes of all sentient beings. This is the meaning of the Transmission of Living Wisdom of the Buddhas. I am going to pray for the Buddha's guidance, and you should make confession and be given the Precepts. Please recite this after me:

> All wrong actions, behaviour and karma perpetrated by me from time immemorial have been, and are, caused by greed, anger and delusion which have no beginning, born of my body, mouth and will; I now make full and open confession thereof.

> *Preceptor:* Now, by the guidance of the Buddhas and ancestors, we can discard and purify all our karma of body, mouth and will and obtain great immaculacy. This is by the power of confession.

You should now be converted to Buddha, Dharma and Sangha. In the Three Treasures there are three merits. The first is the true source of the Three Treasures; the second is the presence in the past of the Buddha; the third is his presence at the present time. The highest Truth is called the Buddha Treasure; immaculacy is called the Dharma Treasure; harmony is called the Sangha Treasure.

The person who has realised the Truth really is called the Buddha Treasure; the Truth that is realised by Buddha is called the Dharma Treasure; the people who study the Dharma Treasure are called the Sangha Treasure. He who teaches devas and humans, appearing in the sky and in the world, is called the Buddha Treasure. That which appears in the world in the sūtras and becomes good for others is called the Dharma Treasure. He who is released from all suffering and is beyond the world is called the Sangha Treasure. This means that when someone is converted to the Three Treasures, he can have the Precepts of the Buddhas completely. Make the Buddha your teacher and do not follow wrong ways.

THE THREE PURE PRECEPTS

Cease from evil.
This is the house of all the laws of Buddha; this is the source of all the laws of Buddha.

Do only good.
The Dharma of the Sammyakusambodai is the Dharma of all existence.

Do good for others.
Be beyond both the holy and the unholy. Let us rescue ourselves and others.

These three are called the Three Pure Precepts.

THE TEN GREAT PRECEPTS

Do not kill.
No life can be cut off. The Life of Buddha is increasing. Continue the life of Buddha; do not kill Buddha.

Do not steal.
The mind and its object are one. The gateway to enlightenment stands open wide.

Do not covet.
The doer, the doing and that which has the doing done to it are immaculate; therefore there is no desire. It is the same doing as that of the Buddhas.

Do not say that which is not true.
The Wheel of the Dharma rolls constantly and lacks for nothing yet needs something. The sweet dew covers the whole world, and within it lies the Truth.

Do not sell the wine of delusion.
There is nothing to be deluded about. If we realise this, we
are enlightenment itself.

Do not speak against others.
In Buddhism, the Truth and everything are the same: the
same law, the same enlightenment and the same behaviour.
Do not allow anyone to speak of another's faults. Do not
allow anyone to make a mistake in Buddhism.

Do not be proud of yourself and devalue others.
Every Buddha and every ancestor realises that he is the
same as the limitless sky and as great as the universe. When
they realise their true body there is nothing within or without; when they realise their true body they are nowhere
upon the earth.

Do not be mean in giving either Dharma or wealth.
There is nothing to be mean with: one phrase, one verse,
the hundred grasses, one Dharma, one enlightenment, every
Buddha, every ancestor.

Do not be angry.
There is no retiring, no going, no Truth, no lie; there is
a brilliant sea of clouds, there is a dignified sea of clouds.

Do not defame the Three Treasures.
To do something by ourselves, without copying others, is
to become an example to the world, and the merit of doing
such a thing becomes the source of all wisdom. Do not
criticise, but accept everything.

These sixteen Precepts are thus.
Be obedient to the teaching and its giving; accept it with
bows.

Sankon Zazen Setsu
THE THREE PERSONALITIES
IN TRAINING

THE PERSON who does Zazen of the highest type has no interest in such matters as how Buddhas appear in this present world, nor does he consider Truths which are untransmittable by even the Buddhas and patriarchs. He does not doctrinalise about all things being expressions of the self, for he is beyond enlightenment and delusion. Since he never considers anything from a dualistic angle, nothing ever enslaves him, even when differences show themselves. He just eats when he is hungry and sleeps when he is tired.

The person who does Zazen of the less high type gives up everything and cuts all ties. Since throughout the entire day he is never idle, every moment of his life, every breath, is a meditation upon Truth; as an alternative to this, he may concentrate on a kōan with his eyes fixed on one place, such as the tip of his nose. The considerations of life and death, or going and staying, are not to be seen upon his face. The discriminatory mind can never perceive the highest Truth of the Eternal, nor can it comprehend the Buddha Mind. Since there is no dualism in his thought, he is enlightened. From the far past to the present day, wisdom is always shining clearly and brightly. The whole universe in all the ten directions is permeated suddenly by the illumination from his head; all phenomena are seen separately within his body.

The person who does ordinary Zazen considers everything from all angles before freeing himself from good and evil karma. The mind expresses naturally the True Nature of all the Buddhas, for the feet of man stand where the Buddha stands; thus are evil ways avoided. The hands are in the position for meditation, holding no scripture. The mouth being tightly shut, it is as if a seal were upon the lips, for no word of any doctrine is ever uttered. The eyes are neither wide open nor half shut; in no way is anything considered from the point of view of differentiation, for the voice of good and evil is not listened to. The nose takes no cognisance of smells as either good or bad; the body relies upon nothing, for all delusion is suddenly ended. Since there is no delusion to disturb the mind, neither sorrow nor joy is to be found. As in the case of a wooden Buddha, both material and form are one with the Truth. Although worldly thoughts may arise, they are not disturbing, for the mind is as a bright mirror in which no shadows move. From Zazen the Precepts arise eternally, whether they are the five, the eight, the Great Precepts of the Bodhisattvas, the Precepts of the priesthood, the three thousand manners, the eighty thousand beliefs, or the Highest Law of the Buddhas and patriarchs. In all training, nothing whatsoever compares with Zazen.

Even if only one merit is gained from doing Zazen, it is greater than the building of a hundred, a thousand or an uncountable number of temples. Just do Zazen for ever, without ceasing, for by so doing we are free of birth and death and realise our own latent Buddha Nature. It is perfect and natural to go, stay, sit and lie down; to see, hear, understand and know are natural manifestations of the True Self: between first mind and last mind there is no difference, and none can make an argument about either knowledge or ignorance. Do Zazen with your whole being; never forget and lose it.

Scriptures and
Necessary Ceremonial

Morning Service

ALL THE TRAINEES enter the ceremony hall and make three bows to the main altar, then turn and make three bows to each other. The disciplinarian intones the name of each scripture and all join in its recitation as follows:

The Scripture of Kanzeon Bosatsu*

All: In verse, Mujinni Bodhisattva asked,
"World-honoured One, possessor of all grace,
What reason is there for the Buddha's son,
Great Kanzeon, to thus be so addressed?"
The Honoured One made answer too in verse,
"Just listen to the life of Kanzeon;
To calls from every quarter he responds;
Of oceanic depth his holy vows.
*A myriad Buddhas has he truly served
For ages past beyond the thought of man
And made for aye great vows of purity.
When people hear his name and see his form
And think of him not vainly in their hearts,
All forms of ill, in all the worlds, shall cease.
If, wishing harm, an enemy should try
To push another in a fiery pit,
The victim should on Kanzeon's great power
Think, and straightway that fiery pit will be
Transformed into a cool and silver lake.
If drifting in the vast great ocean's foam
A man should be in danger of his life
From monstrous fish or evil beings, let
Him only think on Kanzeon's great power;
At once the sea will all compassion be.

* This small star, to be found in various places throughout this ceremony and others, indicates the places where the gong is struck.

If from the top of Sumeru a man
Be hurled down by an enemy's cruel hand,
Just let him think on Kanzeon's great power
And like the sun he will remain aloft.
If, chased by wicked men, a man should fall
Upon a mountain, let him think again
Of Kanzeon's power, and no injury
Will even a single hair of him sustain.
If, ringed by enemies, a man should be
Threatened by them, all with their swords in hand,
Just let him think on Kanzeon's great power;
Compassion then within their hearts will dwell.
When tyrants persecute a man and he
Stands at the place of execution, let
Him only think on Kanzeon's great power;
The executioner's sword will broken be.
If bound in chains in prison, let a man
Just think on Kanzeon's great holy power;
At once the shackles will then set him free.
When poisonous herbs or magic threaten harm,
The power of Kanzeon, if thought upon,
Will quickly send the curse back whence it came.
If poisonous creatures, evil ones, should come,
Upon great Kanzeon's power gently dwell;
Straightway those evil ones dispersed will be.
When snakes and scorpions attack a man,
Exhaling evil poisons, scorching him,
By dwelling on great Kanzeon's holy power
They will be turned away with shrieks of fear.
When lightning flashes and the thunder rolls,
When hailstones beat and rain in torrents pours,
The power of Kanzeon, if thought upon,
Will quickly clear the heavens of the storm.
If struck by cruel disaster's evil hand
Or tortured by interminable pain
A being flees to Kanzeon's gentle arms,
He, being wise and full of mystic power,

Will save him from all worldly grief and care.
With all miraculous powers well endowed,
And widely skilled in knowledge of all things,
In all the world, in all the quarters, there
Is not a place where Kanzeon does not go.
Hells, evil spirits, beastly creatures, all
The evil ways of living, all the pain
That comes from birth, old age, disease and death
Will for eternity all pass away.
Great Kanzeon views all the world in Truth,
Free from defilement, loving, knowing all,
Full of compassion; he must always be
Prayed to, adored, for all eternity.
He is a light pure, spotless, like the sun,
With wisdom does he darkness all dispel,
Subverting all effects of wind and fire;
His all-illuming light fills all the world.
As thunder shakes the universe does he
Control his loving body, and his thought
Of great compassion, like a cloud from which
A rain of Dharma comes as nectar down,
Destroys the flames of evil passions all.
When threatened by court judgements or in camp
The military should a man oppress,
Let him but think on Kanzeon's great power
And all his enemies will be dispersed.
*He is a most exquisite voice, a voice
That all the world encompasses; the voice
Of Brahma, voice of oceans—one that all
The voices of the world does much excel.
Because of this our thought must always dwell
Upon him. Let us never cherish thoughts
Of doubt about great Kanzeon, who is
All pure and holy and a refuge true,
*Protecting in all grief, in trouble, death,
Disaster. He possesses merit all,
Regards all things with a compassionate eye,

And like the ocean, holds within himself
A mass of virtues inestimable.
For this he must for ever be adored."
Then rose Jiji Bosatsu from his seat
To stand before the Buddha, saying thus:
"World-honoured One, they who this scripture hear
Of Kanzeon Bosatsu must indeed
No small amount of merit gain, for here
His life of perfect action is described.
This is the life of one who, all endowed
With powers all miraculous, appears
In all directions." When the Buddha thus
Finished the recitation in the hall
Of this great scripture which makes clearly plain
The life and work of the all-sided One,
All people present then, a great concourse,
In number four and eighty thousand strong,
†With all their hearts cherished a longing deep
†For the Supreme Enlightenment with which
Nothing in all the universe compares.

The disciplinarian or his assistant then recites the offertory alone:

*Wholeheartedly do we recite this scripture. We offer the
merits thereof, candles, flowers and fruit to Kanzeon, the
Great Compassionate Bodhisattva, who is our example.
Whenever this scripture is recited, Great Compassion is
with us and we are searching for it within ourselves. We
pray for peace in all the world; we pray that evil may be
overcome by good; we pray for the peace of this temple
and for the cessation of all disaster.

All recite the following:

*Homage to all the Buddhas in all worlds;
*Homage to all the Bodhisattvas in all worlds;
*Homage to the Scripture of Great Wisdom.

† This mark indicates the use of a small gong.

The disciplinarian announces:

The Scripture of Great Wisdom*

All: When one with deepest wisdom of the heart
That is beyond discriminative thought,
The Holy Lord, great Kanzeon Bosatsu,
Knew that the skandhas five were, as they are,
In their self-nature, void, unstained and clean.
O Śāriputra, form is only void;
Void is all form; there is then nothing more
Than this; for what is form is void, and what
*Is void is form. The same is also true
Of all sensation, thought, activity,
And consciousness. O Śāriputra, here
All things are void, for they are neither born
Nor do they wholly die; they are not stained
Nor yet immaculate; increasing not,
Decreasing not. O Śāriputra, here
In void there is no form, sensation, thought,
Activity or consciousness; no eye,
Ear, nose, tongue, body, mind; no form, no tastes,
Sound, colour, touch or objects; vision none;
No consciousness; no knowledge; and no sign
Of ignorance; until we come to where
Old age and death have ceased, and so has all
Extinction of old age and death; for here
There is no suffering, nor yet again
Is there accumulation, or again
Annihilation or an Eightfold Path;
No knowledge, no attainment. In the mind
Of the Bosatsu who is truly one
With Wisdom Great there are no obstacles
*And, going on beyond this human mind,
He *is* Nirvāna. All the Buddhas True
Of present, past and future, they *are* all,
Because upon Great Wisdom they rely,
The perfect and most high enlightenment.
The Prajñāpāramitā one should know

To be the Greatest Mantra of them all,
The highest and most peerless Mantra too;
*Allayer of all pain Great Wisdom is.
It is the very truth, no falsehood here.
This is the Mantra of Great Wisdom, hear!
†O Buddha, going, going, going on
†Beyond, and always going on beyond,
Always *becoming* Buddha. Hail! Hail! Hail!

The disciplinarian announces:

Sandōkai*

All: From west to east, unseen, flowed out the Mind
Of India's greatest Sage, and to the source
Kept true as an unsullied stream is clear.
Although by wit and dullness the True Way
Is varied, yet it has no patriarch
Of south or north. Here born, we clutch at things
And then compound delusion later on
By following ideals. Each sense-gate and
*Its object all together enter thus
In mutual relations and yet stand
Apart in a uniqueness of their own,
Depending and yet non-depending both.
In form and feel component things are seen
To differ deeply, and the voices in
Inherent isolation, soft and harsh.
Such words as "high" and "middle" darkness match;
Light separates the murky from the pure.
The properties of the four elements
Together draw just as a child returns
Unto its mother. Lo! the heat of fire,
The moving wind, the water wet, the earth
All solid; eyes to see, sounds heard and smells;
Upon the tongue the sour, salty taste.
And yet in each related thing, as leaves
Grow from the roots, end and beginning here
Return unto the source, and "high" and "low"

Are used respectively. Within all light
Is darkness, but explained it cannot be
By darkness that one-sided is alone.
In darkness there is light, but here again
By light one-sided it is not explained.
*Light goes with darkness as the sequence does
Of steps in walking. All things herein have
Inherent, great potentiality;
Both function, rest, reside within. Lo! with
The ideal comes the actual, like a box
All with its lid. Lo! with the ideal comes
The actual, like two arrows in mid-air
That meet. Completely understand herein
*The basic truth within these words. Lo! Hear!
Set up not your own standards. If, from your
Experience of the senses, basic truth
You do not know, how can you ever find
The path that certain is no matter how
Far distant you may walk? As you walk on,
Distinctions between near and far are lost,
And should you lost become, there will arise
†Obstructing mountains and great rivers. This
†I offer to the seeker of great Truth:
Do not waste time.

The disciplinarian announces:

The Most Excellent Mirror—Samādhi*

All: The Buddhas and the patriarchs have all
Directly handed down this basic truth:
Preserve well, for you now have; this is all.
The white snow falls upon the silver plate;
The snowy heron in the bright moon hides.
Resembles each the other, yet these two
Are not the same. Combining them, we can
Distinguish one from other. Supreme mind
*In words can never be expressed, and yet
To all the trainees' needs it does respond.

Enslaved by words you fall into a hole.
If you should go against the basic truth
You come to a dead end. This is as if
A giant fire-ball; never come too close
Or put yourself too far away. If you
Express by fancy words, it is all stained.
The night encloses brightness, and at dawn
No light shines. This truth holds for beings all.
Through this we free ourselves from suffering.
Although not made by artifice, this truth
Can find expression in the words of those
Who teach true Zen. It is as if one looks
Into a jewelled mirror, seeing both
Shadow and substance. You are not he; he
Is all of you. A baby of this world
Is such as this, possessing all his five
Sense organs, yet goes not and neither comes;
Neither arises nor yet stays; has words
And yet no words. Then finally we grasp
Nothing, for words inaccurate will be.
When stacked, six sticks of ri for ever move
In mutual relations in extremes
And centre. Stacked three times, return again
To the first pattern after changes five.
This as the five tastes of the chi-grass seems
And as the diamond sceptre's branches five.
The absolute "upright" holds, as it is,
Many phenomena within its own
Delicate balance. When a trainee asks
A question, matching answer always comes
From the Zen master. So that he may bring
The trainee to the ultimate of Truth,
The master uses skilful means. Trainees
Embrace the ultimate; masters contain
The means. Correctly blended, this is good.
Avoid one-sided clinging. This is all
The natural and superior truth that does
Attach itself to no delusion or

Enlightenment. It calmly, clearly shows
When all conditions ripen; when minute
Infinitesimally small becomes;
When large, it transcends all dimension, space.
Even the slightest twitch will surely break
The rhythm. Now we have abrupt and slow,
And separated do the sects become
By setting up of doctrines, practices,
And these become the standards that we know
Of all religious conduct. Even should
We penetrate these doctrines, practices,
And then delusive consciousness flows through
The 'ternal truth, no progress shall we make.
If outwardly all calm we do appear
And yet within disturbed should be, we are
As if a tethered horse, or as a mouse
Within a cage. So pitying this plight,
The former sages teaching all dispensed.
Because delusions in the trainees' minds
Were topsy-turvy, all the sages true
Did match thereto their teachings; thus they used
All means, so varied, even so to say
That black was white. Delusive thought, if lost,
Abandoned, will all satisfaction bring.
If you in ancient footsteps wish to walk
Observe examples old. That he could take
The final step to true enlightenment,
A former Buddha trained himself for ten
Long kalpas, gazing at the Bodhi tree.
* If thus restrained, freedom original
Is like a tiger that has tattered ears
Or like a hobbled horse. The sage will tell
A trainee, who is feeling he is low
And all inferior, that on his head
There gleams a jewelled diadem and on
His body rich robes hang and at his feet
There is a footrest. If the trainee hears
* This teaching with surprise and doubt, the sage

Assures him that of cats there are some kinds,
As also some white cows, that perfect are
Just as they are. A master archer hits
A target at a hundred yards because
He skill possesses. But to make to meet
Two arrows in mid-air, head-on, goes far
Beyond the skill of ordinary man.
In this superior activity
Of no-mind, see! the wooden figure sings
And the stone maiden dances. This is far
Beyond all common consciousness—beyond
All thinking. The retainer serves his lord
The emperor. His father does the child
Obey. Without obedience there is
No filial piety; and if there is
No service, no advice. Such action and
Most unpretentious work all foolish seem
† And dull. But those who practise thus this law
† Continually shall in all worlds be
Called Lord of Lords unto eternity.

The disciplinarian recites the following offertory alone:

We offer the merits of this recitation of (names of scriptures) to (the patriarchal line follows; the disciplinarian should read down each column, not across):

All:	
* Bibashibutsu Daioshō	Daitaka Daioshō
* Shikibutsu Daioshō	Mishaka Daioshō
* Bishafubutsu Daioshō	Bashumitsu Daioshō
* Kurusonbutsu Daioshō	Butsudanandai Daioshō
* Kunagonmunibutsu Daioshō	Fudamitta Daioshō
	Barishiba Daioshō
* Kashōbutsu Daioshō	Funayashya Daioshō
* Shakyamunibutsu Daioshō	Anabotei Daioshō
Makakashyo Daioshō	Kabimora Daioshō
Ananda Daioshō	Nagyaarajyuna Daioshō
Shōnawashyu Daioshō	Kanadaiba Daioshō
Ubakikuta Daioshō	Ragorata Daioshō

Sōgyanandai Daioshō

Kayashyata Daioshō

Kumorata Daioshō

Shyyata Daioshō

Bashyubanzu Daioshō

Manura Daioshō

Kakurokuna Daioshō

Shishibodai Daioshō

Bashyashita Daioshō

Funyomitta Daioshō

Hannyatara Daioshō

Bodaidaruma Daioshō

Taisō Eka Daioshō

Kanchi Sōsan Daioshō

Daii Dōshin Daioshō

Daiman Kōnin Daioshō

Daikan Enō Daioshō

Seigen Gyoshi Daioshō

Sekitō Kisen Daioshō

Yakusan Igen Daioshō

Ungan Donjō Daioshō

Tōzan Ryōkai Daioshō

Ungo Dōyō Daioshō

Dōan Dōhi Daioshō

Dōan Kanshi Daioshō

Ryōzan Enkan Daioshō

Daiyō Kyōgen Daioshō

Tōsu Gisei Daioshō

Fuyō Dokai Daioshō

Tanka Shijyun Daioshō

Choro Seiryō Daioshō

Tendō Sōkaku Daioshō

Setchō Chikan Daioshō

Tendō Nyojō Daioshō

Eihei Kōsō Daioshō

Koun Ejō Daioshō

Tetsū Gikai Daioshō

Keizan Jōkin Daioshō

Meihō Sotetsu Daioshō

Shugan Dōchin Daioshō

Tetsuzan Shikaku Daioshō

Keigan Eishō Daioshō

Chuzan Ryōhun Daioshō

Gisan Tōnin Daioshō

Shōgaku Kenryu Daioshō

Kinen Hōryu Daioshō

Teishitsu Chisenn Daioshō

Kokei Shōjun Daioshō

Sessō Yuho Daioshō

Kaiten Genju Daioshō

Shūzan Shunshō Daioshō

Chōzan Senyetsu Daioshō

Fukushū Kōchi Daioshō

Meidō Yūton Daioshō

Hakuhō Gentekki Daioshō

Gesshū Sōkō Daioshō

Manzan Dōhaku Daioshō

Gekkan Gikō Daioshō

Daiyu Esshō Daioshō

Kegon Sōkai Daioshō

Shōun Taizui Daioshō

Nichirin Tōgō Daioshō

Sonnō Kyōdō Daioshō

Sogaku Reidō Daioshō

Daishun Bengyu Daioshō

Kohō Hakugun Daioshō

Keidō Chisan Daioshō

The disciplinarian continues the offertory alone:

> We pray that we may be able to show our gratitude to the
> four benefactors, rescue all beings in the Three Worlds,

and make the Four Wisdoms perfect together with all living things. We pray that this priestly family may prosper and all misfortune cease.

If there is a separate meditation hall in addition to the ceremony hall, the *Sandōkai* and *The Most Excellent Mirror—Samādhi*, together with the patriarchal line, are recited in it. The community then goes in procession to the ceremony hall, where they recite the Scripture of Kanzeon Bosatsu and then the Scripture of Great Wisdom, after which the disciplinarian recites the following offertory:

> We offer the merits of this recitation of the Scripture of Kanzeon Bosatsu and the Scripture of Great Wisdom to the Great Master Shakyamuni Buddha; the highest patriarch, Great Master Jōyō; the greatest patriarch, Great Master Jōsai; and the Three Treasures in all the worlds. We pray that we may be able to show our gratitude to the four benefactors, rescue all beings in the Three Worlds, and make the Four Wisdoms perfect together with all living things. We pray that this priestly family may prosper and all misfortune cease.

All: * Homage to all the Buddhas in all worlds:
         * Homage to all the Bodhisattvas in all worlds;
         * Homage to the Scripture of Great Wisdom.

All make three bows to the main altar and three bows to each other, and leave the hall.

Evening Service
Fukanzazengi (Zazen Rules)

The trainees either go in procession into the ceremony hall or else sit in their places in the meditation hall. The disciplinarian rings the *inkin* (small bell) once for each of the Three Refuges and then intones the following:

Zazen Rules*

All: Why are training and enlightenment differentiated since the Truth is universal? Why study the means to attaining it since the supreme teaching is free? Since Truth is seen to be clearly apart from that which is unclean, why cling to a means of cleansing it? Since Truth is not separate from training, training is unnecessary. However, the separation would be as that between heaven and earth if even the slightest gap existed.* When the opposites arise, the Buddha Mind is lost. However much you may be proud of your understanding, however much you may be enlightened, whatever your attainment of wisdom and supernatural power, your finding of the way to mind illumination, your power to touch heaven and to enter into enlightenment, when the opposites arise you have almost lost the way to salvation. Although the Buddha had great wisdom at birth, he sat in training for six years. Although Bodhidharma transmitted the Buddha Mind, we still hear the echoes of his nine years facing a wall. The ancestors were very diligent, and there is no reason why we people of the present day cannot understand. All you have to do is cease from erudition, withdraw within and reflect upon yourself. Should you be able to cast off body and mind naturally, the Buddha Mind will immediately manifest itself. If you want to find it quickly, you must start at once.

You should meditate in a quiet room, eat and drink

moderately. Cut all ties; give up everything; think of neither good nor evil; consider neither right nor wrong. Control mind-function, will, consciousness, memory, perception and understanding; you must not strive thus to become Buddha. Cling to neither sitting nor lying down. Place a round cushion on top of a thick square one on your seat. Some people meditate in the full-lotus position and others in the half-lotus. In the full-lotus position your right foot is placed upon your left thigh and your left foot is placed upon your right thigh. In the half-lotus position the left foot is placed upon the right thigh and nothing more. Do not wear tight clothing. Rest the right hand on the left foot and the left hand in the palm of the right hand with the thumbs touching lightly. Sit upright, leaning neither to left nor right, backwards or forwards. The ears must be in line with the shoulders and the nose in line with the navel. The tongue must be held lightly against the back of the top teeth with the lips and teeth closed. Keep the eyes open. Breathe in quickly, settle the body comfortably and breathe out sharply. Sway the body left and right, then sit steadily with the legs crossed, neither trying to think nor trying not to think. Just sitting with no deliberate thought is the important aspect of Zazen.

This type of Zazen is not something that is done in stages of meditation. It is simply the lawful gateway to carefree peace. To train and enlighten oneself is to become thoroughly wise. The kōan appears naturally in daily life. If you become thus utterly free, you will be as the water wherein the dragon dwells or as the mountain whereon the tiger roams. Understand clearly that the Truth appears naturally, and then your mind will be free from doubts and vacillation. When you wish to rise from Zazen, sway the body gently from side to side and rise quietly. The body must make no violent movement. I myself have seen that the ability to die whilst sitting and standing, which transcends both peasant and sage, is obtained through the power of Zazen. It is no more possible to understand natural activity with the discriminatory mind than it is possible to understand the signs of enlightenment. Nor is it possible to understand training and enlightenment by supernatural means. Such understanding is outside the realm of speech and vision. Such Truth is beyond discrimination. Do not discuss the wise and the ignorant. There is only one thing, to train hard, for this is true enlightenment. Training and enlightenment are naturally undefiled. To live by Zen is the same as to live an ordinary daily life. The Buddha Seal has been preserved both by the Buddhas in the present world and by those in the world of the Indian and Chinese patriarchs; they are thus always spreading true Zen. All activity is permeated with pure Zazen. The means of training are thousandfold, but pure Zazen must be done. It is futile to travel to other dusty countries, thus forsaking your own seat. If your first step is false you will immediately stumble. Already you are in possession of the vital attributes of a human being. Do not waste time with this and that. You can possess the authority of Buddha. Of what use is it merely to enjoy this fleeting world? This body is as transient as dew on the grass; life passes as swiftly as a flash of lightning. Quickly the body passes away; in a moment life is gone. O sincere trainees, do not doubt the true dragon; do not spend so much time in rubbing only a part of the elephant. Look inward and advance directly along the road that leads to the Mind; respect those who have reached the goal of goalessness; become one with the wisdom of the Buddhas; transmit the wisdom of the patriarchs. † If you do these things for some time, you will become as herein described. † Then the treasure house will open naturally and you will enjoy it fully.

The following offertory is then recited by either the disciplinarian or his assistant alone:

> * We offer the merits of this scripture reading to all so that they may be able to obtain the Truth.

All: * Homage to all the Buddhas in all worlds;
> * Homage to all the Bodhisattvas in all worlds;
> * Homage to the Scripture of Great Wisdom.

Mealtime Ceremonial

THE FOLLOWING should be recited at both breakfast and lunch but never at supper, the reason being that Shakyamuni Buddha did not eat after twelve noon. For this same reason the actual begging bowl is never used for supper, but one or two of the other bowls which make up the trainee's set of food utensils. In actual practice, however, this ceremonial is seldom used for lunch, the recitation of the Scripture of Great Wisdom or the *Sandōkai* being preferred together with the special lunchtime verse which is included, as an alternative to the breakfast verse, in the middle of this official ceremony.

The disciplinarian strikes the wooden block once, and everyone opens the covering on his food bowls and begins to spread them out.

All: The Lord Buddha was born in Kabira,
Enlightened in Makada,
Taught in Harana,
Died in Kuchira.
As we spread the vessels of the Lord we pray
That they who eat, the things that are eaten
And the actual eating shall be universally void of self.

Disciplinarian alone, after again striking the wooden block:

We take refuge in the Buddha,
The completely perfect scriptures,
The patriarchs and Bodhisattvas
Whose merit is beyond all understanding.

The following is recited only if a donor has made an offering of food to the community. Disciplinarian alone:

> Today a donor has offered food. I pray you all to understand well his reasons for doing so, which I am about to read to you.
>
> *(The statement of the donor is read.)*
>
> I have read the donor's reasons for his offering, and I call upon the Buddhas and Bodhisattvas to witness its sincerity, for they are endowed with holy eyes which can see beyond both self and other. Now let us chant the Names of the Ten Buddhas in chorus.

If there is no offering from a donor, the foregoing is omitted. All chant the following:

> * The completely pure Buddha, Birushanofū, Dharma itself;
> * The complete Buddha who has been rewarded for his previous training;
> * Shakyamuni Buddha, one of the many Buddhas who has appeared in the many worlds;
> * Miroku Buddha, who will appear in the future;
> * All the Buddhas in all directions and in the Three Worlds;
> * The great and excellent Dharma Lotus Scripture;
> * Holy Monju Bodhisattva;
> * The great and wise Fugen Bodhisattva;
> * The great and kind Kanzeon;
> * All the Bodhisattvas and ancestors;
> * The Scripture of Great Wisdom.

Disciplinarian alone:

> In the beginning the mallet will strike the Buddha on the foot;
> Later it will strike him on the head.
> Having taken refuge in the Three Treasures
> All will be able to grasp them perfectly.

The disciplinarian recites the following at breakfast only, after striking the wooden block:

> The ten benefits bless the breakfast gruel
> And all trainees profit greatly therefrom;
> Since the results thereof are limitless and wonderful
> Pleasure is ours for eternity.

The disciplinarian recites the following at lunch only, after striking the wooden block:

> Since I will give Three Merits and six tastes
> To all the Buddhas and the members of the priesthood,
> All sentient beings within the universe
> Will enjoy this offering.

The disciplinarian strikes the wooden block once, and the chief junior recites the following alone, loudly:

> The two kinds of alms, material and spiritual,
> Have the endowment of boundless merit;
> Now that they have been fulfilled in this act of charity
> Both self and others gain pleasure therefrom.

The disciplinarian strikes the wooden block again to announce the arrival of the food, and all recite the following:

> We will first share the merits of this food with the Three
>   Treasures of the Dharma;
> Second, we will share it with the four benefactors, the Bud-
>   dha, the president, our parents and all people;
> Third, we will share it with the six lokas;
> With all of these we share it and to all we make offering
>   thereof.
> The first bite is to discard all evil;
> The second bite is so that we may train in perfection;
> The third bite is to help all beings;
> We pray that all may be enlightened.
> We must think deeply of the ways and means by which this
>   food has come.

We must consider our merit when accepting it.
We must protect ourselves from error by excluding greed
from our minds.
We will eat lest we become lean and die.
We accept this food so that we may become enlightened.

During the recitation above, food has been served out to the trainees, and at the end of it, the food offering for the spirits of the departed is made. When all have finished eating, including those who have asked for second helpings, the abbot's attendant strikes the wooden block once and the disciplinarian recites the following:

We offer this water to the spirits of the departed so that
they too may be filled.

The abbot's attendant strikes the wooden block again, and the disciplinarian recites alone:

The universe is as the boundless sky,
As lotus blossoms above unclean water;
Pure and beyond the world is the mind of the trainee;
O Holy Buddha, we take refuge in Thee.

Various Short Ceremonies

KESA VERSE

This is used for the putting on of the kesa each morning, and is recited whilst the folded kesa is placed upon the trainee's head:

> How great and wondrous are the clothes of enlightenment,
> Formless, yet embracing every treasure;
> I wish to unfold the Buddha's teaching
> That I may help all living things.

The kesa is then unfolded and the trainee puts it on.

SHAVING VERSE

This is recited by everyone three times prior to the shaving of heads, whilst making gasshō:

> Now, as we are being shaved, let us pray that
> We may leave behind selfish desires for eternity;
> After all, neither birth nor death exists.

TOILET VERSE

Whilst making gasshō, this verse is recited prior to cleaning the teeth:

> I take the toothbrush that all living things may profit;
> May they understand the Truth quickly and become naturally pure.

After the cleaning is over, the following is recited:

> Our teeth have been cleaned this morning so that all living
> things may profit;
> Since they control the fang of delusion, let us crush delusion as this toothbrush has been crushed in the mouth.

BATH VERSE

Before entering the bathroom, three bows are made to Badarobosatsu in front of the altar outside the bathroom, and the following is recited once with each bow:

> I must cleanse my body and my heart.

When the bath is over, three more bows are made to the same altar whilst the following is recited once with each bow:

> I have cleansed my body;
> I pray that I may cleanse my heart.

LAVATORY VERSE

Prior to entering the lavatory the following is recited three times:

> Adoration to all the Buddhas.
> Adoration to the limitless teaching.
> Peace! Speak! Blaze! Up! Open!
> To the glorious, peaceful one for whom there is no
> Disaster whilst upon the water-closet, hail!

LECTURE VERSE

This is recited by all prior to any lecture given by the abbot and is preceded by one stroke of the small bell:

> The unsurpassed, penetrating and perfect Truth
> Is seldom met with even in a hundred, thousand, myriad
>   kalpas.
> Now we can see and hear it, we can remember and accept it;
> I vow to make the Buddha's Truth one with myself.

After the lecture is over all recite the following:

> * Homage to all the Buddhas in all worlds;
> * Homage to all the Bodhisattvas in all worlds;
> * Homage to the Scripture of Great Wisdom.

Meditation Hall Closing Ceremony

THE OFFICIAL NAME of this ceremony is translatable as "Recitation of Prayer," but since it is performed on the day the meditation hall is closed so that the trainees may rest and bathe—that is, on any day of the month in which there is a four or a nine—I have called it the meditation hall closing ceremony.

The wooden block is beaten and the bell struck seven times alternately. When all the trainees are present and standing in front of the meditation hall, the disciplinarian recites the following alone:

> * The Light of Buddha is increasing in brilliance and the Wheel of the Dharma is always turning. These temple buildings and this ground are guarding the Dharma and the trainees. All dhyānas are full of treasure and wisdom, and because of them, we are going to pray to the Ten Buddhas.

All recite the following, and the meditation hall bell is struck at the beginning of each line:

> The completely pure Buddha, Birushanofū, Dharma itself;
> The complete Buddha who has been rewarded for his previous training;
> Shakyamuni Buddha, one of the many Buddhas who has appeared in the many worlds;
> Miroku Buddha, who will appear in the future;
> All the Buddhas in all directions and in the Three Worlds;
> The great and excellent Dharma Lotus Scripture;
> Holy Monju Bodhisattva;
> The great and wise Fugen Bodhisattva;

The great and kind Kanzeon;
All the Bodhisattvas and ancestors;
The Scripture of Great Wisdom.

The chief junior then says in a low voice:

Rest.

General and Special Offertories

GENERAL OFFERTORY 1

This is recited by the disciplinarian in either the meditation hall or the ceremony hall during memorial ceremonies for the dead, after recitation of the scripture chosen by the deceased's relatives:

> The great saint turns the Wheel of the Law and thereby shows many aspects of the Truth. He rescues those who are in distress and brings them to great happiness. Let us pray that the Three Treasures of the Dharma may be always watching clearly. We have offered incense, flowers, candles, lanterns, cakes, tea and other good food in the hope that the merit we accrue in making these offerings will be given to (name of deceased), wherever he may be. We have recited the (name of scripture) for his benefit. We pray that the light of the spirit of Truth shall shine of itself and pierce the darkness of the streets of delusion. We sincerely pray that the mountain of (his/her) karma shall vanish and the flowers of the Mind bloom in the springtime of enlightenment. Let us pray that we may all ascend the brilliant altar and realise the Truth.

GENERAL OFFERTORY 2

This is used as an alternative to the offertory above:

> When we are one with enlightenment, we know that there is complete immaculacy and universal light. Utter quietness embraces the sky. When we return to the world, we know that everything is as a dream. Let us pray that the Three Treasures of the Dharma may be always watching clearly. We have offered incense, flowers, candles, lanterns, tea, cakes and other good food and have recited the (name of scripture). We pray that the merit we accrue in making

these offerings may be given to (name of deceased). We pray that when we are in delusion the jewels of enlightenment shall shine of themselves, and that when we are in enlightenment the circle of japonica shall be high in the blue sky. Let us walk on the way to enlightenment with all living things.

OBON OFFERTORY

This is recited by the priest of any temple when making his yearly visit to the family altars of his parishioners:

Let us pray that the Three Treasures of the Dharma may be always watching clearly. We have made a beautiful altar and offered incense, flowers, candles, food and other offerings and have recited the (name of scripture). We pray that the merit we accrue from making these offerings shall be given to (names of all the family dead). We sincerely pray that (he/she/they) may escape from karma and obtain true freedom, either knowingly or unknowingly. We pray that (he/she/they) may realise that there is neither birth nor death.

OFFERTORY FOR THE FESTIVAL OF HANAMATSURI, THE BUDDHA'S BIRTHDAY, MAY 8

This is recited after the scriptures chosen for the day by the disciplinarian:

* From Great Compassion comes forth the Pure Dharma Body, unborn, uncreated. We pray that the darkness of our delusions may be illuminated by True Compassion. On this eighth day of May we are gathered here to offer sweet tea, flowers, fruit, candles, water and cakes to celebrate the birth of our Great Master Shakyamuni Buddha, and out of gratitude we wish to offer the merits of the recitation of (name of scripture). The wonderful udumbara flower bloomed upon this day, and the meaning of this festival is found within its blossom. Even as its sweet fragrance fills the whole world, so does Buddhism cover the world. The birth of Shakyamuni brought the sun of hope to a world of dark-

ness and illuminated the whole universe. He took upon himself the form of a human being, was born with the thirty-two marks of a Buddha and, for unmeasurable time, pursued works of great compassion. He found and transcended the cause of suffering; all beings, whether saints or laymen, praise this magnificent understanding. His three hundred sermons are for us as rain is for trees and grass. Just as rain causes drooping flowers to flourish, so his words touch our heavy hearts. At this very moment the Rain of the Dharma pours into the Lake of Kindness. The merit of his life may be likened to the wind which, as it bends the grass and fans the leaves, blows the good seed of the Dharma to take root in the hearts of the people all over the world even after two thousand years, and will continue to do so not only in this world but also in the next. We, the followers of our Great Master Shakyamuni, bow in gratitude to him for his goodness and compassion as we celebrate his birthday. We pray that his halo, which is the Light of the Dharma, will illuminate the darkness of the delusion of those beings of this world who have not yet heard his Name. We pray that all beings may be saved and thus prosper for all eternity. We pray that the seed of Buddhahood will bud and blossom into the flower of Enlightenment so that its beauty may fill the universe.

OFFERTORY FOR THE FESTIVAL OF JŌDŌ, ENLIGHTENMENT DAY, DECEMBER 8

The Enlightened One, with knowledge of all things, appeared in the Western Heaven, containing within himself the whole universe, worlds as numberless as the sands of the Ganges. We pray that all may be enlightened as he so that Great Compassion will be eternally ours. We are gathered here to celebrate the Enlightenment of our Great Master Shakyamuni, and we offer incense, flowers, candles, water, cakes and tea and have recited the (name of scripture) out of gratitude to him. Just as a furnace is needed to melt jars, bowls, hairpins, bracelets and other objects into one mass of metal, so the fire of Buddha's Wisdom is needed to bring together the people of the world to the path of Buddhism, for they are of various colours, understanding and position. It takes a master of tonal appreciation to combine musical instruments in harmony in such a way that they produce the six tones of the sun and the six tones of shadow. In the same way a master like Shakyamuni, skilled in producing harmony among men, is needed to produce the magnificent sound of the Dharma. Though all already possess wisdom as great as that of Buddha himself and have the same Dharma Body, their progress is obstructed by greed, hate and delusion. If Buddha had not shown us the way of overcoming these, we would be as insane as Yajñadatta or make the same mistake as was made by the wrestler who lost the diamond that gleamed between his eyebrows by not knowing its value. Were it not for Shakyamuni we would have both forgotten and lost the Truth. When Shakyamuni was enlightened he said, "I was enlightened simultaneously with the universe," and now, as we hear these words, we are assured anew of our own Buddha Nature and our ability to enter the Path of Truth. When Shakyamuni died he told his followers to make his teaching the light of their lives and to make their own lives shine as brilliantly as the sun. The light of Shakyamuni and his followers has shone through many centuries and has been transmitted to countless people. We must follow in the footsteps of those who have gone before us so that our own light shines in the same way, and we must transmit it even as they did, so that it may shine brightly in countless worlds and lives to come.

OFFERTORY FOR THE FESTIVAL OF NEHAN, THE BUDDHA'S DEATH, FEBRUARY 15

The Dharma Body of the Buddha cannot be seen so long as one is within duality, for it is beyond birth and death, filling all things. Out of compassion for all living things the Buddha appeared in the form and figure of a human being. For this great act we bow in gratitude and pray that we may be able to illuminate our minds from delusion. On this fifteenth day of February we have gathered to commemorate our Lord Shakyamuni's entry into Parinirvāna, and we offer incense, flowers, candles, cakes, tea and fruit and the merits of the recitation of (name of scripture) out of gratitude for his Great Compassion. The moon over Mount Ryoju shines miraculously in all directions; the sāla trees bloom and their petals convey the fragrance of the Dharma down to the present time. The Buddha transcended desire and used the blessing of his understanding to help all who are deluded. After all delusion is removed, that which remains is called the True Form, the Form of Buddha, all. The merit of this Form has been a light for all from the far past until the present time. All forms of existence join in the grief of this day and wholeheartedly recite with us the (name of scripture). We are filled with awe at the countless voices and boundless light which proclaim the Dharma, and we vow to propagate it eternally.

OFFERTORY FOR THE FESTIVAL OF DARUMA, BODHIDHARMA DAY, OCTOBER 5

The Dharma Body of the Buddha cannot be seen so long as one is within duality, for it is beyond birth and death, filling all things. Out of compassion for all living things the Buddha appeared in the form and figure of a human being. For this great act we bow in gratitude and pray that we may be able to illuminate our minds from delusion. On this fifth day of October we commemorate the death of the First Patriarch, Engaku Daishi, Bodhidharma. We are gathered here to offer incense, flowers, candles, cakes, fruit and tea and the merits of the recitation of the (name of scripture) out of gratitude for his Great Compassion. Bodhidharma was the son of the king of southern India; he was very imposing in appearance. Although he was the possessor of many jewels, he realised that they were not the true and shining Treasure and were utterly valueless, so he left behind worldly things and began monastic training. He went to China and there became the First Patriarch, showing the others the Way as does Kanzeon Bosatsu. Because of his deep desire to rescue all beings he travelled many roads and crossed the great sea to China. He was the twenty-eighth person after Shakyamuni to receive the Truth, and this highest of all possessions he carried to China with him. He did not try to explain the Dharma in words; instead, by just keeping the Precepts and doing silent Zazen, he taught all around him. It was King Butei who called him to China, and because of their conversation, Bodhidharma sat facing a wall for nine years. When the snow lay deep upon the ground, he received a truly worthy follower. When we think wholeheartedly of the merit of his actions, we see that it has illuminated a thousand autumns and still embraces his uncountable family warmly in the Dharma. Just as one branch of a tree can produce five flowers, so his Transmission has flowered and its perfume fills countless places in which Buddhist training is being truly undergone.

OFFERTORY FOR THE FESTIVAL OF KAISAN, FOUNDER'S DAY,
NOVEMBER I

The Dharma Body of the Buddha cannot be seen so long as one is within duality, for it is beyond birth and death, filling all things. Out of compassion for all living things the Buddha appeared in the form and figure of a human being. For this great act we bow in gratitude, and pray that we may be able to illuminate our minds from delusion. On this first day of November we are gathered to commemorate the death of our Founder, the great Priest Keidō Chisan Kōhō Zenji, and we offer incense, flowers, candles, cakes, tea and fruit and the merit of the (name of scripture) out of gratitude for his Great Compassion. His Dharma Eye was as bright as the moon and his Light of Wisdom lit the darkness of those in delusion. Because of his deep Zen he knew true freedom and his heart was as constant as an iron rock; he could not help but rescue all the deluded and spread the Dharma. Just as Indra pointed a blade of grass at the earth and a magnificent temple sprang up on that very spot, so wherever a True Heart exists, the Dharma springs up also. In the same way has our Founder made possible this temple as our training place. Because of this temple's existence we can gather around our Founder as children around their parents. So that he could lead all seekers of the Way, he was at times as the bright moon and again at times as a voice of thunder. When the rhinoceros tried to reach the reflection of the moon in the water, the moonlight remained upon his horns; when the elephant was alarmed by thunder, flowers suddenly blossomed upon his tusks. The followers of our Founder spread as the branches of a tree, and the Wheel of the Dharma continues to roll; the temple prospers and its gate shall always stand wide open for all who truly seek the Way. The offering that we place in the fathomless begging bowl is formless and unlimited in weight and flavour, for it is the offering of our own Buddhist training that we bring today. Let us eat this daily and pray that all within this temple may be saved thereby.

Short Scriptures

ADORATION OF THE BUDDHA'S RELICS

This may be recited, instead of any of the other scriptures included in the Morning Service, at memorial ceremonies for the dead together with either of the two general offertories in the previous section.

> * Homage to the relics of the Buddha of Complete Merit; Homage to the Body of Truth which is Truth Itself and a Stūpa for the World of the Dharma for the benefit of our present body. Through the Merits of Buddha, the Truth enters into us and we enter into the Truth. Through the excellent power of Buddha we realise the Truth. Let us do only good for all living things that we may possess the True Mind. † Let us do only pure deeds that we may enter the peaceful world which is unchanging, Great Wisdom. † Let us pay homage eternally to the Buddha.

(It is customary to recite this three times.)

REVOLVING THE SCRIPTURES

This is recited by all at the time of the revolving of the numerous books of the Scripture of Great Wisdom, each trainee naming the number of the volume that he personally happens to be revolving.

> This is the Scripture of Great Wisdom, Volume . . . . That which is wondrous appears before us. The True Wisdom embraces both the wise and the foolish; its excellent light shines throughout the universe. That which is evil will for ever be frustrated. Let us overcome all evil and do all that is good.

249

Jūkai. Receiving the Ten Precepts

THIS IS the most important set of ceremonies in the life of a layman, and no person may become a trainee unless he has undergone the week of training that these ceremonies occupy, either before his ordination or within a year of entering a training temple. Jūkai, which is held every spring, comprises four principal ceremonies: the Reading of the *Kyojūkaimon*, Sange, Ketchimyaku and Recognition. Although in the large temples such as Sōjiji a vast concourse of priests and trainees is assembled for these ceremonies and laymen come from all over Japan, only three priests and seven witnesses are actually necessary. Like the other great set of ceremonies, Kessei, Jūkai can be compressed into a much shorter time than a week, frequently taking place in two or three days. This practice is to be deprecated, however, since neither the laymen nor the trainees are then able to benefit from the week-long meditation which occupies their time between these ceremonies, as well as the discipline of having to be strictly vegetarian during the entire period with no possibility of leaving the temple for a quick snack.

Laymen may attend Jūkai every year, if they so wish, but the layman's ordination, Jūkai Tokudō, can be undergone only once. After the laymen arrive at the temple they are set to meditate until six in the evening, when the bell of the ceremony hall is rung. Then all go in procession, preceded by the disciplinarian and his assistant, both carrying small bells, to the main guest hall of the abbot's house, where the preceptor performs the first of the four principal ceremonies.

READING OF THE KYOJŪKAIMON
When all those who are to take the Precepts are assembled in the guest hall in silence and sitting as if in Zazen, the preceptor, to-

gether with his attendant and two candle bearers, comes in procession from the abbot's room and sits in the lecturer's chair. The congregation bows three times, and the disciplinarian requests the reading of the Precepts in the name of the congregation:

> Great priest, I pray that you may administer the Precepts to these worthy persons who wish to practise the Buddha's Way during this week and become the Buddha's sons and daughters.

The attendant carries the Precepts Book to the preceptor, who bows and opens it, but leaves it in the hands of the attendant, who kneels in front of him. The candle bearers hold their candles close to the book on either side of the celebrant so that he may see to read easily. The *Kyojūkaimon* (see Book III) is then chanted by the preceptor. When he has finished chanting he bows again to the book and closes it, and the attendant takes it away, returning to his place slightly to the rear of the preceptor's chair.

> *Preceptor:* From this earthly body to that of becoming Buddha, will you keep these Precepts or not?
> *Congregation:* I will.

All make three bows again as the disciplinarian rings his bell, and the preceptor and his attendants leave the room. The congregation returns to the meditation hall, where all continue to meditate and search their hearts in readiness for the second and most solemn of all Zen ceremonies.

SANGE (CEREMONY OF CONFESSION)

The following night the congregation and trainees scrub the temple thoroughly; no part of it may be left uncleaned. They then make their way to the part of the temple that has been chosen for the commencement of the great procession. Wherever this procession starts from, the participants must go completely barefoot; absolutely no make-up is permitted and no highly coloured clothing; most of the older persons participating wear white rags for clothes. At a little before midnight the disciplinarian and his assistant take their places at the head of the procession with their small bells, which must play two different notes. The disciplinarian intones the following:

Homage to Shakyamuni Buddha.

The entire procession takes up the chant and repeats it constantly as it moves in procession very slowly towards the ceremony hall with the two bells playing alternately. The entire way has been hung with red hangings so that those taking part in the procession will have no knowledge of where they are being led. After a considerable distance, which is usually created illusively by the hangings being so placed that the procession doubles back on itself several times, a small altar recessed into one side of the hangings is reached, where the preceptor, now sitting as the representative of Maitreya, hands each person a small piece of folded paper after censing it. This paper, on which is written a single Chinese character representing all the past evil committed by the person concerned, is received with gasshō and borne reverently by the recipient as the procession and chant continue, usually for another two or three long turns and doublings back, until a second recessed altar is reached, behind which sits the confessor, representing Mañjuśrī. Each member of the congregation bows and hands the paper he is carrying to the confessor, who receives it in acknowledgement of the fact that the person is now solemnly determined to abandon all his past evil and symbolises this by handing it over to the confessor. The procession continues along its red-curtained way to a third altar, behind which sits the ordination master, representing Shakyamuni Buddha, who, in recognition of the fact that the congregation members have now solemnly renounced their past evil, offers incense and bows to each one as he or she arrives in front of him. The procession continues a little further, emerging finally into the ceremony hall, where all sit down in silence. The disciplinarian chants the renunciation prayer as each person passes the ordination master:

> All wrong actions, behaviour and karma perpetrated by me from time immemorial have been, and are, caused by greed, anger and delusion which have no beginning, born of my body, mouth and will; I now make full and open confession thereof.

When all have sat down, the three priests—ordination master, confessor and preceptor—enter the hall, and a huge cauldron is brought by the attendants and placed in front of the altar. The charcoal within it is lighted, and the three priests drop the confession papers one by one into the flames. When all have been thrown into the fire, the three priests stir the coals with pokers to make certain that every paper is reduced to ashes. They then utter a great cry, called a *kwatz,* to scare away any evildoers or demons who may still be lurking in the hall. The preceptor then recites the following:

> Now, by the guidance of the Buddhas and ancestors, you have discarded and purified all your karma of body, mouth and will and have obtained great immaculacy. This is by the power of confession.

The three priests and their attendants go out in procession, and the congregation is led back to the meditation hall along a quick route by the disciplinarian's assistant. After a further day of meditation, the congregation reassembles in the ceremony hall for the ceremony of the Ketchimyaku. (This is during an ordinary Jūkai, where no persons are being given lay ordination. If some persons are to be admitted as actual lay disciples, the lay ordination ceremony, which is a shortened form of the ordination ceremony, is administered first.)

CEREMONY OF THE KETCHIMYAKU

There is a highly elaborate procession, and the congregation enters the ceremony hall together with the ordination master, candle bearers and two thurifers, the latter walking in front. The master ascends the high altar as Shakyamuni's representative and sits as if in meditation. The only lights in the hall are those of the candles. The congregation bows three times, and the ordination master calls for the torch and his Ketchimyaku. A large pine-resin torch is lit and brought to the master's side. The assistant unrolls the silken Ketchimyaku against the master's left arm, and the master holds the top of it against his left shoulder so that it descends the full length of his arm. He then states his lineage from the time of Shakyamuni Buddha to the present, and explains in his own words his understanding of the Truth of the Buddhas that he received from his own master, paying special attention to the fact that the Precepts are the lifeblood of the Buddhas and are represented by the red lifeline of the Ketchimyaku, which, when each of the congregation members' names has been added to it, will return upon itself to Shakyamuni Buddha whence it stemmed. Therefore each member of the congregation is the ancestor of Shakyamuni himself. When the master has finished speaking, the assistant rolls up the Ketchimyaku and a large tray of small paper Ketchimyakus is brought; the master then gives one to each member of the congregation as they come up to him. Each Ketchimyaku bears the name of the person concerned upon the bloodline immediately below that of the master. When all have been given their Ketchimyakus, the master leaves the room in procession, and the congregation, after making three bows, returns to the meditation hall. The following night the ceremony of Recognition takes place.

CEREMONY OF RECOGNITION

The congregation goes in procession to the ceremony hall, and all sit down facing the altar. They are led in batches of from six to twelve around behind the high altar where the three priests, together with any other priests who may be in the temple, are seated in front of the statue or tomb of the founder of the temple, which has its veils removed so the congregation may see it clearly. Each batch of congregation members is then led up the steps to the high altar, where they sit down; the priests bow to them as newly born Buddhas, and the members bow back again. The priests then go in procession around the high altar, one complete circuit for each batch of congregation members, ringing their begging bells or bell-staffs and chanting the following:

Buddha recognises Buddha and Buddha bows to Buddha.

When all the congregation members have thus been recognised by the priests, they are grouped in the centre of the hall, and all the priests and trainees in the building form a circle around them, ringing either begging bells or bell-staffs whilst they continue the chant, and making an extra amount of noise with the bells as they pass each corner of the hall. When they have made three complete circuits of the hall, they leave in procession. The congregation makes three bows to the altar and returns to the meditation hall. The laymen leave the temple early next morning.

Ordination Ceremony

THE ABBOT'S ASSISTANT leads the disciple in front of the Buddha statue, where the disciple burns incense and bows three times. He then goes to the ordination master's chair, burns incense and again bows three times. He kneels upright, making gasshō, and the master holds the *heirō* (censer), burns incense and recites the following three times quietly:

> Homage to all the Buddhas;
> Homage to all the Dharmas;
> Homage to all the Sanghas;
> Homage to our Real Teacher, Shakyamuni Buddha;
> Homage to all the Bodhisattva ancestors;
> I pray that you will all come here as witnesses.

The master puts down the censer, strikes the wooden blocks once and recites the following, continuing to strike the wooden blocks once at the end of each line:

> Let us pray to the Ten Buddhas.
> The completely pure Buddha, Birushanofū, Dharma itself;
> The complete Buddha who has been rewarded for his previous training;
> Shakyamuni Buddha, one of the many Buddhas who has appeared in the many worlds;
> Miroku Buddha, who will appear in the future;
> All the Buddhas in all directions and in the Three Worlds;
> The great and excellent Dharma Lotus Scripture;
> Holy Monju Bodhisattva;
> The great and wise Fugen Bodhisattva;
> The great and kind Kanzeon;
> All the Bodhisattvas and ancestors;
> The Scripture of Great Wisdom.

The master continues:

> You, good (man/woman), the source of the mind is
> completely calm and the Sea of the Dharma is fathomless.
> One who cannot realise it will sink eternally, and one who
> realises it will be enlightened instantaneously. It is by enter-
> ing the priesthood that we unknowingly enjoy enlighten-
> ment. Indeed, do not doubt. To become a priest or priestess
> is the best way to let both mind and body become one with
> the Truth. Why? Because when we cut off our hair and the
> root of human ties, the Truth manifests itself. When we
> change our clothes and live beyond the world, we can attain
> freedom. Therefore, among all the Buddhas in the Three
> Worlds, no one has been able to become a Buddha when
> he or she appeared as an ordinary person. The merit of
> becoming a priest or priestess is the most excellent of all
> merits. For example, there is great merit in building a pagoda
> as high as the thirty-third heaven, but by comparison with
> entering the priesthood, the merit is one-hundredth. We
> cannot measure the worth. A pagoda may become ruined
> and unuseable, but the merit of becoming a priest or priest-
> ess is always increasing towards enlightenment and will
> never lose its power for eternity. Therefore we can be far
> beyond all delusion without throwing away this earthly
> body. Even though we do not yet know our enlightenment,
> we are already the real children of Buddha. We are the
> most excellent among all beings in the Three Worlds.
> Whilst we are dwelling in the six lokas, this is the highest
> life. Please think carefully. Now you are being released from
> eternal wandering and are entering the no-birth country of
> Buddha. Delusion, which is beginningless, has now ceased,
> and the real merit of the Truth has been made complete.
> Therefore, after we enter the priesthood, heaven neither
> covers us nor does the earth sustain. We are not mistaken
> for other beings. We have nothing with which to cover our
> round heads. Our square clothes are the symbol of enlight-
> enment. One who sees us will gain much benefit, and our
> relatives will obtain an excellent reward. Our rank is beyond

the Three Worlds and our merit is the highest of all. Even a king is lower than we are. Even our parents are not more respectable than we. All deities are lower than you. You must worship nothing except your master and your greater self. There is no one whom we should respect except the Buddhas and patriarchs; therefore the verse says:

> In the drifting, wandering world it is very difficult to cut off our human ties.
> Now we are going to throw them away and enter nothingness.
> This is real gratitude.

You, think of your parents' kindness to you and then sincerely say good-bye. Think of the kindness of the ruler of this country and tell him what you are doing. This is the real proof of being apart from the world and a special symbol of being noble. Tell your guardian deity what you are doing and repay his kindness to you. Also tell the deity in the place where you were born what you are doing. They will both guard you.

The disciple bows once and leaves the room. Guided by the abbot's assistant, he goes to the tablets for the ruler, the deity, his father and mother, and bows once to each. He returns to the Buddha and bows three times and then to the ordination master once. He then sits in front of the master, making gasshō. The assistant trainees part his hair in the middle and tie it up in bunches, if it is long. The master holds up the razor and recites the following three times, together with all the trainees:

> Good, you, the (great man/great woman), realise the drifting, wandering world, have thrown it away and entered Nirvāna. This is rare and cannot be realised with the ordinary mind.

The master pours perfumed water on the disciple's hair and begins to shave him. Then he gives the razor to the assistant trainees or his personal attendants, and they continue the shaving; first the left side is shaved, then the right. During the shaving the master, together with all the trainees, recites the following verse three times. They all continue to recite it until the shaving is finished:

> All Bodhisattvas, when converted to the Truth for the first time, search therefor, but their minds are hard and set and cannot be broken. The merit of first mind is the widest and most completely fathomless. Even if Buddhas explain it fully, such explanation can never be enough.

When the shaving is completed except for a small round patch on the crown of the head, called the *shūra*, the assistant dresses the disciple in the koromo. He then bows three times, and the ordination master, again holding up the razor, asks the disciple the following three times:

> This last part is called the shūra. Only a Buddha can cut it off. I am going to cut it off. Do you permit me to do so or not?

The disciple replies once to each of the three repetitions:

> I do.

The master then cuts off the shūra whilst reciting the following with all the trainees:

> I have changed my form but kept my wish, cutting off worldly attachment; being apart from my family in order to seek for the Truth. I vow to help others.

The disciple returns to the master and burns incense in front of him, bows three times, sits down and makes gasshō. The master gives him his new name, written down, saying:

> This is your name.

The master then holds up the mat, censes it and gives it to the disciple, who stretches out his arms to receive it and holds it up. The disciple recites the following:

> Great Bodhisattvas, think wholeheartedly. I, the disciple (name), now have this mat which shall for ever guide my robes.

The master takes back the mat and gives it in a similar manner to the disciple twice more; the disciple recites the same verse twice more, making three times in all. He then spreads the mat, bows three times and again sits in front of the master. The master recites the following verse together with all the trainees:

> This excellent mat has been used by many Buddhas. Let us sit upon it always together with all beings.

The master gives the disciple the rakusu in the same way as the mat, and the disciple says:

> Great Bodhisattvas, think wholeheartedly. I, the disciple (name), have been given this rakusu, which has five stripes. I will always use it.

This is also given and received three times in the same way as the mat, and the preceding verse recited each time. The disciple puts on the rakusu, bows three times, takes it off again and puts it on the altar. The seven-striped kesa is given next three times, in the same way as the other garments, and the disciple receives it but does not put it on. The disciple recites the following three times:

> Great Bodhisattvas, think wholeheartedly. I, the disciple (name), now have this seven-striped kesa. I will always use it.

The disciple puts the kesa on, bows three times, takes it off again and puts it on the altar. The master gives him the nine-striped kesa in the same way as the seven-striped one, and the disciple says three times:

> Great Bodhisattvas, think wholeheartedly. I, the disciple (name), now have this nine-striped kesa. I will always use it.

The disciple puts on the kesa, bows three times, but does not take it off. Everyone recites the following verse together with the disciple whilst the kesa is being put on with the help of the assistant. This also is recited three times:

> How great and wondrous are the clothes of enlightenment,
> Formless, yet embracing every treasure;
> I wish to unfold the Buddha's teaching
> That I may help all living things.

The disciple bows three times again, and then the master gives him the bowls three times in the same way as the other things. The disciple says three times:

> Great Bodhisattvas, think wholeheartedly. I, the disciple (name), now have this begging bowl. I will always use it.

All recite the following:

> How great is this begging bowl which has every merit; I now have it and wish to rescue all beings in the universe.

The disciple puts the bowl on the altar and bows three times. Here follow the Bodhisattva Precepts. These should be given at the same time, or later on the same day. The disciple kneels in front of the master, makes gasshō, burns incense, and bows three times. The master recites the following:

> If you want to be converted to the Precepts you should first make confession. Even though in confession there are two meanings and two ways, there is a confession verse that has been kept by the Buddha. Recite the verse after me, because when you do so, all your past wrongdoing will disappear.

In a higher voice, he recites the following verse three times, clapping the wooden blocks at the end of each line:

> All the evil committed by me
> Is caused by beginningless greed, hate and delusion.
> All the evil is committed by our body, speech and mind.
> I now confess everything wholeheartedly.

The disciple bows once, makes gasshō and kneels as before. The master continues in his ordinary voice:

> You have purified your body and mind from evil and become clean by the power of confession. You should be converted to the Three Treasures, Buddha, Dharma and Sangha. There are three kinds of Three Treasures. When we are once converted the Three Merits are completed.

The master then holds up the asperge bowl and describes three counterclockwise circles with the branch of leaves in the water within it. He takes the spiritual "water" from his head three times and puts it into the bowl, after which he asperges the disciple's head three times. After this he asperges to the right and left three times each, thereafter returning the spiritual "water" to his head. He makes gasshō and recites the following:

> *Disciple (name), from this present human state to that of*
> *Buddhahood,*
> *Give homage to the Buddha,*
> *Homage to the Dharma,*
> *Homage to the Sangha,*
> *Homage to the Highest Buddha,*
> *Homage to the Most Immaculate Dharma,*
> *Homage to the Harmonious Sangha,*
> *Homage to the Buddha,*
> *Homage to the Dharma,*
> *Homage to the Sangha.*

This is repeated by the disciple and then recited again by everyone, making three times in all, the wooden blocks being clapped at the end of each line. The master continues:

> Now you have thrown away the past evil and been converted to the Truth. From this time the Buddha and the truest enlightenment are your true teacher, so call the Buddha your teacher and do not be converted to evil and other teaching. This is my great compassion to you.

The disciple bows three times and kneels upright. The master recites the following:

You have already been given the Three Treasures Precepts. Now you have obtained the rank of a (priest/priestess) and should be given the Three Pure Precepts and the Ten Greater Precepts. Then you will obtain the rank of Buddha. This is to become the real child of Buddha.

The master claps the wooden blocks once at the beginning of each Precept, and recites:

Cease from evil. From this present human state to that of becoming Buddha, will you keep this Precept or not?

The disciple answers:

I will.

The disciple makes the same reply to each of the Precepts listed below as the master recites them:

Do only good. From this present human state to that of becoming Buddha, will you keep this Precept or not?
Do good for others. From this present human state to that of becoming Buddha, will you keep this Precept or not?

These three are called the Three Pure Precepts.

Do not kill. From this present human state to that of becoming Buddha, will you keep this Precept or not?
Do not steal. From this present human state to that of becoming Buddha, will you keep this Precept or not?
Do not covet. From this present human state to that of becoming Buddha, will you keep this Precept or not?
Do not say that which is not true. From this present human state to that of becoming Buddha, will you keep this Precept or not?
Do not sell the wine of delusion. From this present human state to that of becoming Buddha, will you keep this Precept or not?
Do not speak against others. From this present human state to that of becoming Buddha, will you keep this Precept or not?
Do not be proud of yourself and devalue others. From this

present human state to that of becoming Buddha, will you keep this Precept or not?

Do not be mean in giving either Dharma or wealth. From this present human state to that of becoming Buddha, will you keep this Precept or not?

Do not be angry. From this present human state to that of becoming Buddha, will you keep this Precept or not?

Do not defame the Three Treasures. From this present human state to that of becoming Buddha, will you keep this Precept or not?

These Ten Greater Precepts you must keep. From this present human state to that of becoming Buddha, will you keep this Precept or not?

The disciple bows three times, and the master burns incense, makes gasshō and recites the offertory as follows:

Now the universe rejoices. The earth trembles and the flowers fall. The Bodhisattvas of other worlds ask their Buddha what this means, and the Buddha replies that a new disciple has been given the Pure, Great Precepts of the Bodhisattvas and has been converted to the Truth by the master who was given them before in the teaching of Shakyamuni, who is the Buddha of this world. The disciple will become a Buddha in the future through this merit; therefore the universe rejoices. The Bodhisattvas, on hearing this explanation, bow towards you, saying, "If this is so, you are the same as we. You are believing in and taking the Buddha for your master and making the Bodhisattvas your friends." After receiving these Precepts you obtain their unbreakable merit. This is the Permanent Precept. I pray that you may always keep it. You must never lose it. To have attained to such a relationship and to possess such a pure body is surely to have attained the world of the Precepts. Is this not so? To whom do we offer this merit? To where do we offer it? The offering, the donor and he who receives, these three things are completely immaculate. There is nothing to be desired. Let us, together with all living things, offer this common merit to the highest Truth.

All recite the following:

> * Homage to all the Buddhas in all worlds;
> * Homage to all the Bodhisattvas in all worlds;
> * Homage to the Scripture of Great Wisdom.

The master recites alone:

> We live in the world as if in the sky,
> Just as the lotus blossom is not wetted by the water that
>   surrounds it.
> The mind is immaculate and beyond the dust.
> Let us bow to the highest Lord.

The master rises, burns incense in front of the Buddha, and then leaves the room after all have made three bows.

HOW TO ARRANGE A ROOM FOR AN ORDINATION CEREMONY

If a temple is unavailable, the master's room may be used so long as a picture of the Buddha is hung on the wall in lieu of an altar.

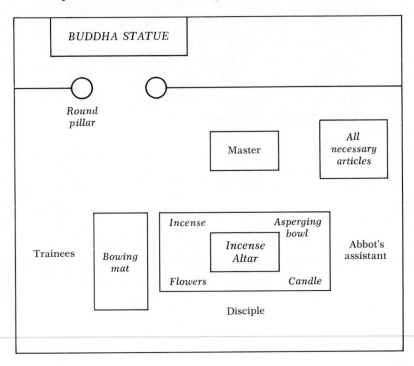

ORDINATION NAME CERTIFICATE

Ordination name	has been given the name of.... kesas, other things and the Precepts.	Temple name	Year
		Master's name (Seals)	Month
			Day

Kessei

THE FOLLOWING four ceremonies make up the whole of Kessei: Shin Zan, or the entrance of a new abbot to a temple; Nyudō-no-hai, or the entrance of a new chief junior to the meditation hall; Hossen, the mondo ceremony for examining the understanding of a new chief junior; Jōdō, the mondo ceremony of a roushi. In a full training temple these ceremonies are performed separately over a period of a hundred days, but they can all be performed in as short a time as two or three days if the occasion requires. They must be performed if the roushi has only just been appointed to a new temple. It is not customary, even in large training temples, to hold more than two training periods of a hundred days each per year, so Kessei is usually held once in spring and once in autumn. Nyudō-no-hai, or the ceremony for entering the meditation hall, does not differ very much from that of an ordinary trainee, except that in the case of a chief junior certain greetings are made which would not ordinarily take place. This ceremony may therefore be used for the entrance of new trainees to the meditation hall, so long as those greetings are omitted.

SHIN ZAN

The new abbot or roushi is met at the house of the chief parishioner of the temple by the five trainees who will perform the duties of his assistants during the whole Kessei period. Each carries one of the new abbot's marks of office, according to length of discipleship, the eldest carrying the begging bowl and kesa box, the next the staff, the third the incense box, the fourth a long, lighted stick of incense, and the fifth anything else that may be needed. The roushi wears either scarlet or such colours as he wishes for the procession from the house to the temple, but must carry either a hossu or a nyoi. The procession consists of all the guest members of the priesthood, who are interspersed between the *chigo*, or children carrying lotus blossoms, followed by the priest, who walks beneath a scarlet umbrella carried by one of the temple council members. The five assistants follow in single file, and all the parishioners follow them. The procession is headed by the remaining members of the temple council, carrying their staffs of office. On arrival at the gate of the temple, where an altar has been set up just inside, the procession halts. The assistant with the incense stick approaches the abbot, who takes the stick, blesses it and offers it on the altar whilst saying the following:

> The gates of (name of) Temple stand open wide. Whilst I remain within this place, this gate shall never be closed to any living thing.

The big drum is then beaten as the abbot leaves the altar at the gate, and the drum-roll gains in volume as he approaches the entrance to the ceremony hall, ceasing with one loud crash as he comes to stand upon the bowing mat in front of the high altar. The assistant brings another stick of incense, which the abbot blesses and holds whilst reciting the following:

> The Light of Buddha shall shine immaculately throughout the whole world.

The abbot goes to the altar, after giving the incense stick back to the assistant. At the altar he takes the incense stick again and places it in the incense bowl. He returns to the bowing mat, and all make three bows. He goes to the altar of the guardians of the building and grounds, offers incense and says the following:

> For eternity you are blessing and guarding this place. I pray that your blessings upon this house may never cease.

The abbot makes three bows to the guardians and then goes to the altar of Bodhidharma, where he again offers incense in the same way as before, saying:

> You came from the west. What is this that is in front of me? Now that I am standing in front of you, what is it that is in front of me?

The abbot makes three bows as before and then goes, with the assistant, to the altar of the founder of the temple. He offers incense as before and says:

> Here is the true fountain of all favour. Even now it will be as it was in former days. For this purpose I pray that I may be able to do all things well, though I am so inexperienced in many matters. I pray your help.

The abbot bows three times and returns to the bowing mat. He does not bow again, but returns to his room.

NYUDŌ-NO-HAI

If the whole of Kessei is being performed in a short space of time, it is usual for this ceremony to take place the night before Shin Zan and for Jōdō to follow Shin Zan within a few minutes. However, since no temple can ever perform Shin Zan more than once in the lifetime of a priest but must perform the other ceremonies of Kessei on numerous occasions, Shin Zan has been put first and the other ceremonies afterwards.

The disciplinarian's assistant strikes the wooden block and all trainees enter the meditation hall. When they are all standing in front of their seats, the treasurer, chief cook and disciplinarian take up their places in front of the gaitan. The assistant brings the new chief junior along the gaitan to stand in front of the treasurer, chief cook and disciplinarian, where they all bow their heads whilst making gasshō. The chief junior also bows his head and makes gasshō. The treasurer, chief cook and disciplinarian recite the following:

> We greet you in the Name of the Buddha. We pray that you may continue in good health.

The assistant then leads the chief junior to the door of the meditation hall, where the disciplinarian is standing by the wooden block. The latter strikes the block once with the mallet and cries in a loud voice:

> The trainee (name) wishes to enter this meditation hall as chief junior. I beg all trainees to greet him cordially.

The assistant leads the chief junior to the censer, where the latter burns incense. The chief junior then removes his slippers, if he happens to be wearing them, and leaves them beside the left pillar of the entrance, which is the side by which he entered the hall. He then spreads his mat and makes three bows to Mañjuśrī. The assistant makes gasshō and, with the chief junior following him, also making gasshō with his head bowed, proceeds up the meditation hall in the direction of the statue, goes around behind it and back down the other side to arrive a little to the right of the abbot's chair. Both the chief junior and the assistant take two side-steps to the left, where, standing exactly in front of the abbot but being careful not to tread on his mat, the chief junior makes the following greeting:

> Great abbot, I greet you in the Name of the Buddha. I pray that you may continue in good health.

The chief junior then places his folded mat on the ground and makes three bows; the abbot makes one bow with the last of the chief junior's. The chief junior recites again:

> Great abbot, birth and death are a grave event and time flies as an arrow flies from a bow. I beg that I may sit within this hall beside you and learn from you.

He places his mat, folded, on the ground as before, and the bowing is done again in exactly the same way. The chief junior continues:

> Great abbot, I thank you for your great compassion.

The chief junior and the abbot both spread their mats. The chief junior again makes three bows and the abbot one. They then pick up and fold their mats and make gasshō to each other, and the chief junior takes one side-step to the left, turns to face the line of trainees with the assistant in front of him and, with head bowed and making gasshō, is led around the entire meditation hall in greeting to all the trainees. At the beginning and end of each line he makes an extra-deep bow; in front of the seats of the vice-abbot, the chief lecturer and the head of the meditation hall he takes two side-steps whilst facing these officials, makes a special deep bow whilst making gasshō, and then takes one more side-step to the left before turning to face the next line of trainees and proceeding down it as before. Having gone all around the hall, the assistant leads him around the gaitan in the same manner and then back into the hall again. He once more goes around behind the Mañjuśrī statue, makes two more side-steps towards the abbot, bows, makes one side-step left, bows to his own seat, spreads his mat, makes three bows to his seat, picks up the mat and stands in front of his seat. The assistant stands in front of him, and they make gasshō to each other with their heads bowed. The assistant returns to his own seat, and the chief junior remains in front of his with his hands in *shashu* (clasped). The disciplinarian strikes the block, saying:

> The chief junior (name) is now officially in charge of all trainees in this hall. I pray that you may all be obedient to his teaching and accept it with gratitude.

The abbot leaves the hall by the right side of the door, and the new chief junior leads all the trainees out of the hall behind him.

JŌDŌ

The drum is beaten in a level rhythm of one loud and one soft stroke alternately, and the procession enters, consisting of the abbot, his assistant and a junior assistant. The abbot carries his staff in his right hand and his hossu is his left. When he is standing in front of the altar, he hits the floor once with the staff and says:

> The white clouds are silent above the altar.

The abbot gives his staff to his assistant and climbs the steps to stand upon the high altar in the centre. He puts the hossu on the incense stand and recites:

> I, (the priest recites his own name and the name and address of the temple), offer this incense with bows of gratitude to Shakyamuni Buddha, to the highest patriarch, Kōsō Jōyō Daishi, and to the greatest patriarch, Taisō Jōsai

Daishi. I pray that, out of their great compassion, they will assist me. Upon this great day of Kessei my spirit kneels before them.

The abbot then makes an offering of incense and recites again:

I offer this incense in memory of the previous priests of this temple and also in memory of the former patriarchs. I pray that, out of their vast compassion, they will this day witness my words.

The abbot makes his second incense offering in the same way as the first, and recites again:

I offer this incense in memory of the Great Master (name of the priest from whom the abbot received his transmission), who is my True Master and the true Shakyamuni Buddha. I bow to his memory; I pray that he may assist me now upon this altar.

The five assistants process from their seats to stand in a line in front of the altar, where they bow to the abbot. The trainees on either side of the hall then bow, beginning with those on the abbot's right hand. The assistants return to their places, and the temple officers process from their places to stand in front of the altar, where they bow to the abbot, and the trainees on the left side of the hall bow. When the officers have returned to their places, the chief assistant climbs upon the altar, kneels down and offers incense, and hands the abbot a kyosaku in place of the hossu. He descends from the altar and goes to the centre of the ceremony hall, where he makes *dai monjin*. The disciplinarian recites the following:

All they who doubt that this is true Buddha, all the great saints and defenders of the faith, stand forth, question and gain proof.

The chief junior comes forward to ask his mondo; he is followed by each of the other juniors in turn, according to their rank and ending with the most senior one present. At the end of each question the trainee concerned makes the same statement:

> Great abbot, I thank you for your great compassion.

When all the questioning is finished, the disciplinarian makes a circle with the mallet and then hits the block once, saying:

> I certify that these answers are true.

The assistant again climbs the altar and takes the kyosaku from the abbot, replacing it with the hossu, and the abbot reveals the teaching that he received from his master at the time of his own transmission, which gave him his understanding. When this is finished, he descends from the altar and leaves the ceremony hall. The drum and all bells are beaten simultaneously.

HOSSEN

The chief junior, his assistant and all the priests who hold any temple office go in procession to the abbot's room, where they make three bows, and then proceed to the ceremony hall whilst the drum is beaten. The abbot sits upon his chair, and the chief junior's assistant sits in front and a little to the left of the abbot. The Scripture of Great Wisdom is recited very slowly, after which the chief junior recites loudly:

> Hear! The emperor of Ryo asked Bodhidharma the following question: "What is the first principle of Buddhism?" Bodhidharma replied, "There is no holiness." The emperor asked again, "What is it that is standing before me?" Bodhidharma replied, "I do not know." The emperor could not understand these answers, so Bodhidharma crossed the river and went to sit facing the wall in Shōrinji for nine years.

The chief junior closes the silk covers over the book in which this discourse is written and which was brought to him by the abbot's assistant during the recitation of the Scripture of Great Wisdom.

He carries it on a raised tray around the ceremony hall, and comes to stand in front of the abbot. He makes two side-steps to the right, holds up the tray, bows, takes two side-steps to the left, and brings the tray down to the abbot after coming to stand at his right side. The abbot takes the tray with both hands and places it on his own private altar. The chief junior returns in front of the abbot, unfolds his mat and makes three bows, placing his fan on the top edge of the mat before bowing. He then picks up the fan, then the mat, makes gasshō, walks to the disciplinarian's seat, places his folded mat on the floor, puts his fan on top of it and makes three bows. The disciplinarian bows once. The chief junior picks up the fan, then the mat, makes gasshō and walks to the seat of his ordination master, where he makes the same bows as he did to the disciplinarian. The chief junior then walks slowly, holding his fan in shashu, around behind the altar and makes the same bows to any official who may be sitting on the opposite side from the disciplinarian, returns around the back of the altar, and comes to stand again before the abbot, making two side-steps to the right before spreading his mat, placing his fan upon it and making three bows again as before. He picks up the fan and mat, in that order, takes two side-steps to the left and comes again to the right side of the abbot, who takes the bamboo sword from the tray where he has laid it on top of the discourse book and gives it to the chief junior, who receives it with both hands (the abbot hands it only with his right hand). Holding the bamboo sword high above his head with both hands, the chief junior returns in front of the abbot, bows deeply after making two side-steps to the right, takes two side-steps to the left, turns inward towards the altar and, still holding the sword high in the air together with the fan, proceeds around behind the altar and back to his own place, where the former chief junior is waiting for him. The latter holds the bamboo sword whilst the chief junior sits down. The chief junior takes back the sword, strikes the floor with it and says:

What say you?

The chief junior's assistant starts the mondo with the following:

Hear! Bodhidharma said there is no holiness; here is an opportunity to gain the Way. Within a garden roses flourish, and the garden is not offended by their invasion. A pound of rice loses nothing when put into a pot, although waste floats to the top. It is rare indeed to sit in the completely cool quietness of Shōrinji undergoing the true discipline. The pure moon of autumn turns within the wheel of mist over the limpid river; night falls in heavy measure. Within the great design the robe and bowl join together the children and grandchildren who follow such a person. This is surely the heavenly medicine that cures all ills. What say you?

Hereafter the chief junior must make answer to satisfy the query in the mind of the assistant, and all the trainees present question the chief junior, according to their ability, on the subject matter first propounded by the chief junior in his preliminary discourse. Each must preface his first question with the word "Hear!" For subsequent questions the opening words are "Unclear" or "Explain"; as a rule, three questions is the limit for each trainee. When a trainee is satisfied with an answer he says, "Congratulations," and the chief junior strikes the floor with the end of the bamboo sword, saying, "I thank you." When all the questioning is over, the chief junior recites a poem he has specially composed for the occasion, which shows his own understanding of Bodhidharma's words. He then rises and carries the bamboo sword back to the abbot, going around behind the altar to reach the abbot's seat. He takes two side-steps to the right, holds up the sword, bows, takes two side-steps to the left and goes to the abbot's right side, where the abbot takes the sword from him with his right hand, saying:

You have done well.

The chief junior returns in front of the abbot, takes two side-steps to the right, spreads his mat, places his fan on top of it, makes three bows, picks up the fan and the mat, makes gasshō and bows his head, takes two side-steps to the left, goes to the disciplinarian and bows as before, proceeds around behind the altar and bows to his ordination master or any other great priest, and then goes directly to his seat, where he sits down. All the senior priests present congratulate him, beginning with the lowest in rank and ending with the disciplinarian and finally the abbot. All of these officials must have previously written a poem for the occasion. The disciplinarian recites the offertory and all make three bows. The procession returns to the abbot's room, where all again make three bows and congratulate both the abbot and the chief junior.

Wedding Ceremony

THE ROOM should be prepared carefully. A celebrant, a celebrant's assistant and an organiser are needed. There should be two vases of flowers, if possible, two baby pine trees or two pine branches, cakes and fruit on the front altar. There should be an asperge bowl, a rosary and the necessary legal papers upon the high altar. The wooden blocks, incense bowl, incense box and writing materials are placed on the side altar. The celebrant's assistant carries the celebrant's ceremony book. If available, the memorial tablets of both families should be placed on the altar. The relatives of the groom are seated on the right side of the room and those of the bride on the left. Musicians may be engaged if desired.

At the sound of the first drum, the candles and three sticks of incense are lighted. At the sound of the second drum, the guests of the two families are led to their seats. At the sound of the third drum, the best man leads the groom to sit on the right, sideways to the altar, and the matron of honour leads the bride to sit on the left, in the same way. The bell is rung, and the celebrant enters the room to stand on the bowing mat. The best man says:

> Let us proceed.

The celebrant goes to the altar, burns incense, returns to the bowing mat and bows three times. All bow together with him. The celebrant recites the following from the book carried by the assistant:

> We worship the Great Lord Shakyamuni Buddha, Kōsō Jōyō Daishi, Taisō Jōsai Daishi, and all the Three Treasures in all directions and in the three periods of time. Here there are an excellent man and woman who are marrying each other since their relationship has been consummated and prepared from ages past. Because of this they now stand

277

before the Lord and beg to attain his benefits. They are praying deeply to the Three Treasures and to all the Buddhas for their protection. I am going to permit them to live together in pleasure and in pain, in happiness and unhappiness, until a ripe old age, and to work for the benefit of both themselves and others and to offer the merits thereof to all creatures. I pray that the True Light of the Lord may shine on their excellent minds, thus purifying both their bodies and their minds.

The assistant puts the papers on the side altar, and the celebrant stands with his back to the high altar whilst the side altar is moved in front of him. The bride and groom then stand together in front of this altar. The celebrant takes the asperge bowl and asperges them in the same way as in the ordination ceremony. The assistant censes the rosary and then hands it first to the groom and then to the bride. The celebrant then says:

I take my refuge in the Buddha; that I may realise the True Way and the Highest Mind, I wish to help all living things. I take my refuge in the Dharma; I wish to help all living things in order to enter the Store of the Scriptures so that I may make the wisdom of this my family as wide as the ocean. I take my refuge in the Sangha; I wish to help all living things so that they and my family shall possess an immaculate and peaceful heart.

This is recited first by the groom, holding the rosary, and then by the bride. The assistant then hands the marriage contract to the groom, who recites it as follows:

We are now being given the Light of the Lord, which is full of grace, so that we have been able to marry each other. From this time we are going to be converted deeply to the Three Treasures and make both our bodies and our minds pure so that we may make no mistakes in human morals. We are going to help each other and make each of us successful in our own way. We offer the merits of all we do for the welfare of all mankind.

The groom hands the contract back to the assistant, who then hands it to the bride, who reads it in the same way. They both sign it, the groom signing first, and if the family has seals, these are used also. The assistant takes the contract to the celebrant, who looks at it, censes it, signs it, and if necessary seals it. He then gives a sermon, and the guests congratulate the bride and groom. The groom expresses his thanks. The celebrant goes in front of the altar and returns to the bowing mat. He recites the following:

> We live in the world as if in the sky,
> Just as the lotus blossom is not wetted by the water that
> surrounds it.

HOW TO ARRANGE THE ROOM FOR A WEDDING CEREMONY

If a temple is not available any room can be used, so long as a picture of Buddha is hung in place of an altar statue.

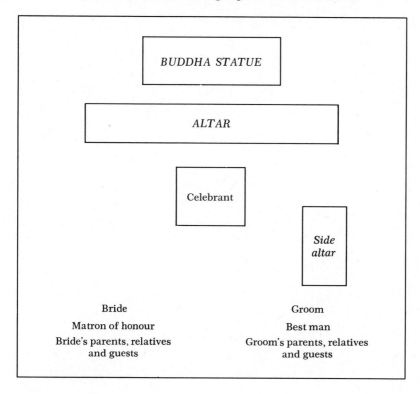

The mind is immaculate and beyond the dust.
Let us bow to the Highest Lord.

All recite the following:

I vow to save others endlessly,
I vow to cease from desire for eternity,
I vow to study the Dharma for ever,
I vow to perfect Buddhism in all lives and in all worlds.

The celebrant leaves the room, and the bride and groom follow.

Funeral Ceremony

THE COFFIN is placed on the highest shelf of the altar with the memorial tablet and a bowl of water in front of it. There is also the Ketchimyaku of the dead, two incense bowls, four white paper flowers (or real ones, if available), food consisting of dough-balls, salt and soup, and a candle. In front of the altar are the bowing mat and a cushion. The celebrant sits in front of the coffin, makes gasshō with one hand and offers incense with the other. He then takes a razor rolled in white paper, makes gasshō with one hand, and recites the following three times:

> Whilst wandering in the world we find many difficulties when we try to cut family ties and dissolve relationships in order to enter the world of no-birth and no-death. To do so, however, is to understand true gratitude.

At the end of the verse the celebrant takes the razor out of the paper and recites the following three times:

> Now you have been shaved; let us all pray that you will leave behind selfish desires for eternity; from now on there will be neither birth nor death.

The celebrant says the following in a low voice, burns incense and holds the rosary, after returning to sit in front of the coffin and washing his hands. (This washing is always done after shaving the corpse, although the shaving is only symbolic:)

Kakoshichi Butsu
Shakyamuni Butsu
Saitenshishichi
Bodaidaruma
Tōdōentososhisho

Eihei Kaisan
Sōji Kaisan
Nichiikidento
(Name of the temple founder)
Rekidaisoshisho
Gorinshōmyo

Having recited the names of the Buddhas of the Dead, the celebrant continues:

Now, if the newly dead, (name), wants to be converted to the Precepts, you should first confess. They who want to confess know that there are two ways of doing it, but there is a confession verse that has been used by every Buddha. Please say it with me:

All: All the evil committed by me
Is caused by beginningless greed, hate and delusion.
All the evil is committed by our body, speech and mind.
I now confess everything wholeheartedly.

The celebrant takes the asperge bowl and touches his head three times with the branch of leaves in it, then makes three triangles in the water. He asperges the congregation to the right, left and centre, then between the centre and the right and between the centre and the left. He returns the branch to his head and touches it there three times, then says in a low voice:

The Precepts that are the True Mind of Buddha sound forth like thunder. The kindness of the Buddha is as the clouds. Now I am pouring the sweet water of the Buddhas upon you so that you may cease from desire unto eternity. You have already confessed your three karmas of body, speech and mind and become immaculate. You should be converted to the Three Treasures. They have three merits. The first is absoluteness, the second is appearance, and the third is the appearance at the present time. When we are once converted to them, all merit is completed. Please repeat after me:

Homage to the Buddha,
Homage to the Dharma,
Homage to the Sangha,
Homage to the Highest Buddha,
Homage to the Dharma that is farthest from the dust,
Homage to the Most Peaceful Sangha
I have given homage to the Buddha,
I have given homage to the Dharma,
I have given homage to the Sangha.

Thus you have made your confession and have received the Three Treasures and become immaculate. From now on the Buddha, the Truth and the enlightened are your Great Master and so you must not be converted to other beliefs. These Precepts have been kept by the former Buddhas and have been transmitted by the previous ancestors. Now the Precepts have come down to me and I am going to give them to you. You must keep them from your present body to that of becoming Buddha.

Homage to the Buddha. You must keep this from your present body to that of becoming Buddha.
Homage to the Dharma. You must keep this from your present body to that of becoming Buddha.
Homage to the Sangha. You must keep this from your present body to that of becoming Buddha.

Cease from evil. You must keep this from your present body to that of becoming Buddha.
Do good. You must keep this from your present body to that of becoming Buddha.
Do good for others. You must keep this from your present body to that of becoming Buddha.

Do not kill. You must keep this from your present body to that of becoming Buddha.
Do not steal. You must keep this from your present body to that of becoming Buddha.
Do not indulge in sexuality. You must keep this from your present body to that of becoming Buddha.
Do not lie. You must keep this from your present body to that of becoming Buddha.
Do not drink the wine of delusion. You must keep this from your present body to that of becoming Buddha.

Do not talk about others. You must keep this from your present body to that of becoming Buddha.

Do not be proud of yourself and blame others. You must keep this from your present body to that of becoming Buddha.

Do not be mean in giving the wealth of the Dharma. You must keep this from your present body to that of becoming Buddha.

Do not be angry. You must keep this from your present body to that of becoming Buddha.

Do not defame the Three Treasures. You must keep this from your present body to that of becoming Buddha.

Because of my compassion, because of my compassion, because of my great compassion. When someone receives these Precepts of the Buddha, he attains to Buddhahood. Buddhahood is equal to enlightenment. Indeed, he truly becomes a baby Buddha.

The precentor announces:

The Litany of the Great Compassionate One

All: Adoration to the Triple Treasure!

Adoration to Kanzeon the Bodhisattva-Mahāsattva
who is the Great Compassionate One!

Om, to the One who leaps beyond all fear!

Having adored Him, may I enter into the heart of Him
known as the Noble, Adored, Kanzeon!

His life is the completion of meaning; it is pure;
it is that which makes all beings victorious and cleanses
the path of existence.

Om, O thou seer, World-transcending One!

O hail to the great Bodhisattva!

All, all is defilement, defilement; earth, earth.

Do, do the work within my heart.

O great Victor, I hold on, hold on!

To Indra the Creator I cry!

Move, move, my defilement-free One!

Come, come, hear, hear,

A joy springs up in me!

Speak, speak, give me direction!
Hulu, hulu, mala, hulu, hulu, hile!
Sara, sara, siri, siri, suru, suru!
Awakened, awakened, I have awakened!
O merciful One, compassionate One,
Of daring ones the most joyous, hail!
Thou art all successful, hail!
Thou are the great successful One, hail!
Thou hast attained mastery in the discipline, hail!
Thou hast a weapon within thine hand, hail!
Thou hast the Wheel within thine hand, hail!
Thou who hast the lotus, hail!
Hail to thee who art the root of eternity!
Hail to thee who art all compassion!
Adoration to the Triple Treasure!
Adoration to Kanzeon!
Hail!   Hail!   Hail!
Give ear unto this my prayer, hail!

The precentor recites the offertory alone:

Thus we have recited the Litany of the Great Compassionate One. We pray we may give the merit thereof to (name) at the time of entering the coffin.

All: * Homage to all the Buddhas in all worlds;
* Homage to all the Bodhisattvas in all worlds;
* Homage to the Scripture of Great Wisdom.

The celebrant continues:

When we think sincerely we find that birth and death are cyclic, as are cold and heat. Now this one who is newly dead has realised that everything is transient; that true peace is in quietude. In the presence of this pure-hearted congregation we are going to recite the names of the great saints. The merit of this recitation will glorify (name's) enlightenment. I ask this good congregation to please pray with me.

All: The completely pure Buddha, Birushanofū, Dharma itself;

The complete Buddha who has been rewarded for his previous training;

Shakyamuni Buddha, one of the many Buddhas who has appeared in the many worlds;

Miroku Buddha, who will appear in the future;

All the Buddhas in all directions and in the Three Worlds;

The great and excellent Dharma Lotus Scripture;

Holy Monju Bodhisattva;

The great and wise Fugen Bodhisattva;

The great and kind Kanzeon;

All the Bodhisattvas and ancestors;

The Scripture of Great Wisdom.

All recite the Adoration of the Buddha's Relics, and the offertory is recited by the celebrant as follows:

Thus we have prayed and recited the Adoration of the Buddha's Relics. With the merit thereof we are going to glorify your way. We pray that you may go to the pure world, that your karma may go beyond dust and dirt, and that you will become as the flowers of the lotus. The Buddha is giving you his blessing.

The celebrant then recites the following prayer:

We are going to take you to the (place of burial/crematorium). Let us recite again the names of the Ten Buddhas and thus help your way.

The names of the Ten Buddhas are recited again, followed by a second recitation of the Litany of the Great Compassionate One. The small bell, drums and cymbals are then played and everyone proceeds to the temple, graveyard or field, where the celebrant again recites the Adoration of the Buddha's Relics three times. He walks around the coffin three times clockwise, and the bell is tolled. Then he goes to the altar, burns incense, takes the torch or hoe, censes it and makes three counterclockwise circles with it, then three clockwise ones, and throws it behind the coffin or gives it to the assistant.

He burns incense at the altar and returns to the chair. The precentor recites the following prayer:

> Returning to the source of Truth this day, this one, (name), who is newly dead, has finished his life according to his appointed time. Now we are going to (bury/burn) his body, which, like a dream, has a span of only a hundred years, and let him go on the way to Nirvāna. We ask this pure-hearted congregation to recite the names of the Ten Buddhas in order to beautify his way to Nirvāna.

The names of the Ten Buddhas are again recited by everyone, and the precentor recites the following:

> Thus we have recited the names of the ten Buddhas and helped you on your way to heaven. We pray that the pure mirror of wisdom will share its light with you and that the True Wind will cover you with the coloured halo so that you may be enlightened in the garden of the Bodhisattvas and work in the waveless sea that is immaculacy itself. We pray that you may receive our offerings as we say farewell to you within the clouds that hide the heavens from our sight. We worship the holy Bodhisattvas and we offer incense to them.

Hereafter any scripture, such as the Scripture of Kanzeon Bosatsu, may be recited. All recite the scripture, and the precentor recites this offertory:

> The merit received from the recitation of the (name of scripture) and from making this procession we wish to give to (name); we pray that we may glorify (his/her) way to heaven.

All: * Homage to all the Buddhas in all worlds;
    * Homage to all the Bodhisattvas in all worlds;
    * Homage to the Scripture of Great Wisdom.

All return to the temple, if the ceremony was held elsewhere, and again recite the Adoration of the Buddha's Relics three times. Then the precentor recites the following offertory:

The merit of the recitation of the Adoration of the Buddha's Relics we are giving to (name). We pray that (he/she) is now in (his/her) own true home in peace.

All: * Homage to all the Buddhas in all worlds;
             * Homage to all the Bodhisattvas in all worlds;
             * Homage to the Scripture of Great Wisdom.

HOW TO ARRANGE THE COFFIN ON THE ALTAR AT A FUNERAL

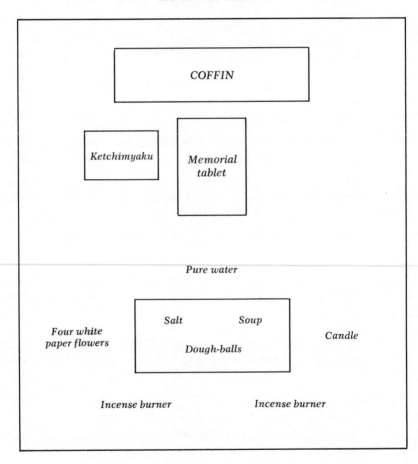

Segaki

AT THE COMMENCEMENT of the ceremony the small bell, drum and cymbals are sounded. After the arrival of the celebrant and the other priests, the Litany of the Great Compassionate One and the Sweet Gate Scripture are recited. During the recitation of the Sweet Gate Scripture the celebrant offers incense and asperges the altar, after which the other priests offer incense and asperge the altar in pairs. When the Sweet Gate Scripture is finished, the precentor recites the following offertory:

> Let us pray that the merits of this recitation may be given to everything within the universe, and that we may attain the Truth.

All then recite any scripture that may be desired, during which the priests process around the ceremony hall. When the scripture is finished, the precentor recites the following offertory alone:

> The Body of the Buddha permeates the universe and manifests itself in front of all of us; there is no place where it does not so manifest itself. It does so for every relationship and in all need, yet it is still in its own true place. The seas of its merit cannot be counted. We pray that the Three Treasures may give us their loving-kindness. We have decorated these altars and offered many things that exist within the sea, the fields and the mountains, and opened the Gate of the Dharma that is the most excellent in all the world. We have made much ceremonial and recited the (name of scripture). We pray that the merit thereof may be turned to the good of all animate things in the endless world, and to the spirits that are lacking in wealth in the nether worlds, and to the evil and wicked in heaven. We

pray that everything may realise the Truth and be released from all bad karma, make the hidden and apparent free, and complete the Right and True Wisdom.

All: * Homage to all the Buddhas in all worlds;
         * Homage to all the Bodhisattvas in all worlds;
         * Homage to the Scripture of Great Wisdom.

This ceremony is frequently held out of doors, with a specially constructed altar, either in the fields, by the side of a river or on the seashore. When it is held in a temple a special altar is constructed near the front door or just outside it, since it is believed that if the ghosts of the dead climb an altar to take food and find thereon a statue of Buddha or of any Bodhisattva, they will not be able to eat. The Segaki altar is therefore placed as far from the main altar as possible, facing outward towards the garden, and those taking part in the ceremony do so with their backs to the main altar— which is, however, usually acknowledged by the offering of incense and three bows prior to the commencement of the Segaki ceremony.

Funeral Ceremony of a Priest

WHEN IT IS APPARENT that the death of any full priest has taken place, the disciples and grand-disciples and his assistant must be called together to discuss how to dispose of his clothing, bowls, seals and other effects. All the temple officers must be informed and all relatives and other necessary persons notified. The assistant must inform the precentor immediately that death appears certain, and the precentor in his turn must inform the chief lecturer. The disciplinarian's assistant rings the meditation hall bell to call the community together, and they all go to the abbot's room to express their condolences after making three bows. They then read the Parinirvāna Scripture and express their condolences to the disciples and grand-disciples. Next they prepare an altar with flowers and candles. If there are any last messages or instructions, these must be written down and pinned upon a board which is hung in front of the founder's hall. The precentor then writes a large notice to be put beside the main gate to inform all persons of the priest's death.

When an abbot dies the same course is followed, but the celebrant for the ceremony should be the abbot of a branch temple or whomever else the deceased may have designated in his instructions. The celebrant sends out a notice of death, written on white paper, to all whom it may concern. On occasion one of the disciples becomes the celebrant. The celebrant next calls together the disciples and others to decide upon the various duties for the ceremony and the sitting in state. The rank of each disciple determines what duty he will fulfil, the five top-ranking persons having the privilege of sitting with the deceased in meditation for the first two days and one night, and the next three performing the same duty for only one day. If the deceased is to be cremated, the celebrant is called the *hinkōshi* (priest who will direct the last words to the deceased before the body is cremated), and if the deceased is to be buried, he is termed a *kokakushi* (priest who performs the whispered ceremony with the deceased before burial). A notice informing all persons concerned of their duties, the time of the funeral, etcetera, is hung in the Buddha hall.

Nyugan (putting the body into the coffin). When the time comes, the disciples, grand-disciples and relatives wash the body with perfumed hot water, shave it and dress it in clean clothes, koromo and kesa. The body is then placed in the coffin in the Zazen position, and the coffin is placed in the sarcophagus and put into the founder's hall. A circle is drawn upon the front of the coffin. When it is placed in the sarcophagus, a funeral kesa is draped over the coffin. An altar is placed in front of the sarcophagus, draped in white, and various ceremonial objects, candles and flowers are placed upon it. When the preparations have been completed, the bell is rung and all the trainees are gathered. The ordinary trainees stand in their respective places according to their rank, and the disciples and grand-disciples line up behind the sarcophagus. The bell ringer comes forward and requests the celebrant to conduct the ceremony. Standing in front of the celebrant, he rings the small bell, and all make three bows. He then proceeds in front of the sarcophagus to lead the procession. The chief celebrant (there should be three for the abbot of a temple) stands in front of the altar at the end of the procession and, together with the two other celebrants, offers incense and makes offerings of tea, cakes and sugared water. The disciplinarian then intones the following offertory:

> Looking back, we see great works, the impressions of which reach both heaven and men. This priest's existence was excellent, surpassing even the foundations laid by the patriarchs. Let us respectfully reflect. (Name of priest), the great priest, possessed wisdom like the full moon which illumined the waters of life. His compassion responded to calls from the ten quarters. We cannot see his face now, but his good works persist. We are all gathered here to recall this.

All then recite the names of the Ten Buddhas, and the disciplinarian recites the following offertory:

> We have recited the names of the Ten Buddhas, offered sugared water, tea, fruit and cakes, and the merit thereof we wish to give to (name). We pray for the enlightenment of all.

All make three bows and leave the hall. The disciples and grand-disciples make special bows to the sarcophagus from behind it; if there is insufficient space, these special bows may be done beside the sarcophagus.

Igan (moving of the sarcophagus). When the bell is rung the sarcophagus is moved from the founder's hall to the ceremony hall, and the room where it is afterwards to be placed is prepared with white hangings. All the ceremonial items belonging to the deceased must be moved at the same time. Whilst the bell, drums and cymbals are sounded, the sarcophagus is moved and all trainees take up their positions. A ceremony exactly similar to the preceding is then performed, except that on this occasion there is no procession. The disciplinarian intones the Litany of the Great Compassionate One and all join in. The disciplinarian then recites the following offertory alone:

> We have moved the sarcophagus, made offerings and recited the Litany of the Great Compassionate One. The merits of this we offer to (name), and pray that (his/her) true position will continue to grow in nobility.

All make three bows, and the disciples and grand-disciples make special bows behind the sarcophagus as before.

Sagan (closing the sarcophagus). This ceremony is usually performed immediately after the sarcophagus is moved, the bell being rung once and the trainees remaining where they are, waiting. The disciplinarian requests the celebrant to perform the ceremony, and the latter takes up his position in front of the sarcophagus. His assistant brings a ceremonial key to him on a tray, and he blesses it and hands it to the sacristan, who locks the sarcophagus. The disciplinarian intones the Litany of the Great Compassionate One as before after the offerings have been made in the same way as for Igan, and all join in the recitation. When it is finished, the disciplinarian recites the following offertory:

> We have locked the sarcophagus, made offerings and recited the Litany of the Great Compassionate One. The merits of this we offer to (name), and pray that (his/her) true position will continue to grow in nobility.

The bows are made exactly as for Igan.

Kashin (hanging up of the portrait of the deceased). When the necessary preparations have been completed, the bell is rung and all the trainees gather in the appointed place. The disciplinarian requests the celebrant to perform the ceremony, and the latter proceeds to the middle of the room, where his assistant presents him with the portrait on a tray. The celebrant blesses and censes it and then hands it to the sacristan, who places it on the high altar. The same offerings are made as in the two previous ceremonies, and the disciplinarian intones the Litany of the Great Compassionate One, in which all join. He then intones the following offertory:

> We have hung the portrait and made many offerings. We have recited the Litany of the Great Compassionate One, and merits thereof we offer to (name). We pray that (his/her) true position will continue to grow in nobility.

The bows are performed in the same way as before.

Taishishōsan (mondo ceremony in front of the portrait of the deceased). This is usually performed on the evening before the actual cremation or burial. The celebrant may be any one of the three who performed the original ceremony. The disciples, grand-disciples and various officials meet in the room of the priest who will perform the ceremony, where they exchange bows with the disciplinarian. At the appointed time the bell is rung, and the trainees stand on either side of the hall in two groups, the persons closest to the deceased being in the main positions. At the sound of the drum the disciples go in front of the sarcophagus and offer incense. The chief one takes a few steps backward and sits on the chair opposite the sarcophagus. The abbot's five assistants line up behind him and perform the usual ceremonial of a normal Shōsan ceremony. There is no actual mondo, however, and at the close of the ritual bowing, the celebrant retires.

Taiyanenju (closing ceremony). When the Shōsan ceremony is finished, the disciplinarian announces the closing ceremony, saying:

> This I say to all trainees. He who has newly entered into Nirvāna, (name), the great priest, has returned to the True Source of all Peace. As this day passes, so his life has come to an end. We are as fish in shallow water; there is no happiness to be found here. You must all devote yourselves wholeheartedly to your training. You must realise the impermanence of everything and not become dissolute or self-indulgent. All of you have respectfully gathered here and stand before this sarcophagus. We repeat the name of (name), which is utterly virtuous, and pray through him for advancement on the road of enlightenment.

The offerings are then made as in the former ceremonies, and the disciplinarian continues:

> We have performed this closing ceremony and made many offerings. We offer the merits of this to (name), the great priest, and we pray that (his/her) true position will increase in nobility.

All perform three bows and leave the hall except the disciples and grand-disciples, who go to the chair of the celebrant and bow in gratitude. After a short interval there is usually a lecture in which the virtues of the deceased are recalled. Those who wish then recite scriptures, one after the other, and thus the night passes quietly.

Kigan (taking up the sarcophagus). The next morning, all the necessary ceremonial items are set out and the funeral procession is planned. At the appointed time the big bell is rung one hundred and eight times, and the small bell is rung for the trainees to line up for the procession. The disciplinarian requests the celebrant to perform the ceremony, and the latter offers incense and makes offerings of food and sugared water. The disciplinarian announces the closing ceremony for the taking up of the sarcophagus, and, according to the old tradition, it is read quickly, instead of slowly as is the case with all other closing ceremonies. The disciplinarian says:

> We lift the golden coffin and go around the great castle of Kushi, whereon the flag waves in nothingness. We proceed now to the funeral pyre. We pray that all trainees shall pay tribute to (his/her) great name as we say farewell.

The Litany of the Great Compassionate One is then recited by all after being intoned by the disciplinarian, and the drums, bell and cymbals are sounded as the procession sets out. A large number of flags are carried by the disciples and grand-disciples as here described: Four coloured flags upon which is written, "The Buddha proves Nirvāna to be the elimination and cutting off of life and death, thus enabling us to obtain supreme peace"; four white flags reading, "Supreme Nirvāna shines in perfect peace. The worldly are dead when all ties outside the Way are cut." Ten red flags bearing the Names of the Ten Buddhas. One white flag on which is written the dead priest's final words or teaching. When the sarcophagus is lifted the disciplinarian announces, in a drawn-out voice, together with the second celebrant:

> The completely pure Buddha, Birushanofū, Dharma itself.

This is repeated by all trainees in time to the small bell, and the small bell, drums and cymbals are sounded. The second line of the Ten Buddhas is then intoned in the same way as the first, all trainees intoning it after the disciplinarian and the celebrant. Again the bell, drums and cymbals are sounded whilst everyone stands still, no one moving again until the disciplinarian intones the third line. In such a way is the whole of the Ten Buddhas recited. There are two groups carrying small bells, drums and cymbals, one in front of the sarcophagus and one behind it; the one in front plays first and the one behind second. On arrival at the funeral pyre or place of burial, the sarcophagus is placed as in the diagram below, and the disciples, grand-disciples and officials group themselves as set out in the diagram following. The Litany of the Great Compassionate One is recited, and no offertory, after all have made three bows. The Dharma disciple lights the funeral pyre, after the sarcophagus has been carried around it three times before being placed on top. All the disciples and grand-disciples sit around the funeral pyre in Zazen until the body has been utterly consumed; they then quietly return to the temple.

Shūshari (receiving the ashes). The morning after cremation or burial, the bell rings after breakfast in the trainees' hall and all trainees go in procession to meet the disciples and grand-disciples returning with the ashes. The ashes are then placed in an urn and taken by the

PLACING OF THE PRIEST'S SARCOPHAGUS

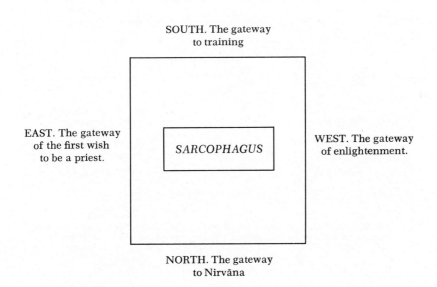

SOUTH. The gateway
to training

EAST. The gateway
of the first wish
to be a priest.

SARCOPHAGUS

WEST. The gateway
of enlightenment.

NORTH. The gateway
to Nirvāna

CEREMONY LAYOUT FOR A PRIEST'S FUNERAL

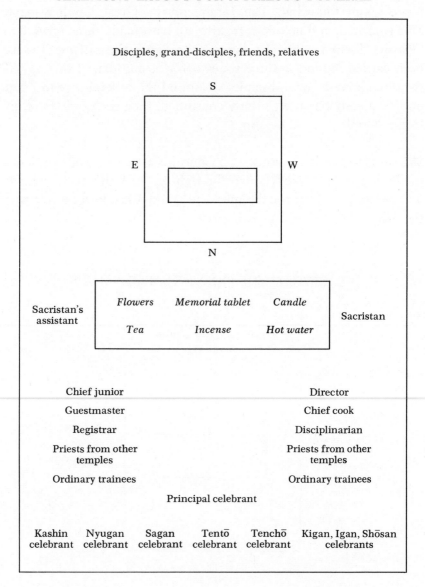

chief disciple to the founder's hall. If the priest has been buried, only the memorial tablet is brought back by the disciples, and this is placed in the founder's hall. The following ceremony is then performed.

Anifugin (placing of the ashes in the founder's hall). The ashes are placed in the founder's hall and offerings of incense, flowers, wine, water and fruit are made. The disciplinarian's assistant sounds the small bell for three bows, and the disciplinarian intones the Litany of the Great Compassionate One. The disciplinarian then recites the following offertory:

> The merits of this recitation are offered to (name), the great priest. Now that he has become ashes we pray that his position may increase in nobility.

All make three bows and leave the founder's hall. At two o'clock food is taken, and at three o'clock ceremonial tea, in the same way as when the priest was alive.

Sessai (offering food). The food-offering ceremony is performed on the same day as the ceremony for receiving the ashes, if possible and if time permits; otherwise it is performed on the seventh day after the funeral. The portrait of the deceased is hung in the ceremony hall, and all the celebrants who took part in the other ceremonies are called to take part in this ceremony. The offerings are made in exactly the same way as in all the other ceremonies. On each successive seventh day all the trainees circulate in order to make incense offerings. The Sessai ceremonies vary according to the temple's position. If an abbot of higher rank than the deceased should come to offer incense, the disciples of the deceased must be at the left-hand side of the altar so as to make special bows to him. If the visiting abbot is of lower rank than the deceased, there is no special bowing. If an abbot from another temple should visit after the funeral rites are concluded and wishes to recite scriptures before the portrait, the guestmaster and officers of the temple make the welcoming and farewell bows. If the visiting abbot does not have his assistant with him to recite the offertory, the disciplinarian recites it on his behalf.

Yuisō (presentation of the keepsakes). When all the ceremonies have been completed, the disciples and grand-disciples, as well as any others who may have been intimate friends or acquaintances of the deceased, come to perform a salutation of gratitude to the various temple officers who took part in the ceremonies. Keepsakes of the abbot are given and exchanged at this time. Customs with regard to this, as well as the manner of salutation, vary according to the tradition of the area.

Glossary

The following abbreviations are used:

> J.   Japanese
> Skr. Sanskrit
> P.   Pali

ācārya (Skr.). A master or teacher; a senior priest of five years' standing.

Amida (J.). A Buddha who is believed to reside in the Western Heaven, or Pure Land. He is called in Sanskrit Amitābha, "Buddha of Fathomless Light," or Amitāyus, "Buddha of Immeasurable Life." Historically, he is believed to have been a king who gave up all to become a monk and, after meditating for five kalpas, made forty-eight vows for the saving of all beings. His eighteenth vow is the basis of Amida Buddhism, which teaches that anyone who calls upon his name with true faith will be reborn in the Western Heaven.

Amitābha. See *Amida.*

Anabotei Memyō. See *Aśvaghosha.*

anattā (P.). "No-soul," the Theravāda doctrine which teaches that there is no permanent individual soul that transmigrates at death to another body. (Skr. *anātman.*)

anicca (P.). Transience, the Theravāda doctrine which teaches that all things are impermanent and subject to change. (Skr. *anitya.*)

Ārāda Kālāma. A highly respected Brahman teacher to whom Shakyamuni Buddha became disciple before his enlightenment.

Arahant (J.). One who seeks, finds and dwells in the realm of Nirvāna without regard to saving others; the opposite of a Bodhisattva, who desires the salvation of all living beings. (Skr. *Arhat.*)

Arūpa Jhāna (P.). The four meditations: upon the Realm of Infinity of Space; upon the Realm of Infinity of Consciousness; upon the Realm of Nothingness; upon the Realm of Neither Perception nor Non-Perception.

Asanga. An Indian master (c. 310–390) of the Yogācāra school of Mahāyāna Buddhism. His works were translated into Chinese in the sixth century. His younger brother, Vasubandhu, is equally famous as a master.

Asita. Asita Rishi, Indian ascetic who visited the future Buddha at the time of his birth and foresaw his destiny.

Asoka. Asoka Maurya, king of Magadha (c. 270 B.C.). One of the great Buddhist rulers of India, under whose reign Buddhist art and architecture flourished. His edicts greatly influenced social structure, and he sent missionaries to various parts of India and Ceylon, as well as to Syria, Egypt and Macedonia. His daughter Sanghamitta took a branch of the original Bodhi tree to Ceylon, as recorded in the *Great Chronicles of Ceylon*. It is said that Asoka was enlightened on his deathbed.

asuras (Skr.). The fighting demons of the realm of dissension, one of the six lokas, or realms of rebirth: one of the eight classes of supernatural beings. In Hindu mythology, the asuras, led by Varuna, fought the devas, headed by Indra. The word means literally "those without wine."

Aśvaghosha. An Indian Buddhist philosopher (c. 100), author of the *Buddhacarita*, which deals with the life of the Buddha, and the *Mahāyāna-śraddhotpāda Śastra*, or *The Awakening of Faith*. In the Zen tradition, he is considered the Twelfth Ancestor, and he appears in Keizan's *Denkoroku* as Anabotei Memyō.

Avalokiteśvara. See *Kanzeon*.

Badarobosatsu (J.). Bhadrāpala, an Indian Arahant who attained enlightenment whilst bathing. There is a small altar dedicated to him in the bathrooms of all Zen temples.

Basō, Basō Dōitsu (J.). Ma-tsu Tao-i (709–788), a Chinese Zen master. He was a disciple of Nangaku Ejō.

Bimbisāra. King of Magadha in India. Prior to the Buddha's enlightenment, Bimbisāra had offered him his entire kingdom. The Buddha refused, but promised to teach first at Rājagaha, Bimbisāra's capital, if he attained enlightenment. When the Buddha returned to fulfil his promise, the king gave him the Bamboo Grove (Veluvana), his own favourite pleasure ground, and came to hear his teachings. Devadatta, the Buddha's cousin, plotted with the king's son Ajātasattu to murder both the king and the Buddha. When Bimbisāra heard of the plot, he abdicated in favour of his son, who, on Devadatta'· insistence, allowed his father to starve to death.

Birushanofū. See *Vairocana Buddha*.

Bishari (J.). Vaiśālī (modern Basarh), a city in India, site of the second Buddhist council in 377 B.C.

Bodhi (Skr.). Enlightenment, understanding, perfect wisdom.

Bodhi tree. See *pipal tree*.

Bodhidharma (Skr.). The First Patriarch of Chinese Zen. The third son of a south Indian ruler, he went to China in 520. It is told that he sat for nine years facing a wall in Shōrinji until his legs withered away, and then transmitted the Dharma to Eka, his disciple. He is said to have died in 528 or 536. In Japan he is known as Daruma, or by his posthumous title, Engaku Daishi.

Bodhisattva (Skr.). One who is in search of enlightenment and on his way to becoming a Buddha. The name indicates one who aspires to Buddhahood or one who desires enlightenment for every living thing. There are three categories of Bodhisattva: Intellectual, Devotional, Energetic. (J. *Bosatsu*.)

bompu Zen (J.). Sitting in meditation simply for physical advantages.

Bonten (J.). (1) Brahmadevaloka (Skr.), first of the four dhyāna heavens in Rūpadhātu, the world of form, where beings have no appetite or sexual desire, consisting of: Brahmapārishadya, the realm of Brahma's retinue; Brahmapurohitā, the realm of Brahma's ministers; and Mahā-brahmā, the Great Brahma Realm. (2) Brahmadeva, God as creator of the universe.

Bosatsu. See *Bodhisattva.*

Brahman. One of the four Indian castes: Brahman, or priest caste; Kshatriya, or warrior caste; Vaisya, or merchant caste; Sudra, or common caste.

Buddha (Skr.). An enlightened person; a person with understanding of the Truth. (J. *Butsu.*)

Buddha Gayā. The place in India where Shakyamuni Buddha sat beneath the pipal tree and gained enlightenment. The Mahābodhi Temple is situated there, as is also a lotus pond in which the Buddha is believed to have bathed.

Buddha hall. See *Butsuden.*

Butsu. See *Buddha.*

Butsudanda Ryū-ō (J.). One of the 185 dragon kings, deities that bring rain; Manda Ryū-ō was another. The Ryū (Skr. Nāga) are one of the eight types of supernatural beings who protect the Dharma.

Butsuden (J.). The Buddha hall, which enshrines the image of either a Buddha or a Bodhisattva. In Zen temples the *honzon*, or principal image, is enshrined in the Butsuden.

Cakravarti Rāja (Skr.). The "Wheel King," a universal ruler whose chariot wheels roll everywhere without hindrance. It also means the king who rules by the wheel, which can be made of gold, silver, iron or copper and is used as a weapon to be hurled at his enemies. He is one of the protectors of the Dharma.

Chidoron, Daichidoron (J.). The *Mahāprajñāpāramitopadeśa*, by Nāgār-juna, a discourse on the Scripture of Great Wisdom comprising 100 fascicles. It was translated from Sanskrit into Chinese (*Ta-chih-tu Lun*) by Kumārajīva.

dai monjin (J.). An invitational bow, before which the hands are spread wide in both directions to include everyone in the ceremony hall.

Daibaijo Zenji, Daibai Hōjō (J.). Ta-mei Fa-ch'ang (752-?), a Chinese Zen master of the Rinzai school. He was a disciple of Basō Dōitsu.

Daie Sōkō (J.). Ta-hui Tsung-kao (1089–1163), a Chinese Zen master of the Rinzai school. His assistant, Enen (Yün-wên) comp'led his sayings into six volumes, originally called in Japanese the *Shōbōgenzō*, but now called *Daie Shōbōgenzō* to avoid confusion with Dōgen's work.

Daijōji. A temple in Kanazawa, Japan, which originally belonged to the Shingon sect but later became Sōtō. Keizan Zenji was chief abbot there for ten years.

Daikan Enō. See *Enō.*

Daioshō (J.). A title meaning "Great Priest."

Daishi (J.). "Great Teacher" or "Great Master," a title given posthumously to Zen masters.

Dandokusen (J.). Dandaka or Dandaloka, a mountain in Gandhāra, India.

Dentōroku (J.). Called in English *The Transmission of the Lamp*, this work was compiled in China in 1004 by another Dogen—Tao-yüan, a Chinese scholar, not the founder of Japanese Sōtō Zen. Its Chinese title is *Ching-tê Ch'uan-têng Lu*. It records the sayings of the great masters from the time of the Seven Buddhas to the tenth century, for a total of 1,701.

Dependent Origination. The doctrine of the twelve-linked chain of causation (Skr. *Pratītyasamutpāda*). The causal links, which form a closed round, are: ignorance (*avidyā*), volitional formations (*samskāra*), consciousness (*vijñāna*), mind and body (*nāmarūpa*), sense organs (*sadāyatana*), contact (*sparśa*), feeling or emotion (*vedanā*), craving (*trishnā*), attachment (*upādanā*), becoming (*bhāva*), birth (*jāti*), ageing and death (*jarāmarana*).

deva (Skr.). A god, a being that possesses supernatural powers. Also, the realm of the gods, or heaven: one of the six lokas, or realms of rebirth.

Dharma (Skr.). The teachings of the Buddha.

Dharmakāya (Skr.). The Dharma Body, one of the Three Bodies of the Buddha in the Trikāya doctrine. The essence of all things; the Cosmic Buddha.

dhyāna (Skr.). Meditation. (P. *jhāna*.)

Dōgen. Kigen Dōgen, also known as Jōyō Daishi, founder of Sōtō Zen in Japan. For further details about his life and work, see the Introduction to the Translations, Book II.

dukkha (P.). Suffering. Birth, disease, death, separation and frustration are all forms of suffering if not transcended. (Skr. *duhkha*.)

Echū, Nanyō Echū (J.). Nan-yang Hui-chung (677–744), a Chinese Zen master and disciple of Daikan Enō, the Sixth Patriarch.

Eiheiji. A large temple situated in Fukui prefecture in Japan; one of the two head temples of the present Sōtō Zen Church.

Eisai. Myoan Eisai (1141–1215), founder of the Rinzai school of Zen in Japan.

Eka (J.). Hui-k'ê (487–593), the Second Patriarch of Chinese Zen, having been the disciple of Bodhidharma. It is said that he cut off his arm outside Shōrinji temple as a proof of the sincerity of his desire to be accepted as a disciple.

Enan, Ōryō Enan (J.). Huang-lung Hui-nan (1002–1069), a Chinese Zen master of the Rinzai school. Since he lived on Ōryūzan from 1036, his teachings were known as the Ōryū (Huang-lung) school.

engaku. See *pratyekabuddha*.

Engo, Engo Kokugon (J.). Yüan-wu K'ê-ch'in (1063–1135), a Chinese Zen master. He was a disciple of Goso Hōyen (Wu-tsu Fa-yen, 1025–1104), and the master of Daie Sōkō.

Enō, Daikan Enō (J.). Hui-nêng (638–713), the Sixth Patriarch of Chinese Zen.

Eshi (J.). Hui-ssu (515–577), the Second Patriarch of the Chinese Tendai sect of Buddhism.

Four Existences. This can mean two things. (1) Monks (Skr. *bhikshu*), nuns (*bhikshunī*), laymen (*upāsaka*), and laywomen (*upāsikā*). (2) Those who requested the Buddha's teaching of the *Lotus Sūtra*; those whom he taught and who responded; those who reflected upon the teaching; those who benefit by seeing and hearing the Buddha but will gain enlightenment in a future life.

Fugen (J.). A Bodhisattva always found at the side of Shakyamuni Buddha, usually seated on a white elephant. He represents truth, love, meditation and practice. His Sanskrit name is Samantabhadra.

funzoe (J.). One of the Twelve Zuda, practices aimed at eliminating attachment. *Pāmśukūlika*, the Sanskrit equivalent, indicates clothing made from discarded rags.

gaitan (J.). The meditation seats placed outside the meditation hall for the use of new trainees, visiting priests and laymen.

Gassan (J.). Chia-shan Shan-hui (805–881), a Chinese Zen master. Also called Kassan Zene in Japanese.

gasshō (J.). The ancient Indian salutation, which consists of placing the palms together, the right hand representing the holy, or higher nature, and the left hand the world, or lower nature; the two hands together thus make up the "One Mind" of human beings.

gedō Zen (J.). Meditation done solely for the purpose of gaining supernatural powers.

Goi theory. The Five Levels of Understanding, as explained by Tōzan Ryokai.

Gunin. (J.). Hung-jên (601–674), the Fifth Patriarch of Chinese Zen, who lived at Ōbai (Huang-mei). He is also called Daiman Kōnin in Japanese.

han (J.). The wooden board which is struck with a hammer to signal various happenings in a temple.

Harana (J.). Baranasi (Benares), a city in India where the Buddha taught the five ascetics who were with him before his enlightenment.

heirō (J.). A thurible for powdered incense, used by an abbot.

Hinayāna. See *Three Vehicles*.

Hipparakutsu (J.). The Pippala Cave near Rājagaha, where Makakashyo is believed to have meditated whilst the Buddha was entering Parinirvāna. After the Buddha's death the first meeting for the gathering of the doctrines was held there.

Hōgen, Hōgen Buneki (J.). Fa-yen Wên-i (885-958), founder of the Hōgen (Fa-yen) school of Chinese Zen. He was the disciple of Rakan Keishin (Lo-han Kuei-ch'en, 867–928).

honshi (J.). The "true master" with whom a Zen trainee does his transmission.

Hossen (J.). Literally, "Dharma Battle," a ceremony in which the other trainees test the understanding of a new chief junior in a question-and-answer session called *mondo*; it is part of the set of ceremonies known as Kessei.

hossu (J.). A ceremonial fly-whisk.

Hui-nêng. See *Enō.*

Hyakujō, Hyakujō Ekai (J.). Pai-chang Hui-hai (720–814), a Chinese Zen master of the Nangaku line; also known in Japanese as Daichi Zenji. His eight-volume *Hyakujōshingi (Pai-chang Ch'ing-kuei)* contains rules for training temples and is one of the most important of all Chinese Zen writings on the teaching of trainees.

Igyō. See *Isan.*

Indra. The Hindu god who controls wind, rain, lightning and thunder. Introduced into Buddhism, he is known in Japanese as Taishakuten, the ruler of the Tuśita Heaven. See also *asuras.*

inkin (J.). A small bell used in temple ceremonial.

inō (J.). The disciplinarian of a Zen training temple.

Isan, Isan Reiyū (J.). Kuei-shan Ling-yu (771–853), a Chinese Zen master and disciple of Hyakujō. In conjunction with his disciple Kyōzan Ejaku (Yang-shan Hui-chi, 814–890), he founded the Igyō (Kuei-yang) school of Zen.

Jiji Bosatsu (J.). In Sanskrit, Dharanimdhara Bodhisattva, meaning "Holder of the Earth."

jikidō (J.). A meditation hall monitor.

Jinshū Jōza (J.). Shên-hsiu (606–706), a disciple of Gunin, the Fifth Patriarch of Chinese Zen. Before becoming Gunin's disciple at the age of fifty, he had studied Confucianism, the Buddhist scriptures and other texts, especially the *Kegon Sūtra*; his erudition precluded his direct experience of Gunin's teaching.

Jizō, Jizō Bosatsu (J.). A Bodhisattva who is said to save all beings between the time of Shakyamuni's death and the coming of Miroku Buddha. As he is hard at work saving beings in all six realms of existence, he appears in six different forms. In Japan he is regarded as the protector of children, especially of those killed in auto accidents; stone statues of him as a monk with shaved head and robes are erected by roadsides wherever a child has been killed. His name in Sanskrit is Kshitigarbha.

Jōdō (J.). The Pure Land, or Western Paradise, of Amida Buddhism. The place of enlightenment.

Jōdō (J.). A ceremony in which an abbot is tested in *mondo* (question and answer) on his realisation of the Truth; part of the Kessei set of ceremonies.

Jōsai (J.). A title meaning "Great Master": for example, Keizan Zenji is referred to as Jōsai Daishi.

Jōshu Jūshin (J.). Chao-chou Ts'ung-shên (778–897), a Chinese Zen master and disciple of Nansen Fugan (Nan-ch'üan P'u-yüan, 748–834). He is famous for the kōan known as Jōshu's "Mu."

Jōyō (J.). Another title meaning "Great Master": for example Jōyō Daishi is one of the titles of Dōgen Zenji.

Jūkai (J.). The special period of a week set aside for the ceremonies involving the receiving of the Precepts.

Jūkai Tokudō (J.). The lay ordination ceremony.

Kabira (J.). Kapilavastu.

kalavinka (Skr.). A bird with a wondrously beautiful voice, said to be found in the Himalayan valleys.

kalpa (Skr.). An incalculable period of time, usually described as the time it would take a ten-cubic-mile rock to be worn out by the touch of the robe of a heavenly being once every three years, or the time it would take to remove all the mustard seeds from a ten-mile-square area at the rate of one seed every three years.

Kanzeon, Kannon (J.). The Bodhisattva who is the personification of compassion. The word *kanzeon* means, literally, "hearing the calls of living beings," or "hearing the sound of the suffering world." His name in Sanskrit is Avalokiteśvara.

Kapilavastu. The capital of the country where the Buddha spent his childhood. It is in the Terai district of present-day Nepal.

karma (Skr.). Actions; the law of consequences which inevitably follow upon actions. (P. *kamma.*) See also *vipāka.*

Kashikoku (J.). Magadha.

Kegon (J.). The Kegon (Hua-yen) sect, also known as the Hōzō sect, was founded in China by Hōzō (Fa-tsang, 643–712), who was also known as Genjū. The Kegon teachings are based on the *Avatamsaka Sūtra.*

Kegon Sūtra. In Sanskrit, *Avatamsaka Sūtra;* in Chinese, *Hua-yen Ching.* Translated into Chinese by Buddhabhadra in 418–420 and by Śiksānanda in 695–699, this sūtra is the basis of the teachings of the Kegon sect of Buddhism.

Keidō. Keidō Chisan Zenji, or Kōhō Zenji (1879–1968), former chief abbot of Sōjiji, the head temple of the Sōtō school in Japan. Reverend Jiyu Kennett was one of his main disciples.

Keisoku (J.). Mount Kukkutapāda.

Keizan. With Dōgen Zenji, the co-founder of the Sōtō Zen Church in Japan. For details concerning his life and work, see Introduction to the Translations, Book III.

Kenninji. One of the head temples of the Rinzai school in Kyoto; founded by Eisai in 1202. Dōgen trained there under Eisai and later under Myozen, and himself became abbot there on his return from China.

kenshō (J.). The experience of enlightenment; literally, "to see one's own nature."

kentan (J.). The inspection of trainees on their meditation seats by the abbot prior to the commencement of the meditation period.

kesa (J.). A monk's robe. (Skr. *kāśāya*.)

Kessei (J.). The series of ceremonies performed when a priest has a trainee whom he considers ready for the rank of chief junior. It is also performed when a priest becomes the new abbot of a temple.

Ketchimyaku (J.). The line of ancestors from the Seven Buddhas to the present master in a temple. It is recited daily in most Zen temples, always ending with the master's master. A copy of this bloodline is given to each disciple when he or she is ordained and transmitted. The ancestor line given in this book ends with Keidō Chisan Daishō, Jiyu Kennett's own master.

kinhin (J.). "Mindful walking," or walking meditation, within the meditation hall in Sōtō Zen and outside it in Rinzai. It is performed in remembrance of the day that Shakyamuni Buddha spent walking round the Bodhi tree after his enlightenment, in gratitude for the tree's shade.

Kinnara (Skr.). A heavenly musician, part animal and part human, sometimes described as having a horse's head and a human body. The Kinnaras are one of the eight classes of supernatural beings.

kōan (J.). A catalyst that brings a trainee to full understanding of the Truth. It can be either a saying or an action upon which the trainee meditates until he finally learns to transcend it.

koromo (J.). The formal robe of a trainee, or of a full priest.

Kōsei. Basō Dōitsu.

Koun Ejō. A Japanese Sōtō Zen master (1198–1280). After studying Tendai on Mount Hiei and then Jōdo, he finally changed to Zen under Dōgen. He helped to found Eiheiji and was its second abbot in 1253. He is the author of the *Shōbōgenzō Zuimonki*, which records the interviews and lectures of Dōgen, and of the *Ejōroku*, a collection of his own sayings.

Kshatriya. See *Brahman.*

Kuchira (J.). Kushinagara or Kusinara in India, where the Buddha passed into Parinirvāna on the banks of the river Hiranyavatī. A stupa marks the spot where the Buddha was cremated and the relics divided among the mourners.

Kukkutapāda. A mountain in Magadha, India, where the Buddha's disciple Makakashyo died. It is said that Makakashyo is still on that mountain, awaiting the coming of Miroku Buddha.

Kūō Buddha (J.). In Sanskrit, Dharmagahanābhyudgata Rāja, a Buddha mentioned in the *Lotus Sūtra* as having taught understanding of the absolute.

kutsujun (J.). A fine-textured cloth resembling cotton. The kesa conveyed from Bodhidharma was of blue-black kutsujun.

kyosaku (J.). The "awakening stick," carried by a monitor during meditation for the purposes of encouraging the trainees to greater efforts, massaging away stiffness in the shoulders and testing the depth of a trainee's meditation. In Rinzai Zen it is called *keisaku,* or "policing stick."

kyoshi (J.). A divinity degree received from the temple where a priest has undergone his training. Kyoshis are of different grades, from third up to first and on to *sei,* which is roughly the equivalent of a doctorate.

Lankāvatāra Sūtra. A scripture attributed to Shakyamuni, who is said to have delivered it on the Lankā mountain in Ceylon. Three parts were translated into Chinese (*Lêng-chia Ching*) from Sanskrit by Gunabhadra (394–468), Bodhiruci (arrived China 508), and Sikshānanda (652–710). It is called *Ryogikyo* in Japanese.

lokas (Skr.). The six worlds, or six realms of rebirth or illusion: heaven; the world of humans; the world of asuras, or dissension; the world of animals; the world of hungry ghosts; hell. We fall into these various forms of existence as a result of our actions.

Lumbinī Garden. Rummindei, a place in Nepal about six miles from the Indian border, where the Buddha is said to have been born in a grove of sal trees.

Magadha. The kingdom of King Bimbisāra, whose capital was Rājagaha (modern Rajgir). It was here that King Asoka began his reign about 270 B.C.

Mahā Māya. The mother of Prince Siddhārtha, the future Shakyamuni Buddha.

Mahāprajñāpāramitā. See *Prajñāpāramitā.*

Mahāsattva (Skr.). A perfect Bodhisattva, ranking second only to a Buddha.

Mahāyāna (Skr.). The "Greater Vehicle": the northern form of Buddhism, developed in northern India and surviving in China and Japan. Its scriptures are in Sanskrit.

Maitreya. See *Miroku.*

Makada. (J.). Magadha.

Makakashyo (J.). One of the ten great disciples of Shakyamuni Buddha and the First Ancestor in the Zen tradition. Born to a Brahman family, he became Buddha's disciple and reached Arahantship in only eight days. When Shakyamuni winked and held up a flower, Makakashyo smiled and the Truth was transmitted to him, thus beginning the Zen tradition of transmission. It is said that Makakashyo is still on Mount Keisoku, awaiting the coming of Miroku. His name in Sanskrit is Mahākāśyapa.

makyo (J.). Obstructions to meditation, such as visions, strange mental states, and physical discomforts caused by incorrect posture or breathing or other incorrect functioning of the body.

Manda Ryū-ō. See *Butsudanda Ryū-ō.*

Mangalama. Maudgalyāyana. See *Mokkenren.*

Mañjuśrī. See *Monju.*

mantra (Skr.). In Esoteric Buddhism, a *mantra* or *dhāranī* is a mystical

(magical) formula in sounds, represented by Sanskrit letters and sylla-
bles. Also, a spell or a charm, a power embodied in sound. It is called
in Japanese *shingon*, or "true words."

Māra (Skr.). The spirit of evil or of death; the Great Tempter, who used
many tricks to try to prevent the enlightenment of Shakyamuni
Buddha.

Miroku (J.). The Buddha who is to come and who is now teaching all
beings in the Tuśita Heaven. His Sanskrit name, Maitreya, also means
the highest rank of Bodhisattvahood.

Mokkenren (J.). In Sanskrit, Maudgalyāyana, one of the Buddha's ten
great disciples. A good friend of Śāriputra, he was recognised as having
the greatest supernatural powers of all the disciples.

mokugyo (J.). A wooden drum shaped in the likeness of a fish, used to
accompany chanting in a temple.

mondo (J.). A question-and-answer session for testing the understanding
of a trainee.

Monju (J.). In Sanskrit, Mañjuśrī, a Bodhisattva whose name means
"Deep Virtue" or "Great Fortune." He is always seated at the side of
Shakyamuni Buddha, riding on a lion, and represents wisdom; he
holds the delusion-cutting sword.

Mujinni Bosatsu (J.). In Sanskrit, Akshayamati, a Bodhisattva whose
name means "Unfailing, Unending Devotion."

Myozen. The chief disciple of Eisai, founder of the Rinzai school in Japan.
After Eisai's death, Myozen was the teacher of Dōgen Zenji for nine
years and went to China with him, where he died in 1225.

Nāgārjuna. An Indian Buddhist philosopher, considered the Fourteenth
Ancestor in the Zen tradition. Born a Brahman c. 200, he became the
founder of the Mādhyamika, or "Middle Way," school of Buddhism,
and is the author of its principal scripture, the *Mādhyamika Śastra.*
His biography was written by Kumārajīva.

Nagyaarajyuna (J.). Nāgārjuna.

Nangaku, Nangaku Ejō (J.). Nan-yüeh Huai-jang (677–744), a Chinese
Zen master and disciple of the Sixth Patriarch, Daikan Enō. After
Enō, the line divides into the Seigen (Hsing-ssu) and the Nangaku,
which became the two great lines of Zen in China. Basō Dōitsu was one
of Nangaku's disciples, and the Rinzai and Igyō schools come from
this line.

nembutsu (J.). Repetition of the Buddha's name. The term generally
refers to the Shin Buddhist practice of reciting "*Namu Amida Butsu*"
(I trust in Amida Buddha), which is used instead of meditation as a
form of concentrated prayer.

ni-oshō (J.). A female priest, or priestess.

Nirvāna (Skr.). Extinction of attachment to desire and delusion. (J.
Nehan.)

Nyojō Zenji, Tendō Nyojō (J.). Ju-ching (1163–1228), abbot of Tendōzan
Keitokuji (T'ien-t'ung-shan) in China and the master who transmitted

Dōgen Zenji. One of the five great temples in China, Keitokuji was the headquarters of the Sōtō school of Zen.

nyoi, nyoibo (J.). A staff shaped like a lotus flower, occasionally with a dragon twisted about its length, carried by a celebrant during great ceremonies symbolising the Nyoi jewel.

Nyoi jewel. The jewel which removes all the pain that comes from suffering; the symbol of the Buddha's merit.

Nyudō-no-hai (J.). The ceremony in which a new trainee is officially admitted to the meditation hall. Also, the induction ceremony of a new chief junior.

Ōbai. See *Gunin.*

Ōbaku, Ōbaku Kiun (J.). Huang-po Hsi-yün (?–850), a Chinese Zen master and disciple of Hyakujō Ekai, founded the Ōbaku school of Zen. His writings, known in English as *The Transmission of the Mind* and in Japanese as *Denshinhōyō* (*Ch'üan-hsin Fa-yao*), are famous, but his fame rests primarily upon his being the master of Rinzai Gigen, founder of the Rinzai school of Zen.

Obon. See *Segaki.*

Ōryūnan. Enan.

Ōryūzan (J.). Huang-lung Shan, the Yellow Dragon Mountain, so called because the Chinese believed that a yellow dragon dwelt at the top which brought rain. See also *Enan.*

oshō (J.). A priest.

Parinirvāna (Skr.). Complete or final extinction (*pari* means "complete" or "all round"). This term usually refers to the death of the Buddha.

Parinirvāna Scripture. In the Pali Canon, the *Mahā-parinibbāna Suttanta,* included in the *Digha-nikāva,* deals with the last days of the Buddha. In the Sanskrit scriptures, the *Mahāparinirvāna Sūtra* is said to be the last discourse of the Buddha.

paryanka (Skr.). The full-lotus position, the Buddha's meditation posture. (J. *kekka-fuza.*)

pipal tree. The tree (*Ficus religiosa*) under which the Buddha sat at the time of his enlightenment; now known as the Bodhi tree.

prajñā (Skr.). Wisdom: the wisdom brought by enlightenment, not by discrimination. Also, one of the three types of learning, the other two being *śīla* (rules) and *samādhi.*

Prajñāpāramitā (Skr.). Supreme Wisdom. Also, the name of a group of scriptures of Mahāyāna Buddhism, one of which is the Scripture of Great Wisdom, or the *Heart Sūtra* (*Prajñāpāramitā-hridaya Sūtra*).

pratyekabuddha (Skr.). One who has reached enlightenment as a result of his own efforts, but who does not teach others in order to save them. (J. *engaku.*)

Rāhula. The son of Prince Siddhārtha Gautama, so named—Rāhula means "Hindrance" in Sanskrit—because his father regarded the child as an impediment to his resolve to leave the world and enter the priest-hood. Rāhula later became one of his father's disciples.

rakusu (J.). A small token kesa, given to a confirmed layman or a priest, and worn at all times during both work and sleep.

Rei-un (J.). Ling-yün, a Chinese Zen master who gained enlightenment upon seeing blossoms.

Rinzai, Rinzai Gigen (J.). Lin-chi I-hsüan (?–867), a Chinese Zen master and disciple of Ōbaku Kiun, founded the Rinzai school of Zen. The *Rinzairoku* (*Lin-chi Lu*) comprises his sayings. He is also known in Japanese as Eshō Zenji.

Roushi or *Roshi* (J.). A title usually translated as "Respected Master" and frequently used when addressing priests. It has the connotations, however, of noble, old and useless.

rūpa (Skr.). Body, matter as opposed to *nāman*, or mind. Also, form or shape.

Ryogikyo. See *Lankāvatāra Sūtra*.

Ryogonkyo. See *Śūrangama Sūtra*.

Ryoju (J.) Grdhrakūta, or Vulture Peak, a mountain in India whereon the Buddha lectured. It is situated northeast of Rājagaha.

Ryozen (J.). Mount Ryoju.

samādhi (Skr.). One-pointedness of mind; concentration; meditation.

Sammyakusambodai (J.). The peerless and full enlightenment of a Buddha. (Skr. *samyak-sambodhi*.)

Samsāra (Skr.). The cycle of birth and death; the world of ignorance and delusion.

Sandōkai (J.). A scripture written by Sekitō Kisen and read each day in Zen temples. The Chinese title is *Ts'an-t'ung-ch'i*.

Sangha (Skr.). The Buddhist priesthood.

Śāriputra. One of the Buddha's chief disciples.

Sattva (Skr.). Sentient Being.

Scripture of Great Wisdom. See *Prajñāpāramitā*.

Scripture of the Three Thousand Manners. A scripture dealing with rules of behaviour for monks. Actually there are 250 rules, which are multi-plied by 4 to cover the conditions of standing, walking, sitting and sleeping, and then by 3 to cover past, present and future.

Segaki (J.). A ceremony held at the time of Obon, the Japanese equivalent of Halloween, during which the hungry spirits of the departed are ceremonially fed.

Seigen, Seigen Gyoshi (J.). Ch'ing-yüan Hsing-ssu (?–740), a Chinese Zen master and disciple of Daikan Enō, was the founder of the Seigen (Hsing-ssu) line, one of the two great lines of Zen in China. The Sōtō and Ummon schools came from this line.

Sekitō, Sekitō Kisen (J.). Shih-t'ou Hsi-ch'ien (700–790), a Chinese Zen master who trained under Daikan Enō and then under Seigen Gyoshi. He received his name (Shih-t'ou means "Stone Head") because he always meditated upon a large flat stone. He is the author of the *Sandōkai*.

Sekkō (J.). Sekkō loved and painted dragons, but fled when he was visited by their king.

Seppō, Seppō Gizon (J.). Hsüeh-fêng I-ts'un (822–908), a Chinese Zen master and disciple of Tokusan (Tê-shan, 780–865).

Sesson (J.). World-honoured One: a name for Shakyamuni Buddha.

Seven Buddhas. Shakyamuni and the six Buddhas who preceded him. In Japanese and Sanskrit, they are as follows: Bibashibutsu (Vipaśyin Buddha), Shikibutsu (Śikhin Buddha), Bishafubutsu (Viśvabhū Buddha), Kurusonbutsu (Krakucchanda Buddha), Kunagonmunibustu (Kanakamuni Buddha), Kashōbutsu (Kāśyapa Buddha), Shakyamunibutsu (Śākyamuni Buddha).

Shakyamuni (J.). In Sanskrit, Śākyamuni, meaning "Wise Man of the Śākyas." The name given to the historic Buddha, Siddhārtha Gautama.

Sharihotsu (J.). Śāriputra.

shashu (J.). Holding the hands clasped whilst walking or standing still.

Shin Buddhism. Jōdō Shin or Jōdō Shinshu, Pure Land Buddhism, a sect founded by Shinran (1173–1262) which relies on faith in the vows of Am'da Buddha.

Shingon Buddhism. This Buddhist sect was introduced into Japan in 806 by Kūkai (also known as Kōbō Daishi, 774–835). Its teachings are based on *Mahāvairocana Sūtra* and the *Vajraśekhara Sūtra*.

Shin Zan (J.). "Ascent of the Mountain": the ceremony of induction of a new abbot.

Shō, Zō, Matsu (J.). The three periods into which Buddhism is divided after Shakyamuni's death: Shōbō, when the True Teaching is actively spread and practised; Zōbō, when the True Teaching still exists and is still practised, but no enlightened persons appear; Mappo, when only the teaching exists but no one practises it and no one becomes enlightened.

shōmon. See *śrāvaka*.

Shōrinji (J.). Shao-lin-ssu on Sung Shan, or Mount Sung (J. Shūzan), the Chinese temple where Bodhidharma is said to have sat nine years facing a wall, and his disciple Eka to have cut off his arm to prove his sincerity of purpose.

shōsan, taishishōsan (J.). A mondo (question and answer) ceremony performed by disciples before the portrait of a deceased abbot as part of the funeral ceremony.

shuryō (J.). The trainees' hall in a Zen temple, where all studying takes place.

shuryogon-zammai (J.). Particularly powerful samādhi. (Skr. *śūramgama-samādhi*.)

shusōshō (J.). A chief junior.

Shuzan, Shuzan Shōnen (J.). Shou-shan Hsing-nien (926–993), a Chinese Zen master and disciple of Fūketsu (Fêng-hsüeh, 896–973).

six supernatural powers (six extraordinary senses). The ability to appear wherever one desires; the ability to see what the ordinary human eye cannot; the ability to hear what the ordinary ear cannot; the ability to read minds; the ability to know various events in the past; the ability to know the cause of all suffering and thus have a disposition void of passions and craving. Also called the "six sorceries."

six worlds. See *lokas.*

skandhas (Skr.). The five aggregates which make up a human being: matter (*rūpa*), feeling (*vedanā*), perception (*samjñā*), mental states (*samskāra*), and consciousness (*vijñāna*).

Sōjiji. One of the two head temples, with Eiheiji, of the Sōtō Zen Church in Japan. Originally situated in Ishikawa prefecture, it was moved to Kanagawa prefecture in 1884 after a disastrous fire had destroyed the original temple.

Sonja (J.). A senior or superior, a holy one.

Sōkei (J.). Ts'ao-ch'i, the name of the locality where Enō, the Sixth Patriarch, had his monastery. The name is also used to refer to the Sixth Patriarch himself.

Sōtō (J.). The southern school of Chinese Zen flourished during the time of Daikan Enō, the Sixth Patriarch, and it was from this school that Tōzan Ryokai (Tung-shan Liang-chieh) came. Since he spent much of his time with Sōzan Honkaju (Ts'ao-shan Pên-chi, 840–901), the school they founded was named Sōtō (Ts'ao-tung), Sō from Sōzan and Tō from Tōzan.

śrāvaka (Skr.). This term originally meant a person who heard the Buddha's teaching, and is now applied to trainees in general. (J. *shōmon.*)

stūpa (Skr.). Hemispherical or cylindrical mound, usually of earth, erected above the relics of a Buddha or a saint, or over a consecrated place that pilgrims visit. Also, a monument.

Subhūti. One of the ten great disciples of Shakyamuni Buddha.

Suddhodana. The father of Shakyamuni Buddha.

Sumeru (Skr.). Mount Sumeru is believed to be the centre of all the worlds. Hell and the realm of the hungry ghosts are below it; the realm of the asuras and that of animals are located in the sea and land at its base; heaven and the realm of human beings are upon its slopes; the highest heaven is above it.

Sūrangama Sūtra. The ten volumes of this scripture were translated from Sanskrit into Chinese by Haramittai in 705. The seventh volume is read in Japanese Zen temples and is known there as the *Suryogonkyo, Ryogonkyo* or *Ryogonshū.*

sūtra (Skr.). A Buddhist scripture incorporating the teachings of the Buddha, supposedly in the actual words of the historical Buddha. The sūtras form one division of the Pali Canon, or *Tripitaka* ("Three Baskets"): *Sūtra-pitaka; Vinaya-pitaka,* or monastic rules; *Abhidharma-pitaka,* or higher doctrine.

Sweet Gate Scripture. A scripture that is read during the Segaki ceremony, or the feeding of the hungry ghosts. In Japanese it is called *Kanrōmon* and in Sanskrit *Amrita-dvāra* (*amrita* means "nectar"). The Sweet Gate is the gateway to Nirvāna.

taikō (J.). A senior member of the priesthood who has undergone at least five years' training.

Taisō (J.). A title meaning "Great Patriarch." Taisō Jōsai Daishi is the posthumous title of Keizan Zenji.

tan (J.). The raised platform along the sides of the meditation hall, upon which the trainees sit.

Tathāgata (Skr.). Literally, "He Who Has Thus Arrived"—that is, arrived like the Buddhas before him: an epithet used by the Buddha when referring to himself.

Teijo (J.). A famous Chinese priestess who began her training under Isan Reiyū at the age of twelve and became a very excellent trainee.

ten quarters. The ten directions: the four cardinal compass directions, the four intermediate directions, and the zenith and the nadir. (Skr. *daśa diśah.*)

Tendai (J.). The Tendai (T'ien-t'ai) sect of Buddhism was founded in China by Chigi (Chih-i, 538–597). Its philosophy is traced back to Nāgārjuna in the second century, and he is regarded as its founder.

tengentsu (J.). The ability to see what the ordinary human eye cannot: one of the six supernatural powers.

tenkien (J.). The senior on night duty in a Zen training temple.

tennitsu (J.). The ability to hear what the ordinary human ear cannot: one of the six supernatural powers.

tenzo (J.). The priest in charge of cooking in a Zen temple.

Theravāda (P.). The "Way of the Elders." The southern form of Buddhism, based on the Pali scriptures and prevalent in Ceylon, Burma, and Thailand. It stresses attainment of salvation by each person for himself alone instead of for all beings.

Three Vehicles. (1) Hīnayāna, or Śrāvakayāna, the "Lesser Vehicle" by which one reaches Arahantship through understanding the Four Noble Truths; (2) Pratyekabuddhayāna, by which one reaches understanding by one's own efforts and does not teach in order to save others; (3) Mahāyāna, or Bodhisattvayāna, the "Greater Vehicle" by which one attempts to save all beings. (Skr. *Trīni-yāyāni.*)

Three Wisdoms. This can refer to two things. (1) Sammyo (J.), Tisro Vidyāh (Skr.): remembrance of former births; knowledge of the future destiny of all beings; understanding of the origin of pain and misery and how to eliminate it. (2) Sanchi (J.): the wisdom of the śrāvaka or pratyekabuddha; the wisdom of the Bodhisattva; the wisdom of the Buddha.

Three Worlds. This can refer to two things. (1) Sanze (J.): the worlds of past, present and future. (2) Sangai (J.), Trayo Dhātavah (Skr.): Kāmadhatu, the realm where beings have desire for food and sexual pleasure; Rūpadhatu, realm of form, where beings have neither appetite nor sexual desire: Arūpadhatu, the formless realm of spirit.

tokudō (J.). Ordination as a trainee for the priesthood.

Tosotsuten (J.). The "Heaven of the Satisfied," where dwells Miroku, the Buddha who is to come. It is the place of waiting for all Bodhisattvas who are to appear in the world as Buddhas. Shakyamuni Buddha waited there. (Skr. *Tuśita.*)

Tōzan Ryokai (J.). Tung-shan Liang-chieh (807–869), a Chinese Zen master and disciple of Ungan Donjō. It is believed that the second part of the name of the Sōtō school was taken from his name.
Tōzan Shusho (J.). Tung-shan Shou-ch'u (?–990), a Chinese Zen master and disciple of Ummon Bunen. He is famous for the kōan of the three pounds of flax, found in the *Hekiganroku* (*Pi-yen Lu*) and the *Mumonkan* (*Wu-mên Kuan*). He is not to be confused with Tōzan Ryokai, one of the founders of the Sōtō school in China.
Tuśita Heaven. See *Tosotsuten.*

Udayana. King of Kosambi, in India, who lived around the time of Shakyamuni Buddha. He is said to have made the first statue of a Buddha.
Udraka Rāmaputra. A teacher of Shakyamuni Buddha prior to his enlightenment. With him the Buddha attained the N'eva Sañña N'āsañ-ñayatana, or the stage of meditation that reaches the Realm of Neither Perception nor Non-Perception. After his enlightenment Shakyamuni wanted to teach the Truth to Udraka, but discovered that the latter had died the evening before.
udumbara (Skr.). A tree which is said to flower only once in three thousand years, symbolising the appearance of a Buddha.
Ummon, Ummon Bunen (J.). Yün-mên Wên-yen (?–949), a Chinese Zen master. A disciple of Seppō Gizon, he founded the Ummon (Yün-mên) school of Zen, which takes its name from the mountain where he lived and taught.
umpan (J.). The "cloud-plate," or meal gong in a Zen temple, so called because it is shaped like a cloud.
Ungan, Ungan Donjō (J.). Yün-yen T'an-ch'êng (772–841), a Chinese Zen master of the Seigen line, and a disciple of Yakusan Igen.
unsui (J.). A Zen trainee. The word comes originally from *gyoun-ryusyu*, or "floating clouds, running water." Clouds have no form, for they are constantly changing; water has no form, for it fits into a square or round container at will. Yet water has the strength to move mountains and clouds wander free. Thus must be the Zen trainee.
upādhyāya (Skr.). A priest; a senior priest of ten years' standing.
Uruvelā. A village in India on the banks of the river Nairanjanā, where Shakyamuni Buddha stayed prior to his enlightenment.

Vairocana Buddha (Skr.). The Illuminator. He is the central figure of the Kegon scriptures, is considered the essence of the universe by the Shingon sect, and is the Dharmakāya of the Tendai sect. In Japanese he is called Birushanofū, Biroshanubutsu, or Dainichi Nyorai.
Vajrasattva. An Indian Bodhisattva who is regarded as Shingon's Second Patriarch, as he is believed to have received the Shingon teachings directly from Vairocana Buddha.
Vasubandhu. An Indian master of the Yogācāra school of Mahāyāna Buddhism; the younger brother of Asanga. He wrote the *Abhidharmakośa Śastra* and other works.

Vimalakīrti. A model layman and an elder of Vaiśālī in India; a contemporary of Shakyamuni Buddha. Known in Japan as Yuima, he is considered a Bodhisattva of deep spiritual attachment. The *Vimalakīrti Sūtra* (*Yuimakyo*) consists of his discourses.

Vinaya (Skr.). The rules of discipline for Buddhist monks.

vipāka (Skr.). Action and its result. *Vipāka* can be called the fruit of our actions, whilst *karma* is the seeds that we ourselves sow.

Vishnu. A Hindu god, called Nārāyana in the Upanishads. The chief deity of the Vaishnava, he has the power of changing himself into ten different forms in order to save all beings.

Yajñadatta. A madman in ancient India who thought he had lost his head because he could not see it in a mirror, although he could see his eyes and eyebrows.

Yakusan, Yakusan Igen (J.). Yao-shan Wei-yen (751–834), a Chinese Zen master of the Seigen line.

Yasodharā. The wife of Prince Siddhārtha Gautama, the future Shakyamuni Buddha.

Yoga (Skr.). A means of attaining salvation by finding the unchanging within oneself as a result of various meditation practices. Yoga recognises an individual soul which helps one on the way to finding the Truth.

Yōka Genkaku (J.). Yung-chia Hsüan-chio (665–713), a Chinese Zen master. Officially of the Tendai sect, he became a disciple of Daikan Enō, the Sixth Patriarch. He wrote the *Shōdōka* (*Chêng-tao K'ê*), or *Odes on Enlightenment*.

Yuima. See *Vimalakīrti*.

Zazen (J.). Seated meditation.

Zen (J.). Meditation. (Skr. *dhyāna*.)

Zenji (J.). Literally, "Zen Master," a title usually given only by the emperor of Japan to patriarchs.

Zuda (J.). The twelve practices whose purpose is to control worldly desire and eliminate attachment. (Skr. *Dvādaśa Dhūtagunāh*.)

Zuisse (J.). A special congratulatory ceremony performed only at Eiheiji and Sōjiji by new priests on reaching the priestly rank.